Picturing Disability

Critical Perspectives on Disability
Steven J. Taylor, Beth A. Ferri, and Arlene S. Kanter, *Series Editors*

Books in the Critical Perspectives on Disability series, launched in 2009, explore the place of people with disabilities in society through the lens of disability studies, critical special education, disability law and policy, and international human rights. The series publishes books from such disciplines as sociology, law and public policy, history, anthropology, the humanities, educational theory, literature, communications, popular-culture studies, and diversity and cultural studies.

Picturing Disability

Beggar, Freak, Citizen, and Other Photographic Rhetoric

∼

Robert Bogdan

with Martin Elks and James A. Knoll

Syracuse University Press

For a listing of books published and distributed by Syracuse University Press,
visit our website at SyracuseUniversityPress.syr.edu.

ISBN: 978-0-8156-3302-0

Library of Congress Cataloging-in-Publication Data

Bogdan, Robert.

Picturing disability : beggar, freak, citizen, and other photographic rhetoric /
Robert Bogdan, with Martin Elks and James A. Knoll. — 1st ed.

p. cm. — (Critical perspectives on disability)

Includes bibliographical references and index.

ISBN 978-0-8156-3302-0 (cloth : alk. paper) 1. People with disabilities—Portraits.
2. People with disabilities—History. 3. Sociology of disability. I. Elks, Martin.
II. Knoll, James A.   III. Title.

HV1568.B64 2012

305.9'08—dc23   2012033977

Manufactured in the United States of America

Contents

Illustrations

TABLE

Acknowledgments

A work of this nature involves many people's efforts. I thank those who helped me.

Martin Elks researched and wrote chapter 6, "Clinical Photographs." James Knoll contributed chapter 9, "Art for Art's Sake." These chapters are based on Elks's and Knoll's outstanding doctoral dissertations, completed at Syracuse University (Elks 1992; Knoll 1987). Not only are these chapters important contributions to this book, but the work of these two talented scholars provided some of the inspiration that sustained my efforts in completing it.

Research on asylum postcards in chapter 5 was done with the assistance of Ann Marshall (Bogdan and Marshall 1997). She skillfully worked the data and contributed important ideas. Some of the material on movie stills in chapter 8 is derived from work I published with Douglas Biklen, Arthur Shapiro, and D. Spelkolman (Bogdan et al. 1982).

I also thank those who helped in obtaining the illustrations found here. Leonard A. Lauder, Bruce Nelson, and Joel Wayne have been most generous over the years in allowing me access to their significant collections. Others who have contributed images to this book include Doug Aikenhead, Carl Griffin, Mike Maslan, Jim Matthews, Don and Newly Preziosi, and Robert Wainwright. I am indebted to Lynda Klich, archivist for the Leonard A. Lauder Collection; Nicolette Dobrowolski, archivist in the Special Collections Research Center at Syracuse University; Craig Williams, senior librarian at the New York State Library; David W. Rose, archivist for the March of Dimes; Carin Johnson at the Fraenkel Gallery; Meredith Lue at Mary Ellen Mark Library/studio; and Susan Thomas at the Wolfensberger Collection. Meg Bogdan, my daughter, helped with clarifying and researching copyright restrictions and other legal dimensions of the book.

A special thanks to my colleague Steve Taylor, who prodded me to start as well as to complete this project. He provided insightful commentary at various stages in the preparation of this manuscript, including a careful reading of an early draft. In addition to making general suggestions about the manuscript, John Moeschler applied his medical expertise to an early draft to point out classification, diagnostic, and language concerns. Phil Ferguson read the manuscript and made helpful suggestions for revisions. Annie Barva did a fine job copyediting the manuscript.

I have worked with Mary Selden Evans, former executive editor at Syracuse University Press, on a number of projects over the years. With all of these projects, she has been a supportive and insightful collaborator as well as a joy to work with. My experience with her and others at the press—including Alice Pfeiffer, Kay Steinmetz, Victoria Lane, Fred Wellner, Lynn Hoppel, Lisa Kuerbis, Mona Hamlin, and Jennika Baines—has filled me with admiration for them. Their support of authors has produced a long list of interesting and important books.

Throughout our years together, Janet Bogdan has served as an editor and a supportive critic of my work. Thanks to her for continuing to serve in that role here. My work and life have greatly been improved by her presence.

Abbreviations

Aikenhead Coll.   Douglas Aikenhead Collection, Ann Arbor, Michigan

Becker Coll.   Ronald G. Becker Collection of Charles Eisenmann Photographs,
                               Special Collections Research Center, Syracuse University Library

Blatt Coll.   Burton Blatt Collection, Syracuse University Archives

Coll. of Leonard A. Lauder   Collection of Leonard A. Lauder, New York City

March of Dimes Coll.   March of Dimes Collection, White Plains, New York

Maslan Coll.   Michael Maslan Collection, Seattle

Matthews Coll.   Jim Matthews Collection, Los Angeles

B. Nelson Coll.   Bruce Nelson Collection, Portland, Maine

Preziosi Coll.   Don and Newly Preziosi Collection, Medham, New Jersey

Joel Wayne, Pop's Postcards   Joel Wayne, Pop's Postcards, Los Angeles

Wainwright Coll.   Robert Wainwright Collection, Point Pleasant, New Jersey

Picturing Disability

1 Introduction
Picturing Disability

1.1 People with disabilities on the steps of a shack, ca. 1907. Photo postcard.

In this book, I examine historical photographs and old printed images derived from photos of people we would now say have disabilities.[1] When

1. Rather than continue to use the awkward phrase "photographs and printed images derived from photographs" and similar expressions, I substitute just "photographs." I include Martin Elks' and James Knoll's chapters in my discussion of aims and approaches in this introduction. I use *I* and *my* for simplicity's sake and because I am the book's primary author.

the images were produced, the people depicted were referred to by many terms, including such outmoded words as *handicapped* or more specific dated descriptors such as *insane, epileptic, idiot, midget, feebleminded, crippled, lame, deaf,* and *blind.* The photographers who shot the pictures as well as their associates, the subjects, and the viewers were embedded in particular milieus and historical times. I examine the worlds in which they operated to decipher the relationship between

1

the images and the picture makers' perspectives. I cover photographs produced for sideshows, begging, charity drives, asylum reports and promotional texts, eugenics texts, advertising, movies, art galleries, and family albums.

I am not the first to tackle the topic of the visual representation of people with disabilities in photographs. There have been important predecessors. Some of these writers instruct us about whether particular disability images are positive or negative—whether they demean or in other ways malign people with disabilities or portray them in complimentary ways (e.g., Hevey 1992; Norden 1994; Millet 2004; B. Haller 2010). Others develop classifications schemes of the various ways people with disabilities are depicted (Garland-Thomson 2001). Scholars with a more theoretical bent focus on how the images relate to aesthetics, ethics, race, class, gender, and oppression of particular groups (Garland-Thomson 2002, 2004; Snyder, Brueggemann, and Garland-Thomson 2002; Chivers and Markotic 2010; Sandell, Dodd, and Garland-Thomson 2010; Siebers 2010). These approaches are concerned with broad and abstract cultural meanings and tend to use predetermined theoretical lenses that most often do not capture the meanings of the images to those who produced them.[2] It is important that the study of images of people with disabilities not stop with the pictures but include the historical and cultural circumstances of the people who created them.[3] That is my approach here.

As described in subsequent chapters, photographers employed different visual conventions in their pictures, and these conventions varied depending on their social circumstances. All photographs, be

they of people with disabilities or of other subjects, contain visual rhetoric, patterns of conventions that have a distinct style that cast the subject in a particular way. As others have studied written text to examine verbal rhetorical techniques, I examine the visual rhetorical techniques in photographs.

There are many ways photographically generated pictures can vary. How the subject is posed, what props are used, whether others are included in the picture, and the background and other dimensions of the shoot's setting are subject to manipulation as part of photographic production. How the subjects are dressed, their facial expressions, their posture, the lighting and angles employed, the printing of the picture, and other such details contribute to photographic variation (Knoll 1987; Bogdan 1988; Elks 1992). I am concerned with particular patterns that evolved in the kinds of photos produced, such as those employed for sideshows, disability advertising, begging, art galleries, scientific display, and other situations. How did pictures of people with disabilities produced for the sideshow, for example, differ from those produced for medical textbooks? How did the images relate to the settings that produced them?

As you will see, no single doctrine for photographing disabled people existed in the past. Rather, different sets of guidelines were typical of different institutional arrangements. I call these guidelines "genres." I use phrases such as "modes of presenting" and "photographic conventions" to refer to the visual rhetoric within genres. Nuanced as well as blatant rhetorical differences exist between and within each genre. The impressions given by images within the same genre are sometimes contradictory. For example, sideshow images vary from casting exhibits as wild savages to portraying them as refined royalty. These apparent inconsistencies seem to undermine the idea of genre, but, as I show, they make sense when seen within the framework of the people involved in the picture making.

Who was behind the creation of the visual disability rhetoric examined in this book? In addition

2. Some of this work favors postmodern and critical theories, whereas my analysis is based on social constructionism and related approaches that pay attention to context, meaning, and agency.

3. Martin Norden's work on movie depictions of people with disabilities (Norden 1994) is the one example where the historical and cultural context of picture production is an important part of the analysis.

to photographers, other actors in the picture making included those people who hired the picture takers, artistic directors, writers, and others directly and indirectly involved in picture production. The subjects themselves sometimes helped shape the images. Although people with disabilities were on occasion coerced to pose in particular ways, they often were willing and active participants; they were in some cases the initiators and designers of their own photo opportunities. There were many agents of image production. The conventions they employed did not originate with them. The visual rhetoric was part of the institutional arrangements and larger culture in which the participants were enmeshed, and so it developed over time.

What about the people who saw the images? The pictures in this book could be found in postcard albums, textbooks, family photo collections, magazines, newspapers, and other places. What did the viewers living in the period in which the photographs were taken make of them? Did they respond to the visual rhetoric in the way that the producers hoped they would? Did they share the picture makers' perspectives? What citizens of the times thought of the images is an important and vital part of understanding the images' meaning. Here and there I try to address audience perceptions, but its main focus is deciphering what the makers were up to.[4]

As we now look at these photographs produced at an earlier time, how do we see them? What cultural lens do we apply?

Some readers will undoubtedly see some of the images as deplorable even though they were produced to show what at the time were considered favorable versions of people with disabilities. For example, the pictures that show happy, submissive people with disabilities gathered together in isolated institutions will not today be seen as positive depictions, as they were meant to be, but rather

as evidence of mistreatment and oppression. At various points, present-day perspectives of various images are given, but such commentary is not the book's primary aim.

In researching this book, I did not study just pictures. I read memoirs, diaries, notations on photographs, and other written work in order to decipher the perspectives of those who produced the pictures. But the verbal record was often missing; there was little direct evidence about what was going on in the creators' minds. My knowledge of the history of photography and of how various formats were produced and fit into the producers' lives helped fill in the gaps in understanding what the producers might have intended (Bogdan 1998, 2003; Bogdan and Wesloh 2006). An additional source of information, especially in the case where the images are postcards, were the captions as well as the messages written on the back. All of this information was important, but I relied heavily on inferences drawn from examining the pictures. Here the persistent patterns that emerged were important.[5]

Most people who study visual representation focus on a small number of images within a limited range of subject areas (Garland-Thomson 2004; Millet 2004; Hevey 2006).[6] I have examined thousands of images from a wide variety of sources, and

---

4. See Apel and Smith 2008 for a discussion of the various meanings and uses of lynching photographs.

5. A disclaimer: Because the material I have used for the research reported here is so diverse and dispersed, there was no way of doing systematic sampling. Although I have been rigorous in seeking out material, I do not know how representative the material I reviewed is of all that was produced. In addition, I have chosen the most graphic examples to illustrate points. Some might argue that I am producing visual rhetoric rather than reporting it. The reader should factor this issue into making judgments about the accuracy of my assertions.

6. David Hevey (2006) based his article on a visit to a book store where he examined four photo books and lamented the lack of disability images in photographs. Norden's book *Cinema of Isolation* (1994) is devoted to motion picture depictions of people with physical disabilities. He is the only author I have encountered whose writing is based on the study of thousands of examples.

I have been collecting historical photographs of people with disabilities since 1985 (Bogdan 1988). I seek images at antique shops, flea markets, eBay, postcard shows, and other venues to expand my collection. When I started my research on "freak shows" (as discussed in chapter 2) in 1985, I discovered that the most extensive disability-related photographic collections were private ones. Most major archives in public museums and university libraries had overlooked disability as a collecting area, or they had conceived of the topic in such a narrow way that their holdings where insufficient for my interests. In doing the research for this book, besides using the images from my own collection, I visited many private collectors, who allowed me to scan relevant photographs.

Special Collections at the Syracuse University Bird Library has collections pertaining to my topic: the Becker Collection is perhaps the largest collection of nineteenth-century "freak" photos in the world,[7] and the Margaret Bourke-White Collection has many images taken at Letchworth Village, an asylum that housed people with developmental disabilities.[8] A third source at Syracuse University, its institutional archives, contains the images and information pertaining to Burton Blatt and Fred Kaplan's exposé of state schools for the developmentally disabled published in their book *Christmas in Purgatory* (Blatt and Kaplan 1966).[9]

The images I have studied provide both the illustrations and the insights in this book. I approached the images with the following question: What can

be learned from studying a very large number of images in which people with disabilities appear? My idea was to apply in this context the same logic and techniques I have used as a qualitative sociologist to analyze interview transcripts and field notes (Glaser and Strauss 1967; Glaser 1978; Bogdan and Biklen 2007; Arluke and Bogdan 2010).

For practical reasons, I have focused my collecting and searching on photographs taken in the United States from the 1860s to the 1970s. With the exception of some of the images in chapter 6, "Clinical Photographs," and one illustration in the concluding chapter, all the illustrations are from the United States. The period covered ranges from when photographs became widely available and part of popular culture to the decade in which the modern-day disability rights movement became a significant force of social change. The years covered are different in each chapter because particular types of renderings occurred only during certain years or are best illustrated by images from certain years. For example, the prime years for freak show images were during the late nineteenth and early twentieth centuries. The increased use of images of people with disabilities in modern art photography occurred in the 1960s and 1970s.

The book's scope is wide. Given the limitations of the material available and what can be accomplished in one book, not all topics are covered. In addition, in each chapter only certain aspects of the topic it investigates are included, and some dimensions of the subject are dealt with only superficially. What I offer here can be taken as a start in exploring the social context of disability's image construction—a sampler rather than an encyclopedic presentation.

Why did I choose the particular illustrations included in this book? Those that generated understanding of particular types of depictions had to be incorporated, but I utilized other considerations as well. In some instances, I had many examples of the idea I was trying to convey. When that was the case, I chose illustrations that were the most aesthetically engaging.

7. When working on my book *Freak Show* (Bogdan 1988), I visited Ron Becker at his home and was instrumental in getting him to donate his collection to Syracuse University.

8. Although I studied this collection, I did not use any of the images from it as illustrations. The Bourke-White images reproduced in chapter 5 were taken directly from New York State annual reports of Letchworth Village published in the 1930s and available at the New York State Library in Albany.

9. Burton Blatt was chairperson of the Special Education Department at Syracuse University, and his interest in what was to become disability studies is what brought me to the faculty.

The images in some chapters are more common and easier to find than others in the marketplace of collectibles and in archives. For example, the horror movie stills were manufactured in multiple copies and can be easily found on eBay and in film collections. But the images found in chapter 10 on family and citizens are not easy to come by. Most family pictures are one of a kind, the remnants of family photo albums. I included more examples of the rarer photographs than those that are easy to locate because I felt that making more of these images available is in itself a contribution to the field of disability studies.

The images' reproduction quality varies from chapter to chapter because the formats of the pictures I used were not uniform. For example, those in the chapter on family and citizens are scanned from original real photos, whereas those in the chapters on clinical photographs and advertising were scanned from half-tone textbooks and magazines. Prints of original photos reproduce much more clearly than half-tones.

In all the chapters except chapter 6, the caption under each illustration includes a descriptive title, the approximate date the photograph was taken, the photographer, the format of the photograph, and an acknowledgment of where the image is collected. Quotation marks around caption text means that the wording was taken from the caption on the photograph itself. If the photographer's name is not included, I do not know who took the picture. If there is no acknowledgment to a collection, the illustration is taken from my own collection. The geographic location where the photograph was taken is occasionally named after the description. When it is not, either I do not know, or its location is irrelevant to the discussion. In chapter 6 on clinical photographs, the captions roughly follow the formatting of the captions of images in other chapters, but they also include a reference to the book where the picture appeared.

In regard to the format or the type of photographs, the illustrations fall into the following categories: *cartes de visite,* tintypes, cabinet cards, postcards, news photos, movie publicity photos (stills), and photos printed in books, magazines, and pamphlets. The *carte de visite* was the most common photographic format from 1860 to 1885. Each was a photograph printed from a negative and mounted on a piece of thin cardboard. The size of the mount was approximately two and a half by four inches with the picture itself being slightly smaller. Tintypes were photos formed on a coated piece of thin iron. They varied in size but were typically about the size of the *carte de visite.* The tintype was introduced in the United States in 1856 and remained relative popular until the end of the nineteenth century. It was never as popular as the *carte de visite* or cabinet card, however. The cabinet card was similar to the *carte de visite* but was three times larger and did not become popular until later in the nineteenth century. In the last two decades of that century, they surpassed the *carte de visite* as the most popular photographic format. Postcards include two types, printed and real photo. Both were most popular between 1905 and 1930. News photos and movie stills came into production in the early part of the twentieth century. They are typically eight and a half by eleven inches.

Although the technology to produce half-tone and other mechanical printed versions of photos was present prior to 1900, photos did not regularly appear in newspapers, books, magazines, and pamphlets until a few years after the turn of the century.

When I first became interested in the idea of picturing disability and writing a book about it, some of my colleagues were shocked by how demeaning or ugly some portrayals were. A few advised that the topic might be offensive to people involved in the disability rights movement. One review of the book I wrote about freak shows (Bogdan 1988) accused me of promoting the exhibition of such people by writing about it (Gerber 1992). Interestingly, it is most often people *without* disabilities who are most offended when confronting ugly vestiges of the past, whereas people with disabilities embrace images of their oppression as documents of their struggles for equality.

Other illustrations may be upsetting to those not used to seeing photographs of people with severe and profound physical and mental anomalies. It is not my intention to shock or cause distress. I hope that some of the pictures will bring rarely seen images of people with disabilities into the light, out of the dark places where they have been hidden.

Most people think that to understand social life it is better to know the facts than to experience it emotionally and aesthetically, but these dimensions of understanding can be complementary. A compelling photograph possesses the dual function of instruction and affective impact (Asma 2001, 244–45). A good photograph can make social science issues clearer, and good social science analysis can make photographs more compelling. This book brings these aspects of knowing together to bear on the subject of picturing disability.

Although the book is filled with illustrations, it is not a "picture book." Each chapter is a photo essay. The words and pictures are interdependent. People often look at photo books by thumbing through them and stopping only at the images that catch their eye. They ignore the text or read it only when an image raises questions they want clarified. In contrast, people read text-based books by concentrating on the words, only occasionally paying casual attention to the photographs and the relationship between the sentences and the images. To read my book effectively, you need a different approach. When an illustration is referred to in the text, please stop and study it. Go back and forth between what is stated about the images and what your own scrutinizing brings to light.

A word about the vocabulary used in the book. There is no universal agreement about the language that should be used in referring to the people pictured in this book. The words and phrases considered appropriate have changed over time and vary from group to group. *People with disabilities* and similar phrases are currently favored. Although this phrase is used in the book, others are used as well because of issues of style and

historical appropriateness. For example, you will see words such as *feebleminded, crippled, blind,* and *beggar* when those were the words used during the period in which the images discussed were produced. Words such as *anomaly, deformed,* and *amputee* are used when the current vocabulary is inadequate to capture what is being discussed, to vary language, or to improve the flow of the discussion and remain true to a particular historical period.

Each chapter addresses a particular genre of disability image and the contexts that created it. As with illustration 1.1, not all photographs easily fit within the genres discussed. I conclude by discussing images that do not neatly fit into the categories discussed and reflect on what my coauthors and I have learned from the project.

2 Freak Portraits
Sideshow Souvenirs

2.1. Charles Tripp, "The Armless Wonder," 1885. Photo by Charles Eisenmann. Cabinet card.

From the mid–nineteenth to the mid–twentieth century in America, the public exhibition of people with real and alleged physical anomalies in museum, circus, carnival, world fair, and amusement park sideshows for amusement and profit was widely popular and for the most part respectable.[1] People displayed as "freaks" included those without arms and legs, dwarfs, unusually large individuals (obese people as well as the very tall), conjoined twins, and others with physical and mental differences that we call "disabilities" today.

Starting in the early 1860s, when large-scale commercial production of photographic images became technically possible, and ending with the demise of this form of entertainment, the people on exhibit sold photographs of themselves to patrons both to supplement their income and to advertise their appearances. Because of these photos' popularity, thousands of them still remain in archives and in the hands of private collectors.

Illustration 2.1 is an 1885 studio portrait of Charles Tripp, a man born without arms. Charles Eisenmann, a well-known New York City photographer who specialized in "freak" portraits, took it (Mitchell 1979). Tripp was a famous sideshow performer and sold this portrait to people who came to view him while he toured as the "armless human wonder" (Bogdan 1988). Note the fancy Victorian parlor wallpaper on the studio backdrop. Tripp is shown performing with his versatile feet and prominently displaying the props he used in his appearances. Examples of his penmanship and other footwork are in the foreground. Central in the composition is his limbless torso. The images make clear that his lack of upper appendages has

---

1. For a more comprehensive history, see Bogdan 1988.

7

not impaired his ability to function. Tripp is holding a dainty cup with his toes over a fragile table covered with an ornamental cloth and bearing a China tea set. He is dressed in a spiffy but conventional suit and tie, and his hair and moustache are neatly combed.

Illustration 2.2 is also an Eisenmann portrait of another freak show exhibit that was sold in conjunction with the subjects' appearances. "Maximo" and "Bartola" were the subjects' stage names, and the two were exhibited as the "Last of the Ancient Aztecs" in freak shows in the 1880s (Bogdan 1988, 127–34).

The unusual physiology that made Maximo and Bartola a potential attraction was microcephaly, a condition characterized by an abnormally small head and typically accompanied by a mental deficiency, or what is today called a developmental disability. Both the Tripp image and this one were taken in the same studio at approximately the same time. In the Maximo and Bartola illustration, the background studio screen depicts the out of doors, nature; the props consist of papier-mâché decorative stones and plants. Maximo and Bartola are dressed in loose-fitting ornamental robes that mimic Aztec dress. The tailors who made the outfits crafted a representation of the sun on Maximo's chest that is meant to be emblematic of the Aztecs. Their hair is not neatly combed; rather, it has been frizzed and is unruly.

Although at first glance the two images are very different, they have underlying similarities. Both were produced for the same purposes by a photographer who knew the ways of the amusement world. Charles Eisenmann probably took more commercial freak photographs than any

2.2. Maximo and Bartola, "The Last of the Ancient Aztecs," ca. 1885. Photo by Charles Eisenmann. Cabinet card. Ronald G. Becker Collection of Charles Eisenmann Photographs, Special Collections Research Center, Syracuse University Library.

2.3. Charles Eisenmann with Colonel Goshen, ca. 1885. Photo by Charles Eisenmann. Cabinet card. Robert Wainwright Collection.

other American photographer. The best known freak exhibits came regularly to his studio in New York City's Bowery whenever they and their managers were in town, where they posed for him and placed their photo orders.

Illustration 2.3 shows a self-portrait of Eisenmann standing with the very tall Colonel Ruth Goshen, in sideshow lingo "a giant," who had dropped into Eisenmann's studio for a shoot.[2]

In this chapter, I explore Eisenmann's and other freak show photographers' depictions and investigate the underlying motivation and culture that produced them.

FREAK SHOWS AND PRESENTATIONS

Freak shows were part of the popular-amusement industry, and the people associated with that enterprise had their own distinct culture (Dennett 1997). Those in the industry referred to themselves as "with it"—they were superior, more worldly, more interesting, and free of the humdrum life they judged was typical of small town America. They characterized those outside their circle with such derogatory terms as *townies, suckers,* and *rubes.* Freaks were part of the amusement industry world. They sat on their platforms looking down on those who came to see them and not just in a literal sense: they shared a contempt toward the audience.

In the traveling amusement industry, this disdain was manifested in particular deceptive, dishonest, and illegal practices. Out-and-out cheating, law breaking, and lying were common. Professional pickpockets employed by circuses and carnivals traveled with the shows and stole from the clientele, splitting the take with management. Ticket sellers regularly and systematically shortchanged

customers. The circuses and carnivals rigged games of chance and sold banned commodities and services such as liquor and sex.

In the freak show, this tendency toward fraud was reflected in how exhibits were presented to the audience. Gaffs or out-and-out phony freaks were common. People exhibited as Siamese twins ("conjoined twins" in today's language) were really people held together with a girdle. Illustration 2.4 is a case in point. As you can see by examining the two men's faces, they are not identical; they are impostors. In illustration 2.5, the "legless woman's" legs are not missing; they are cleverly concealed by a manipulation of the setting.

2.4. Fraudulent conjoined twins, ca. 1900. Cabinet card. Ronald G. Becker Collection of Charles Eisenmann Photographs, Special Collections Research Center, Syracuse University Library.

2. This image is extremely rare. Until now there were no pictures of Eisenmann in print. This one came from the Eisenmann family collection. I thank Robert Wainwright for sharing it and allowing me to included it here. Note that "my father" is written on the left, an attribution by Eisenmann's daughter.

materials, inches were added to the height of giants and subtracted from dwarfs. The professed background and circumstances surrounding the exhibit were very likely bogus, fabricated tales to enhance interest in the exhibit. The photographs sold at exhibits incorporated the fraud that accompanied freak presentations by utilizing particular conventions. Dwarfs were photographed next to tall people, even giants, a juxtaposition designed to make the dwarfs seem shorter and the giants taller (illus. 2.6). As in the photo of Colonel Goshen (illus. 2.3), giants wore high hats and thick-bottomed shoes to appear taller than they actually were.

When we look at freak show pictures, we are looking at attempts to make the exhibit more appealing to the audience in a manner that fit the fraudulent presentation of the exhibit when they

2.5. Gaff, woman with missing legs, ca. 1890. Cabinet card. Ronald G. Becker Collection of Charles Eisenmann Photographs, Special Collections Research Center, Syracuse University Library.

Gaffs were the most blatant forms of deception, but all exhibits to some degree were misrepresented to the public. Elaborate lies were made up to embellish the freak front. For example, Maximo and Bartola, pictured in illustration 2.2, were not "Aztecs" whose heads resembled those of ancient Central American humans. They were born and raised in a coastal village in Central America and, as noted earlier, were developmentally disabled. Although Charles Tripp, in illustration 1.1, had mastered foot skills, rather than being an "armless wonder" he was quite ordinary in that he did what other people with this same disability accomplished.

Other, more minor forms of fraud were present in the freaks' presentations. In the publicity

2.6. Dwarf and giant juxtaposed, ca. 1889. Cabinet card. Photo by Obermiller.

appeared on the freak show platform. The pictures were publicity images, and in most cases the subjects actively and willingly participated in photo sessions.

Two ways of presenting exhibits on the stage and in photographs predominated: the aggrandized mode and the exotic mode. By "mode," I mean how the exhibits were presented: standard poses, backdrops, props, costumes, and compositions. Each is an element of a photograph that freak photographers—guided by showmen, some of whom were exhibits themselves—used to construct freak images. The photograph of Charles Tripp is a good example of the aggrandized mode, and the one of Maximo and Bartola fits well into the exotic category. In the former type of photo, the subject is presented in a way that inflates his or her status or flaunts his or her high-achieving normal lifestyle while celebrating his or her embellished talents, whereas in the latter type the emphasis is on the disabled person's inferiority, his or her strangeness or abnormal origins, and the alien land where he or she allegedly was born and raised.

THE AGGRANDIZED MODE

The thrust of the aggrandized mode was to claim that the exhibit in the picture, in spite of his or her particular physical, mental, or behavioral anomaly, was an outstanding person. In some cases, the disability was played as the source of the person's greatness. The freak was pictured as an upstanding person with conventional or highly regarded social status. Such attributes as social position, achievements, talents, family, taste, intelligence, and physiology were fabricated, elevated or exaggerated, and then flaunted.

Within the aggrandized mode, there were subtle differences in the form the embellishment took. In one variety, the exhibit was cast, on the one hand, as being a regular upstanding citizen and, on the other, as excelling in the enactment of those normal values and lifestyle. The way Charles Tripp was pictured fits this description— his dress, the

backdrop, the props, the paraphernalia of his performance, and his general demeanor personify the typical, all-American, above-average freak.

One exhibit that consistently used this presentation was another "armless wonder," Ann E. Leak Thompson, shown in illustration 2.7. The photo contains many of the elements we saw in the Tripp photograph; Thompson is well dressed and groomed, the backdrop is a Victorian parlor, and items that show her foot dexterity are placed in front of her. She has a firm grip on a pair of scissors, which tells the viewer that she is in charge. She produced the embroidery and crocheting that is prominently displayed.

Ann E. Leak Thompson's needlework is an important part of the image not just because it testifies

2.7. Ann E. Leak Thompson, "The Armless Wonder," ca. 1884. Photo by Charles Eisenmann. Cabinet card. Ronald G. Becker Collection of Charles Eisenmann Photographs, Special Collections Research Center, Syracuse University Library.

to her abilities, but because of the symbols it contains: the Christian cross and the Masonic sign. A Bible is displayed in some photos of her. Thompson's above-average persona was tied to her piety. She presented herself as a God-fearing, Bible-toting, scripture-quoting Christian. In addition to the religious and the Masonic symbols, her embroidery contains phrases from scripture: "Holiness to the Lord," "To Thee I cling," "A Lamp unto My Feet."

In a strategy to confirm her above-average normality, Thompson often posed with her family. Her husband, bearded William R. Thompson, and their son appear in many of the photos she sold at her appearances (illus. 2.8). Family group photos

were a common aggrandized mode convention. After all, a base line for being an average adult was a spouse and children.

When Chang and Eng, the so-called original Siamese twins, were first photographed for publicity photos, they appeared in exotic Asian costumes. When they came out of show business retirement after the Civil War, they were pictured in Western dress and with two of their many children (illus. 2.9).

One stellar example of the incorporation of family in his photographs is the case of Eli Bowen, "the legless wonder." We can trace Bowen's history and the growth of his family through the photographs he sold. He started his career as an exhibit when he was thirteen. The earliest images Bowen sold show him as a slick bachelor. When he

2.8. Ann E. Leak Thompson and family, 1884. Photo by Charles Eisenmann. Cabinet card. Ronald G. Becker Collection of Charles Eisenmann Photographs, Special Collections Research Center, Syracuse University Library.

2.9. Chang and Eng with two of their sons, ca. 1870. *Carte de visite*. Ronald G. Becker Collection of Charles Eisenmann Photographs, Special Collections Research Center, Syracuse University Library.

was twenty-six, he married an attractive sixteen-year-old woman, with whom he had four children. After his marriage, his wife and children were featured in the pictures he sold. As each new child was born, he returned to the studio to have a new family portrait done. Each child was a testimony to his normal but above-average presentation. The most contemporary family portrait I have seen was taken around 1890 (illus. 2.10). In it, we see Bowen with his wife and four children, the oldest of whom is a young adult. This family portrait casts Bowen and his family in a formal arrangement shot against a respectable Victorian parlor backdrop, with the patriarch in the center and his family arranged about him. His wife stands at his

side with her hand on his shoulder, and the children encircle him. Why the goat is in the portrait I do not know.

Remember, a showman's scheme lay behind the elegant, complimentary poses taken in the thousands of photo portraits of freaks, including those of Bowen and his family. But even though the "legless wonder" presentation was patronizing, the pictures also portray dignity and independence. Some exhibits, such as Bowen, actually did give up the ways of the showman, marrying outside the amusement world and having typical families. They made enough money to dress well and settle down comfortably in typical communities; Bowen retired to Ogden, California.

Many armless and legless wonders appeared before freak show audiences and sold their images. The practice continued into the middle of the twentieth century. The format for the photos that the twentieth-century exhibits sold was the photo postcard. Frances O'Connor, the "Living Venus de Milo" was one of the last widely known armless wonders. She was photographed as the typical girl next door, albeit also as a modern woman (illus. 2.11). O'Connor was one of the stars in Tod Browning's classic and controversial film *Freaks* (1932) in which a number of people with disabilities played roles similar to their own occupation as sideshow performers.

2.10. Eli Bowen with his family, ca. 1890. Photo by Swords Brothers. Cabinet card. Ronald G. Becker Collection of Charles Eisenmann Photographs, Special Collections Research Center, Syracuse University Library.

Perhaps the best known aggrandized presentation was that of the world-famous dwarf General Tom Thumb. P. T. Barnum, the king of humbug, was his manager and promoter. Tom was actually Charles Stratton, born in Bridgeport, Connecticut, to a poor carpenter and a barmaid. The truth of his origins did not fit Barnum's ideas of how to promote him, however, so he named Stratton after a character in an English folktale, called him "general," and taught him to sing and dance and behave like a proper English gentleman. Stratton first went on tour in America when he was five years old. In an attempt to make his small stature even more remarkable than it really was, Barnum said he was twelve (Harris 1973).

2.11. Frances O'Connor, "armless wonder," ca. 1932. Photo postcard.

Tom Thumb married the diminutive Lavinia Warren, who had also found her way to the freak show platform. Their wedding was a lavish affair and milked for all the publicity it could generate. Their appearance as husband and wife brought new interest to the pair, and attendance at their appearances soared. But when Stratton and his wife's revenue from exhibition began to decline, they devised a plan to attract more customers. They began exhibiting a little Thumb, an infant whom they claimed was their birth child. Illustration 2.12 is a likeness of the couple and their alleged baby taken at Mathew Brady's studio around 1868 and sold while they were on tour. The infant was not

theirs, though, because they were infertile.[3] When they toured Europe, they used different babies from different countries, and when in the United States they changed babies as each grew too large to handle.

Tom Thumb and Lavinia Warren were early in a long line of little people who appeared in freak shows. Little people typically presented themselves in the high aggrandized mode; their claims

3. In her autobiography (Saxon 1979), Lavinia never mentions the child, and the child never appears in later photographs.

TOM THUMB, WIFE & CHILD.

2.12. "Tom Thumb, Wife & Child," ca. 1868. Photo by Mathew Brady. *Carte de visite.*

Bailey Circus. During these years, she sold printed postcards such as the one seen in illustration 2.14. She, too, took on the mien of a high-society woman dressed in an evening gown and was accompanied by her manager, who is wearing a vested suit. The painted backdrop for this image includes an elaborate fireplace.

The aggrandized mode of photographic presentation employed various forms of dress to raise the exhibit's status as well as to bring people's attention to the person's disability. The giants wore tall hats and high-heeled boots. The "human skeletons," or people who were extremely thin, appeared in outfits that enhanced their claim to fame. Male human skeletons often wore tights and tightly fitting shirts. Females adorned themselves with low-cut, armless evening gowns that revealed their scrawny physiology. Eisenmann captured a lady "human skeleton" in illustration 2.15. She is wearing a dress that reveals not her bust, but rather her gaunt condition. Some "human skeletons" were anorexic; most suffered from tuberculosis and other body-wasting diseases.

THE EXOTIC MODE

The aggrandized approach paraded the exhibits' alleged positive attributes: their talents, competence, superior status, and normal lifestyle. The exotic took the opposite tact. On show in the exotic photos were the exhibits' strange features and their alleged alien backgrounds.

The images of Maximo and Bartola, the "Last of the Aztecs," as in illustration 2.2, reveal an obvious exotic freak show presentation and one of the oldest. The fake story used to explain their appearance declared that the brother and sister were discovered by an American explorer in an ancient Aztec temple. The children, so the lie went, were on a temple alter being worshiped by the natives when the explorer spied them. What made the story plausible was that their elongated heads resembled those of the figures in stone reliefs that

of status went beyond just being above-average typical citizens. They took on airs and the titles of royalty and high society. This claim is captured and promoted in their many publicity photos. The Horvath Midgets also presented themselves in the high aggrandized mode. "The smallest People in the world" were photographed, as we see in illustration 2.13, decked out in formal attire—lavish gowns, jewelry, tuxedos, high hats, and medals.

Princess Wee Wee, a diminutive African American woman, appeared for ten years at Coney Island's Dreamland and in 1910 in the Barnum &

2.13. Mr. Horvath with his "midget troupe," ca. 1900. Photo by Frank Wendt. Cabinet card. Ronald G. Becker Collection of Charles Eisenmann Photographs, Special Collections Research Center, Syracuse University Library.

decorated Aztec ruins. As I have said, these early Aztec exhibits were not what they were alleged to be. A showman had lured them from their parents with a small cash payment and promises of forthcoming riches.

The "Last of the Aztecs" were not the last exhibit to appear on the freak show stage to make this claim. Their popularity spawned a long line of imitators, including Hutty and Tain, the "ancient Ethics" *(Ethics* was a corruption of the word *Aztec).* Shown in an Eisenmann photograph in illustration 2.16, the "Ethics" are wearing South American–style clothing and stand in front of a background that suggests the untamed outdoors.

The exhibition of people with developmental disabilities as Aztecs continued well into the twentieth century. In illustration 2.17, a circus pitchman is outside a tent in which two "Aztecs" were on exhibit. Note the sign on the stand: "The Aztecs from Mexico."

Two other postcards were sold in conjunction with the 1910 version of the "Ancient Aztecs" shown in illustration 2.16. One shows the "Aztecs" with their manager Max Klass (illus. 2.18). Their

PRINCESS WEE-WEE
Age 23 years. Weight 12 lbs.

2.14. Princess Wee-Wee, 1910. Printed postcard.

2.15. "Human Skeleton," ca. 1889. Photo by Charles Eisenmann. Cabinet card. Ronald G. Becker Collection of Charles Eisenmann Photographs, Special Collections Research Center, Syracuse University Library.

loose-fitting outer garments were meant to resemble Central American–style serapes, with the swastika used as a symbol of an ancient religion. When the picture was taken, they were traveling with the Sells-Floto Circus Sideshow.

Further into the twentieth century, the deceitful way of presenting people with microcephaly was recharged by another outrageous tale: that the people on exhibit were from head-binding tribes in Africa. A number of freak show exhibits feigning African origins went on the road, borrowing from *National Geographic* stories of certain African tribes that wrapped infants' heads tightly in cloth to make them elongated, supposedly an attractive attribute. In 1929, an enterprising showman

convinced the poor Memphis, Tennessee, parents of four young, developmentally disabled African American siblings with microcephaly to tour with a circus sideshow as "Iturian Pygmies from the Iturian Colony in darkest Africa." They were later labeled as "Pigmy's from Abbyssinnia," with a misspelling of both "Pygmies" and "Abyssinia," the former name for Ethiopia. Illustration 2.19 is a promotional photo postcard sold in conjunction with their appearance.

As the freak shows continued into the twentieth century, the pseudo-anthropological, scientific, and religious stories that framed the exhibits lost

2.16. "The Ancient Ethics," ca. 1890. Photo by Charles Eisenmann. Cabinet card. Ronald G. Becker Collection of Charles Eisenmann Photographs, Special Collections Research Center, Syracuse University Library.

their credibility, so showmen added a mocking comic dimension to the exotic presentations. In the late 1920s and 1930s, for example, Kiko and Sulu appeared in the combined Ringling Bros. and Barnum & Bailey sideshow as "Pinheads from Zanzibar." In one photo postcard, they are draped with animal skins, and their heads are shaved to leave only a small patch of hair on top (illus. 2.20). The sideshow manager, Clyde Ingalls, stands next to them smoking a cigar. Their over-the-top costumes were meant to add a ridiculous twist to what had become an obviously bogus presentation.

In another postcard of Kiko and Sulu, sold at the same time as the earlier one of them dressed in animal skins, they are photographed in a way that breaks with the exotic presentation (illus. 2.21). They are dressed in formal attire, clothes more appropriate for an aggrandized presentation than for an exotic motif.

This mocking depiction, where the exotic is mixed with the aggrandized, created a mode of presentation in which people with developmental disabilities were cast as comic fools. Dropping all exotic pretentions, the three developmentally disabled people with small heads in Tod Browning's film *Freaks* (1932) were pictured in typical childlike dress.

2.17. Outside talker for the exhibit "Aztecs from Mexico," 1910. Photo postcard. Joel Wayne, Pop's Postcards.

2.18. Max Klass, manager of a twentieth-century version of the "Ancient Aztecs," 1910. Photo postcard.

Not just people we would now call mentally retarded or developmentally disabled were presented in the exotic mode. Although people of small stature were most often presented in the aggrandized mode, physiology was not a strict determiner of presentation. Some dwarfs, especially achondroplasic dwarfs—whose body parts are disproportioned when compared to typical physiology—were often presented as exotics. Olof Krarer, shown in illustration 2.22, was dressed in furs and surrounded by fabricated icebergs, thus claiming an exotic background. The tale that accompanied her presentation was a cock-and-bull story (Bjornsdottir 2010). Although really born and raised in Iceland, she said she was a descendant of an ancient group of Danish colonists who were cut off from civilization in Greenland. In her tale, she was confined to an igloo during her childhood, and her diet consisted of raw meat, blood, and animal oils. The outrageous story went on: her family had been discovered by Icelandic shipwrecked sailors, and after a treacherous trip by sled dog she arrived in Iceland.

Other showpersons of short stature jumped on the Arctic bandwagon. Perhaps the best known was "Chief Debro, the Eskimo Midget," who was

2.19. "Pigmy's from Abyssinnia [sic]," ca. 1935. Photo postcard.

2.20. "Kiko and Sulu, Pinheads from Zanzibar," ca. 1935. Photo postcard.

2.21. Kiko and Sulu dressed up, ca. 1935. Photo postcard.

actually Frank Shade of Kendalville, Indiana. He appeared with his diminutive wife, Sarah, decked out in animal skins, their hair long and disheveled.

OTHER FORMS OF EXHIBITION

I have concentrated on the two most common ways of presenting people with disabilities in freak shows: aggrandized and exotic. Although these modes dominated freak photographs, there were others. As my discussion of the evolution of exotic presentations suggests, some exhibits were staged in a mocking mode. One body type in particular, rotund, was presented almost exclusively in a mocking mode. Going along with their stage

appearance, very obese women were photographed wearing dainty short dresses and in coy, flirtatious poses. Their stage names, which appeared in the photo captions, had a mocking ring: "Dainty Dotty," "Sweet Heart Susie," and "Baby Ruth."

CONCLUSION

Freak show photographic images were peddled as part of the flimflam presentation of people with disabilities to the public in various amusement world venues. Pity was not part of freak photography. Audience members were meant to buy the images as souvenirs to remember and advertise the show—for entertainment. The photo depictions of the exhibits were not pitched as donations to charity cases, nor were the exhibits presented as needy,

2.22. Olof Krarer, "The Little Esquimaux Lady," ca. 1890.
Cabinet photo card. Ronald G. Becker Collection of Charles
Eisenmann Photographs, Special Collections Research Center,
Syracuse University Library.

weak, and destitute. Quite the opposite: at least in
the aggrandized mode, exhibits were shown as and
often were better off financially than the people
who purchased their pictures.

3 Begging Cards
Solicitation with Photographs

3.1. John Rose, beggar in goat cart, ca. 1910. Photo postcard.

People with disablements have always been overrepresented in the ranks of beggars.[1] In many people's minds, begging goes hand in hand with disability. In some communities, so-called ugly laws prohibited disabled panhandlers from seeking alms. In other localities, they were more or less given free reign (Schweik 2009).[2] Many famous photographers have produced well-known portraits of people with handicapping conditions in the act of panhandling. Some of these photographs are icons of art photography,[3] but I do not

1. This overrepresentation is linked to a number of factors, including lack of other occupational opportunities, employer discrimination, and choice.

2. In the late nineteenth and early twentieth centuries, several cities adopted "unsightly beggar ordinances," also referred to as "ugly laws," to keep people with incapacities

from asking for handouts in public. Some of these laws remained on the books until the second half of the twentieth century (Garland-Thomson 2009, 72; Schweik 2009).

3. They include Jacob Riis's "Blind Beggar" (1888); P. Strand's "Blind Woman" (1916); A. Kertesz "Legless Man Selling Flowers" (1928); B. Shahn "Accordion Player" (undated); and Garry Winogrand's "American Legion Convention, Dallas, 1964" (1964) (see Marien 2006, 203, 346; Winogrand's photo is also discussed in chapter 9).

look at art museum photographs in this chapter, saving them for chapter 9. Here, I examine a genre of beggar photography that mendicants themselves used to raise money. The photo of John Rose in illustration 3.1 is an example.

Americans have always been distressed by people asking for a handout—in terms of both the abstract concept of seeking alms and the face-to-face encounter it involves. Beggars are an assault on capitalism in that they reveal that many people are unable to find gainful employment under that economic system. Especially in America, beggars are a contradiction of the belief that everyone should and can provide for themselves by working. These abstract considerations may contribute to visceral reactions to beggars and our resistance to contributing. Even though the beggar's physical act of soliciting can involve laborious effort and long hours in dangerous settings, most Americans do not think of panhandling as work or a legitimate vocation. Many citizens view all beggars as offensive, unworthy hustlers to one degree or another. They are often cast as "scroungers," "sponges," "freeloaders", "bums," and "moochers."

Begging on the street is more nerve racking to the person who is asked to give than to the solicitors. People are not used to being approached for a handout by a stranger, especially one with a demonstrable physical or mental anomaly (Goffman 1963). Out of fear, disdain, indifference, or the desire just to move on, many of those approached by beggars develop strategies designed to manage the encounter without forking over cash. Others are more sympathetic and deal differently with those looking for a handout. They establish rules for themselves about the interaction—criteria for whom to give to, under what conditions, and how much to give.

Beggars have their own ways of thinking about these encounters. Most beggars are experienced in confronting people. They have conventions to manage such meetings. Although some merely passively sit at their stations, others are more active. They size up potential benefactors, deciding whom to approach and what tactics to use. They realize the discomfort they may cause. They are also aware of the strategies their patrons use to avoid them and so develop their own methods of manipulation to increase their chances to score.[4]

Talking about beggars in the way I have, as manipulators, might offend some readers. I do not mean to single out beggars as operators. All people present themselves in strategic ways, especially in occupational roles (Goffman 1959). Not to acknowledge that people with disabilities manipulate the alms situation is paternalistic and denies them agency as well as their real connection to other human beings. Beggars' deceptions rely on some citizens' assumption that people with disabilities are too helpless, too nice, too disabled to be devious. My wary approach does not mean that I do not believe many people who beg are needy and use what they receive for real needs. The cat-and-mouse game between beggars and their potential benefactors is an interaction that has a deeply rooted history in our culture. Beggars' performances and scripts evolved in concert with Americans' values, and those patterns have been handed down through the generations. People learn how to beg—not necessarily through tutorials in an apprenticeship relationship with an experienced beggar, but sometimes in indirect ways such as watching from a distance, hearing people talk about beggars, and acquiring their own deep understanding of American norms and values.

BEGGING CARDS

For more than 150 years in the United States, beggars with disabilities have used photographs and printed pictures derived from photos as part of their solicitation schemes. Much less common today than a hundred years ago, beggars selling or

---

4. In some urban locations, beggars negotiate with each other for territory and share common understandings about acceptable tactics. Some are loosely tied to a street subculture.

giving away likenesses of themselves to potential marks was formerly a regular begging practice. Begging cards served solicitors as a way of making initial contact with people, engaging them in interaction, and pitching them their case. Presenting potential contributors with begging cards also created the pretense of an exchange, with the giver getting something in return for his or her contribution.[5] These images most often include captions or printed text on the back of the card describing the beggar's circumstance and making a case for a donation—the plea. The image and the pitch reinforced each other.

The images and accompanying text were typically distributed face to face on the street and in other public places. An alternate and an often more refined approach was for the beggar to send his or her image through the mail along with the request that money be returned via post. (For some, the mail approach was a way to circumvent antibegging ordinances and face-to-face confrontation.) In this chapter, I share some of these historical images and explore the embedded messages as well as the accompanying text.

I cover the period from approximately 1870 to 1930. In reviewing the visual material, I did not detect varying historical trends in how people presented themselves. That is, the beggar images remain similar throughout the period. Based on the evidence in my collection, the number of people with disabilities who used begging cards dropped off in the 1920s and 1930s. This decrease parallels the general decline in personal begging and the rise of charity organizations. Starting in the early decades of the twentieth century, formal charities opposed begging and campaigned to control and eliminate it (Schweik 2009, 41). In addition, they actively engaged in their own solicitations through charity fund drives. I explore these activities in chapter 4.

The pictures I display here were produced for the beggars by local commercial photographers or by small printing companies who used photos to create plates to print the images. The beggar was almost always an active participant in the production of the cards. Sometimes with a collaborator,[6] the beggar would present himself or herself to a photographer and describe how he or she wanted to appear. He or she would review the proofs, pick the one he or she thought was most appropriate, tell the photographer how many to produce, and wait a day or two to pick up the order.[7] The resulting images represented roughly how the beggar wanted to be presented.

In some localities, people with disabilities had a special claim to the role of beggar. Their physical or mental condition legitimated their asking for a handout. People without a disability would often feign impairment as a begging tactic (Schweik 2009, chaps. 3 and 5).[8] Some were so clever at their ruse that the deception is impossible to detect in photographs. For the images in this chapter, I have no way of knowing whether the people depicted were frauds or authentic—that is, with real disablements. Whether beggars were truly disabled or impostors did not change the way they appeared on their cards. Both groups shared the strategies

5. In some municipalities, selling begging cards made beggars eligible for peddler licenses, which then legalized their activity.

6. Some beggars were assisted by family members or associates, including people who served as their managers.

7. There are two main types of images: images printed on printing presses from plates made using original photographs and real photos printed from negatives directly on photographic paper. Because of the expense of making the initial print, the former were printed in large numbers. The real photos were usually done in smaller runs.

8. Early films often used a seeing person posing as a blind beggar as a source of humor. In one of the earliest, *Fake Beggar* (1898), a man with a sign "Help the Blind" quickly reaches down to pick up a coin that landed on the floor after missing the cup. A similar routine has been present in films to the present day (Norden 1994, 14).

and forms of presentation that would induce giving. The issue of fraud is complicated.[9] Just as people who were relatively healthy and unimpaired faked disabilities, people with actual impairments sometimes fabricated stories about themselves and posed in deceptive ways. The latter exaggerated the nature and the extent of their condition and told lies about how they became disabled and about what they planned to do with the donations. They carried crutches and wore bandages or eye patches or other accessories even when they did not need them. In one sense, all beggars shared a degree of fraud. It was the degree of deception that separated the liar from the deceitful.

PITY

Chapter 2 focused on freak portraits and the motivation behind their production: to supplement the freaks' income, to publicize exhibits, and to render the freaks inviting to the public. Whether in the aggrandized mode or in the exotic, the people photographed were cast in a way that would advance curiosity, wonder, and amusement. In the hundreds of freak photos I have studied, none seems to hint that the viewer should pity the person in the picture or buy the image as an act of charity to contribute to the person's livelihood.

Begging images are quite different. They typically parade helplessness and call for pity. Although there are minor exceptions, the beggars did not brag of competence, as in the aggrandized photos; they instead claimed that they were dependent and posed in ways to appear so. The aim was to appear needy and grim and to ask directly or indirectly for alms.

Harry T. Petry's begging card in illustration 3.2 is a striking example of the pity approach to

..Harry T. Petry..
AM PERFECTLY HELPLESS.
MY LEGS ARE BOTH OFF ABOVE
THE KNEES AND HAVE TO
BE FED LIKE A BABY.

THIS IS THE ONLY WAY I
HAVE TO MAKE A LIVING

3.2. "Harry Petry . . . Am perfectly helpless," ca. 1926. Printed postcard.

begging. Given the card's small size, two and a half by four and a half inches, and the absence of an address to send funds to, Petry probably handed it out to passersby on the street.

Petry is sitting in a wheelchair in the picture. His face and posture convey gloom. The image effuses misfortune, or at least the message on the card asks the viewer to draw the conclusion: "AM PERFECTLY HELPLESS. MY LEGS ARE BOTH OFF ABOVE THE KNEES AND HAVE TO BE FED LIKE A BABY." As with most images of beggars, Petry appears well groomed and wears clean clothes. His

9. In their relationship, beggars with disabilities and nondisabled people ranged from street colleagues to adversaries (Schweik 2009, 5).

attire is arranged to display his missing legs and dysfunctional arms.[10]

The image of Petry is constructed to support the assertion at the bottom of the card: "THIS IS THE ONLY WAY I HAVE TO MAKE A LIVING." On the back of the card is additional text. "Good Luck to the Purchaser of this Card. . . . Please Give What You Wish." These words, along with the earlier reference to "making a living," are significant because they embody a begging strategy. Note the use of the word *purchase,* which normally means a real exchange of goods or services for money. Petry also uses the word *give.* The card thus creates ambiguity regarding whether he is merchant or panhandler.[11] Or, to put it another way, the appeal for charity is finessed by the idea that the giver is receiving an object, the picture of Petry, in return. Further, Petry's begging is cast in the language usually reserved for people who are employed—"make a living."

In small print on the back of his card, Petry offers a poem that captures his misery:

I was once happy, the same as you;
But now I'm a cripple and nothing can do.
I am compelled to ask strangers some
    assistance to give,
So please give me something—"Live and Let
    Live."
I pray God will reward you, my wants you
    will relieve,
And remember it is more blessed to give than
    receive.

Petry's verse adds another element to the exchange; he is giving away or selling his poetry. To top it off, he offers a religious justification for giving: God will reward those who give to the less fortunate.

10. Although Petry does not describe his condition in detail, his comments suggest that he, in addition to being legless, does not have use of his arms.

11. In some locations, begging was illegal, but peddling was not, which may in part explain some of the duel presentations.

And in general, Petry's presentation embodies many aspects of the visual and verbal pity rhetoric that was a standard part of begging cards.

RELIGION

Petry's reference to Christian charity is not unusual; religion was often evoked in beggars' cards. In an early example (illus. 3.3), a *carte de visite* photograph from 1875, Nathan P. Van Luvanee assumes a sympathetic pose in his wooden wheelchair. He is touching a Bible.

The text printed on the back of the card is too long to include in its entirety here, but a summary of the relevant parts emphasizes the subject's religiosity. The text is not by Van Luvanee; it is

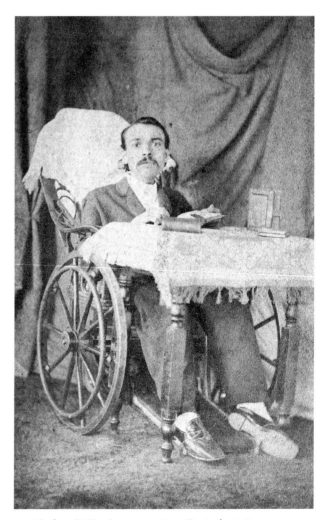

3.3. Nathan P. Van Luvanee, 1875. *Carte de visite.*

a testimonial allegedly written by his pastor. We are told that Van Luvanee was born in 1848 and became a "helpless invalid" when he was fifteen years old. In 1871, he was "blessedly converted" to the Lord and at the time of the picture, 1875, was "constantly and sweetly resting in Jesus."

Some people were leery of beggars, suspecting that they were not what they claimed to be, but impostors rather than the afflicted.[12] Van Luvanee's approach was to deal with that concern directly by having a minister testify for him. The message from the minister ends with the following backing: "I have known him for more than two years. He is a faithful and devoted Christian and a true follower of Jesus, whose blood cleanses from all sin." The choice of the minister to vouch for Van Luvanee was tactical of course. It is difficult to dismiss a minister as a liar. Further, a viewer might hesitate to think that Luvanee composed the statement himself, which he might well have done.

Beggars made use of the charity sentiments embedded in Judeo-Christian text and tradition, including "I am my brother's keeper." They regularly called upon or fabricated statements by ministers and other church authorities to bolster their claims. But one never knows whether the religious vouchers were heartfelt messages from authentic religious people or fraudulent fabrications devised to grease the flow of money.

FAMILY

Another unhappy soul, A. Souslin, appears on a printed postcard begging card in illustration 3.4. His back and neck brace is clearly visible in the picture. His address is given at the bottom, presumably so that people could mail in donations.

Souslin's card illustrates a number of additional begging strategies. He employs his family to evoke

THEIR ONLY SUPPORT

Neck broken October 23, 1906, while decorating new office building, N. C. R., Dayton, Ohio. Was stooped over in the act of removing rubbish, plank fell striking edgewise on back of neck.

A. Souslin, 2530 W. Third St., Dayton, Ohio

3.4. A. Souslin, "Their only support," ca. 1908. Printed postcard.

sympathy for his plight. Notice the stoic look on Mrs. Souslin's face and the child's somber gaze. Souslin takes on the persona of someone in distress. The phrase that appears at the bottom of the card, "THEIR ONLY SUPPORT," has a double meaning: in his role of father provider, Souslin was the sole support of his family, but now begging is the only way for them to survive. Note how this pitch is different from the intent of freak family images in the previous chapter. In the latter, families were included to normalize and enhance the disabled person's status; in the former, they were used as a ploy to provoke sympathy.

Souslin used another begging card as well (illus. 3.5). In it, he features his two-year-old son, Marion.

12. See Norden 1994, chap. 1, for a discussion of disability fraud in early movies.

WILL PAPA EVER BE ABLE TO BUY ME ANY MORE TOYS?

Only a boy with his noise and fun,
One of the veriest mysteries under the sun,
Who troubles his neighbors' dogs and cats;
Tears more clothes, spoils more hats,
Loses more tops, kites and bats
Than would stock a store for a year or more.

Marion G. Souslin, age, 2 years, 7 months; weight, 51 pounds. Son of A. Souslin, who was so unfortunate as to get his neck broken October 23rd, 1906, while decorating the new N. C. R. office building, Dayton, Ohio.
A. SOUSLIN, 2530 W. THIRD ST., DAYTON, OHIO.

3.5. Marion Souslin, ca. 1908. Printed postcard.

The boy is holding a baseball bat and is surrounded by toys. The lead line in the caption is: "WILL PAPA EVER BE ABLE TO BUY ME ANY MORE TOYS?" The maudlin plea is a graphic illustration of the use of family as central to the beggar's appeal, but, strangely, what the boy is concerned about seems rather insignificant—toys, extravagant when compared with the basics, food and shelter.

The text of the first Souslin card, showing the whole family, also reads: "Neck broken October 23, 1906, while decorating new office building, N. C. R. Dayton, Ohio. Was stooped over in the act of removing rubbish, plank fell striking edgewise on the back of neck." The specificity of the account adds detail and compelling credibility to

the narrative, but it also introduces another theme prevalent in many begging cards: the beggar was formerly a hard worker who had been actively engaged in making a living but now, owing to no fault of his own, he cannot work—making him one of the deserving poor.

All my examples of begging cards have so far featured adult men as solicitors. Men were disproportionately represented among those who employed begging cards, but women also used them and engaged in the same tactics men did. The woman in illustration 3.6, who is allegedly sightless, included a young child, presumably her own, in her photographic handout. In the text, the beggar tells of her plight. She does not provide the

3.6. Blind woman with child, ca. 1907. Photo postcard.

details of her disability but rather relies on prose and a religious appeal: "As you behold the light of day think of me who is blind / I need your prayers as well as your support / I come too in Jesus name turn me not away."

As the previous two examples indicate, adult beggars' appeals to potential donors often involved children, thus indicating that giving to the beggar would result in benefits to his or her children. The only example I found of the image of a child with an alleged disability who is soliciting funds for his or her own welfare is the case of George Harton, shown in illustration 3.7. The caption on this photo postcard, from around 1907, declares that George is "a cripple for life" and that he is asking for money to "help me school myself." The boy

shows no visible evidence of being disabled aside from the crutches that are apparently supporting him. This begging card raises suspicion and questions about what viewers of the time were really witnessing. Was it a scam? Who was behind this boy's presentation? To whom was the money raised actually going?

As we shall see in the next chapter, although depictions of children with disabilities seeking funds for their own welfare are almost absent in begging cards, children dominate the imagery in charity drives by philanthropic organizations.

NO FAULT OF THEIR OWN

The begging card of Theordore Peters (illus. 3.8) has a presentation that is similar to Souslin's in that it emphasizes that Peters would work if he could and that resorting to begging is no fault of his own. It uses the phrase "Wonder of the World," but the meaning is decidedly different from its use in freak shows; Theordore Peters is presented as a hero.

According to the text, Peters was a union iron worker who fell 350 feet into a river when he tried to save a coworker's life. We are also told that his wife died from shock after hearing about her husband's injuries. She left five children. The recipient of the begging card is asked: "PLEASE BUY ONE OF MY CARDS."

Illustration 3.9 provides another example of an injured worker's begging card. Barney Brooks poses here with his family in his solicitation card. The appeal is less colorful. The portrait is well composed, and were it not for the message printed on the back and the uniformly sad faces, one would think the photo was just a family picture produced for inclusion in the family album. (I take up family or citizen pictures in chapter 10.)

Mr. Brooks, however, makes a special appeal to fellow workers: "Would you kindly help a brother who has had misfortune to lose the power of his limbs by falling from an electric pole[?] I am a lineman and will appreciate any thing you give or buy." Although the ambiguous "give or buy"

3.7. "George Harton, Cripple for Life," ca. 1907. Photo postcard.

Wonder of the World
NECK IS BROKEN

THEORDORE WILLIAM PETERS
Structural Union Iron Worker
Local No. 16; Baltimore, Md.
Tried to save a fellow-workingman's life and fell 350 feet into the St. Lawrence River, Quebec, Canada; ninety of his fellow-workmen were killed. His wife died from the shock, leaving five orphan children.

PLEASE BUY ONE OF MY CARDS.

3.8. Theordore Peters, ca. 1914. Printed card.

3.9. Barney Brooks, ca. 1909. Photo postcard.

seems to be an appeal to a specific audience, fellow workers, Brooks's address is included at the end of the message, suggesting that he might have been soliciting in general through the mail.

"NOT LICKED YET"

Beggars extensively used the presentation of a down-and-out, helpless condition, but, probably realizing the limitations of this depressing and downbeat appeal, some of them also added a positive element to their plea. In the 1920s, Mr. George Washington had a "keep your sunny side up" avowal (illus. 3.10).[13]

The basics of the picture are the same as others we have examined. Washington looks cheerless, is clean and respectably dressed, and has a disability: a missing lower left leg and mangled right leg are prominently displayed. In the first sentence of the text, he tells us of his plight: "40 Years Since I Have Walked," but in a turn of tactic he states: "But Not Licked Yet: Anyone Can Quit." Not Washington, though. He goes on:

> From the minute we are born
> Until we ride in a hearse
> No matter what ails us
> It might be worse
> *"Keep smiling and Trying"*

13. His name is given on the back side of the card, and he makes no connection between his own name and that of the first president of the United States.

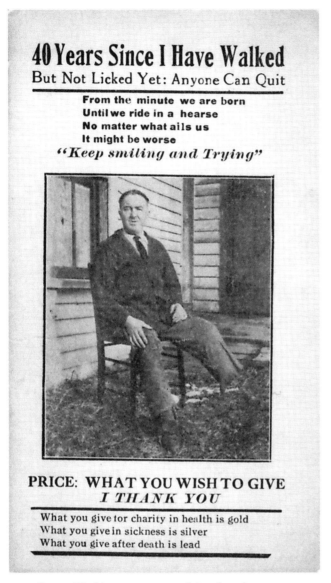

40 Years Since I Have Walked
But Not Licked Yet: Anyone Can Quit

From the minute we are born
Until we ride in a hearse
No matter what ails us
It might be worse
"Keep smiling and Trying"

PRICE: WHAT YOU WISH TO GIVE
I THANK YOU

What you give for charity in health is gold
What you give in sickness is silver
What you give after death is lead

3.10. George Washington, ca. 1924. Printed card.

Washington's overtly buoyant message is more positive and direct than one typically finds on begging cards, but there many examples of others who use a less understated version of the message "not licked yet."

VETERANS' BEGGING CARDS

As far back as the Revolutionary War, veterans who were injured in service to their country received pensions and were some of the first people with disabilities to receive government services. Even so, some former soldiers who were mutilated chose or

had to resort to begging as a method of support. The number of those who chose to beg with the assistance of photographic images was apparently small; I came across only two in my research.

The oldest veteran begging card I found is of two Civil War amputees (illus. 3.11). One has a war medal pinned to his lapel and grasps a large American flag with his remaining hand, and the other holds a gun. The flag and the medal are part of the solicitation's appeal. They remind the potential donor that these men served their country and should be rewarded with a contribution. At the bottom of the card is the hand-written notation

3.11. Civil war veterans' begging card, ca. 1869. *Carte de visite.* Joel Wayne, Pop's Postcards.

"25 cents," which suggests it was distributed as a begging card.

The second veteran begging card I came across shows Captain Lewis Satterfield, who was wounded in World War I. In the card, which I found in the Harvard Medical School Library, he flaunts his military service and appeals to people's patriotism in his solicitation. He is pictured in his uniform. On the back is a poem about his war experience. In the text, he presents himself as a "Disabled Veteran of World's War, making his way by the sale of a ballad."

QUASI-ARTISTS AND PERFORMERS

The beggars who declared themselves to be artists or entertainers used a less overt positive presentation. In that role, the person asking for a handout was not merely a panhandler; he or she was engaged in a productive activity, creating art or playing a musical instrument. The disability was central to the request for money, but the begging was accompanied by evidence of being productive.

Take the case of Daniel Rose, a man with cerebral palsy pictured in his home in Johnstown, Pennsylvania (illus. 3.12). The image shows examples of his whittling. Rose most likely distributed "The Expert Whittler" postcards through the mail as well as when people visited his home to see his carvings—miniature cars, houses, and other objects he created out of wood. The objects he allegedly created were special not because of their exceptional quality, but because they were produced by a person with a demonstrable disability. The display and sale of pedestrian self-made objects showed that Rose and others who engaged in such crafts were trying to make a living for themselves, not just sitting around begging.

Rose was featured in a number of different postcards. In a photo postcard, illustration 3.13, he is shown with a woman he claims is his twin sister in the text in the back of the card. He makes no mention of his whittling in this card, and it appears to be a begging card stripped of his claims to being an artist.

Although I have been rather skeptical regarding the artistry of Daniel Rose's whittling, in the second half of the twentieth century a form of art referred to as "outsider art" became popular and

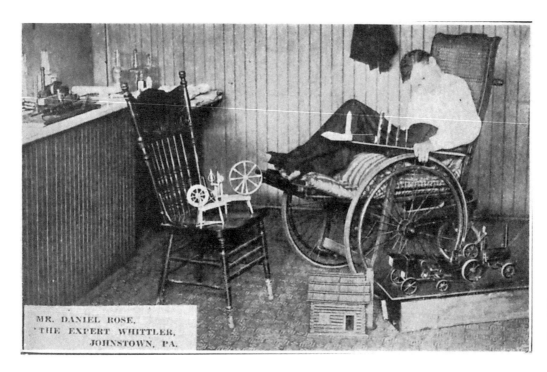

MR. DANIEL ROSE,
THE EXPERT WHITTLER,
JOHNSTOWN, PA.

3.12. Daniel Rose, "Expert Whittler," ca. 1925. Printed postcard.

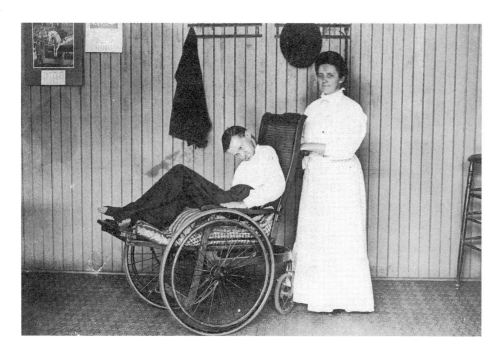

3.13. Daniel Rose in a wheelchair with his sister, ca. 1925. Photo postcard. B. Nelson Collection.

collectible and made headway in being accepted as part of the establishment art world (Becker 1982; Fine 2004). Artwork by people with various physical and mental disabilities who had no formal art training as well as work by those with unconventional lifestyles found an audience and began selling for high prices. Some of these artists started as local oddities, and some of them, like Rose, were beggars. They were "found" and championed by dealers and collectors and were lifted to the status of artist (Fine 2004). Although this transformation from beggar to artist is uncommon, its occurrence reminds us that people with disabilities can and do have careers; they do not necessarily remain in the same role all their lives. Beggars become artists or move on to some other status. For most, begging is not a lifetime pursuit. It can be seasonal or just one of the many roles a person fills during the course of his or her life.

In the studio portrait in illustration 3.14, a photo postcard of a blind beggar provides another example of the mixing of begging and artist performance. The person pictured here apparently distributed this card to pedestrians as he played his harmonica and dulcimer. Although the

3.14. Man with a sign, "Please Help the Blind," ca. 1908. Photo postcard.

image seems bleak, and the sign around his neck, "PLEASE HELP THE BLIND," indicates he was a beggar, the fact that he also played musical instruments puts him in another league of beggar—that of the street performer.

Street entertainers solicit money just as beggars do. We do not know how talented the person in illustration 3.14 was or what the quality of his performances was, but even if he were a terrible musician, the fact that he was doing something in addition to asking for a handout put him in a different league of beggars. The beggar as performer was more active and probably seen more favorably than the run-of-the-mill beggar. Performance was another form of the assertion "But not licked yet."

3.15. "W. C. Williams One Arm One Man Band," ca. 1914. Printed postcard.

In the case of the blind man with a harmonica, the begging aspect is clear. He has a sign around his neck asking for help. In another card, however, distributed by W. C. Williams, the balance between musician and beggar is less clear (illus. 3.15). Mr. Williams is dressed in a band uniform and is surrounded by an array of musical instruments. The caption identifies him as a "ONE ARM ONE MAN BAND." It is difficult to place Williams in the world of beggars. Typical of begging cards, Williams's address is included in the caption. Not a circus sideshow performer, not a legitimate musician, Williams was likely a beggar with a twist, a novelty act whose music brought him attention, which in turn brought donations not least because of his self-help attitude.

ON THE ROAD

Another genre of begging images demonstrates that some beggars with disabilities were willing literally to go the extra mile to enhance their fund-raising success. Richard E. New, the "Legless Motor Cycle Rider," is a flamboyant example (illus. 3.16). Originally from Akron, Ohio, Mr. New traveled about the country at the beginning of the twentieth century collecting money in a vehicle made especially for him in order to support his roving lifestyle. A small insert of him on the postcard displays stumps where once there were legs. The lettering on the side of the cycle brags that he had driven "TWICE ACROSS THE GREAT AMERICAN DESERT," presumably the Great Basin Desert, located primarily in Nevada. A portion of the text reveals that New met his expenses by selling photographs of himself according to a system we have seen before: "Price. What You Choose."

The first illustration shown in this chapter is another postcard of a legless man who used pictures of himself to beg. Rather than getting about on a motorized vehicle, however, he employed a goat cart to accomplish his travel. The sign next to him reads: "Dear Friend, My name is John Rose driver of the only goat team in the world pulling 475 lbs averaging 16 miles per day. I was crippled

3.16. Richard New, ca. 1914. Printed postcard.

3.17. L. J. Bogart, ca. 1912. Photo postcard.

in a R. R. wreck 12 yrs. ago. Someone Help Me." By handing their begging cards to passersby, John Rose and Richard New solicited money as they traveled about the country.

L. J. Bogart, a legless eighteen-year-old, solicited donations with his photo postcards as he traveled by covered wagon and goat team "FROM JUDSONIA ARK. TO LIMA OHIO" (illus. 3.17). Like New's approach, Bogart's appeal to the potential giver asserts that he is not a lazy beggar; he is on the move, creating and completing challenges to show his spirit and willingness to go the extra mile.

Goats were not the only draft animal people with disabilities used to promote their solicitation.

3.18. Max Engel and his dog,
Carlo, ca. 1895. Cabinet card.

3.19. Fred Vaillancourt, ca. 1907. Photo
postcard.

One of the oldest images I have come across of beggars going the extra mile in pursuit of donations is that of Max Engel of Buffalo, New York. In 1890, after a railroad accident that left him legless, Engel hitched his dog, Carlo, to a handmade rig and set off begging.[14] Engel sold the likeness of himself in his travels (illus. 3.18). Stamped on the back of the photo taken in Buffalo is a message from Engel stating that he has been on the road for five years and is on his way to New York City. In the picture, Engel is well dressed and has wooden blocks strapped to his hands to increase his mobility.

Fred Vaillancourt, shown in illustration 3.19, was a former railroad breakman who also lost his legs in a train accident. He traveled about the country in a rig pulled by two dogs. Vaillancourt distributed a variety of photo postcard portraits in his travels. Illustration 3.19 is one of eight different images I have seen of him and his dog team.

14. For a discussion of disability and railroad workers, see Williams-Searle 2001.

These travelers' begging strategy was to show visually that they were willing to go to great lengths to make a living. Given the high number of postcards available today in the antique postcard market that document beggars with disabilities touring in both motorized and animal-driven vehicles, this method of solicitation was apparently quite common.

BEGGAR MERCHANTS

I discussed earlier how distributing images set up a quasi–exchange relationship that resulted in a more subtle form of begging. Images were not the only items beggars gave out or sold. Cards with printed prayers and inexpensive items such as pencils were offered to passersby. Milton Clewell, a man who claimed that he could not walk owing to an injury to his spine, used the card in illustration 3.20 to solicit funds during the holiday season. He sent out his "Wishing you a Merry Christmas and a Happy New Year" card with a return envelope enclosed to encourage donations. Rather than give away an object of dubious value, he also sent an inexpensive knife. The card states that he is selling the knife. The price was the familiar "What You Wish to Give." Note how, in addition to the selling ploy, Mr. Clewell notes a specific need he has: his wheelchair needs repair. An aspect of the picture that is unique among the begging cards I have seen is the presence of Clewell's dog. At the bottom of the card, he reminds the card's recipient: "KEEP SMILING."

In the early 1930s, Homer Minor of Plainview, Texas, used a tactic similar to Clewell's in soliciting funds. He mailed a box of engraved Christmas cards to potential donors and asked that they either send a dollar or return the cards in a self-addressed, stamped envelope. He waited a week and then sent a follow-up postcard asking the recipient if he had received the package and urging him to send the money or the cards so that his account could be settled. In the message, he suggests that the recipient buy more cards and sell them to others. Minor

3.20. Milton Clewell, Merry Christmas card, ca. 1924. Printed card.

does not mention his disability in the text, but on the address side of the card there is a picture of him sitting in a wheelchair with his proportionately small legs tucked in close to his body.

Besides offering marginal gifts, people with disabilities also offered real products—items sold in stores and available from other merchants. Some of these sellers with a disability acted as any merchant would, but others promoted their wares by emphasizing their disability and suggesting that buying from them had added value–charity. They typically priced their items higher than other sellers, trading on the buyer's sympathy as their promotional technique.

One of the earliest examples I found of this approach, from around 1875, included a photograph of L. D. Sine and a message on the back telling the reader that Mr. Sine had lost his sight in 1851 and had started his own business, "Gift Enterprises," soon thereafter (illus. 3.21). The message is not clear about what Mr. Sine is selling, but it encourages people to send for a circular with a full list of items and prices. Interestingly, the printed message in the back is in the third person, suggesting that another party might have been involved in the promotion of the business.

Another ambiguous beggar card shows L. W. Prettyman, the "Shut-in-Magazine Man," who appears to be selling a product: subscriptions to magazines (illus. 3.22). Though a real merchant, he

uses pity and other begging strategies to improve his market position. Prettyman's approach is that of an aggressive salesperson: "Yes, its [sic] a fight— a fight against disease, pain, and COMPETITORS. In my condition the fight seems unusually hard. I must win, for I have to earn my own living. Will YOU help me win? Help me to succeed. You can by sending me each and every one of YOUR magazine and newspaper subscriptions." On the back of his postcard, he notes that his subscription sales are "our only means of support, both mother and I."

Illustration 3.23 shows the card distributed by a John Concilio, who, from the text on the back of the card, appears to have been very self-conscious of the distinction between being a beggar and being a merchant. His pitch contains many of the elements of finessed begging mentioned earlier, but with twists and contradictions. The picture shows a well-dressed man striking a pose as an organ grinder, a person who hauls around a mechanical musical instrument that produces tunes when the operator turns a crank. In this case, the large organ is ornate and mounted on wheels. Organ grinders were often immigrants and were common on streets in the United States through the first third of the twentieth century. These itinerant street people would solicit money by holding out a cup or hat to encourage donations. The solicitor would sometimes be accompanied by a monkey who did tricks and held the cup.

What about Mr. Concilio? The back of his card shows the headline sentence: "This Man Does not Play for Money But Gives Full Value For Contributions." The text states emphatically, "He is not playing for pennies but gives full value for any donations. For 35¢ he gives you one of the latest and most popular song books containing 181 of the most popular songs." The text goes on to say that he lost the use of his right leg and has been crippled for forty-nine years. Although he offers little detail, even which leg he is talking about, he mentions that he recently broke his leg and was "laid up" for two months, during which time he "lost everything he had." Finally, he states that any

3.21. L. D. Sine, "Gift Enterprises," ca. 1869. *Carte de visite.*

3.22. "L. W. Prettyman, Shut-in-Magazine Man," ca. 1920. Printed advertisement card.

3.23. John Concilio, organ grinder, ca. 1911. Printed card.

donation will be used for the support of his family—his wife and two small children—and himself.

Sound familiar? His presentation contains many of the themes we have already discussed. Unlike the presentation on other begging cards, however, on his card Concilio does not show his alleged disability. He must certainly want the viewer to think it is hidden behind the hand organ. There apparently are other elements of deception in Concilio's presentation.

Illustration 3.23 is one of two cards I have that Concilio used. Both cards seem to have been distributed around 1911 and have similar text in the back. But the second card gives a Dubuque, Iowa, address rather than the La Crosse, Wisconsin, location given on the first. No mention is made in the second card of his having a family. In the second card, he states that he is an amputee, whereas the first says he lost the use of his right leg. The second card states that he has been crippled for twenty-six years, but the first states that it has been forty-six years. The disparity between the two pitches is so blatant that the story on one or both is obviously contrived.

I end this chapter with an image that illustrates that the line between begging and regular commerce

3.24. Billy McGogan, peanut vendor, ca. 1910. Photo postcard.

was fuzzy. Billy McGogan traveled around White Cloud, Minnesota, selling candy, popcorn, peanuts, cigars, and postcards. The postcards show him sitting in his goat-drawn mobile store. In the picture, he is nicely dressed, wearing a straw hat, and parked in front of his favorite haunt, the railroad station where he would meet the trains and sell to travelers.

McGogan was an entrepreneurial beggar who had lost the use of his legs early in his life when he was shot by a local farmer while attempting to steal chickens. As the book's conclusion indicates, many people with disabilities had the status of local characters—that is, they were widely known in a particular geographic area for their peculiar behavior and lifestyle. McGogan filled that role in his town and capitalized on his notoriety by selling postcards and other goods.

CONCLUSION

Certain messages are repeatedly conveyed in these begging images and the accompanying prose. Beggars' presentations of the period covered were rooted in centuries-old British laws that

distinguish between the worthy poor and those not deserving charity (Katz 1990, 1996). According to this distinction, the worthy poor want to fend for themselves but cannot. The unworthy are slackers, people who are too lazy to do the hard work of supporting themselves. We show pity for the worthy by providing charity and contempt for the unworthy by requiring that they take care of themselves or be punished. Beggars pitched their appeals with knowledge of these sentiments and so worked to establish themselves as worthy.

In addition to the worthy/unworthy distinction, beggar imagery was laced with ideas of rugged individualism and American capitalism. Aspects of the begging lineup included quasi-entrepreneurial exchanges and upbeat salesmanship. Beggars approached their task with an understanding of the Christian imperative for charity. "Give to the least of us" was translated into "Make yourself look as needy as you can." Promote pity, and people will respond. One particularly effective approach in this appeal was to include dependent children.

As the United States moved into the twentieth century, organized charities laid claim to being the respectable and wise collectors and distributors

of funds for the needy. Professional social workers came to guide charity organizations, claiming that they could best separate the worthy from
the unworthy and tend to the needy in ways that
would lead them out of poverty. Social workers
undermined the freelance beggars' appeal because
people felt more comfortable giving to an organized group in the business of charity than dealing
with beggars who approached them in the street.

4 Charity
The Poster Child and Others

4.1. Kenny Foundation poster child, ca. 1947. Printed postcard.

organizations, but charities increasingly turned to fund-raising. At first, they relied primarily on gifts from the well-to-do, but as the middle class grew, charities launched widespread campaigns designed to appeal to the general public.[1] In this chapter, I look at how disability-related organizations used photography in these fund-raising drives.

Charity campaigns featuring disability became so ubiquitous as the twentieth century progressed that it is impossible to cover the variety and extent of the publicity that was produced. Many charities became national organizations with branches across the country. Each branch participated in both the national and local fund-raising campaigns for their own chapter. In most cases, a percentage of what the branch raised went to the national organization, and the rest remained with the local. Some charities were affiliated with a local group that had no national organization, and there were regional charity organizations. Masonic organizations such as the Shriners and the Elks focused on children with disabilities and engaged in rigorous fund-raising, too.

Further enlarging the fund-raising pool were organizations such as the Community Chest that were established to coordinate services and

During the second half of the nineteenth and continuing into the early years of the twentieth century, organizations whose goal was either to serve people with disabilities or to prevent disability or both prospered, grew, and proliferated. Religious institutions supported some of these

1. Some of the earliest charity fund-raising involved providing for Civil War soldiers who were injured during the war. In 1917, giving was sanctioned by the US government, when charitable gifts were made a tax deduction. For a general history of philanthropy in the United States, see Bremner 1988.

fund-raising in communities across the country.[2] The Community Chest, later called the United Way, was effective in tapping funds from corporations and in getting corporations to sponsor fund-raising among their employees with the offer of matching funds. By 1948, one thousand communities had United Way–type organizations. With the growth of advertising agencies, charity organizations increasingly relied on marketing companies to design their appeals.

Year-round fund-raising was typical, but certain charities concentrated their efforts at particular seasons of the year. The National Lung Association Drive begun in 1907 and keyed its drive around the Christmas holiday season and the sale of Christmas Seals. The March of Dimes major fund drive was during the month of January to coincide with the birth date of Franklin Delano Roosevelt, founder of the organization. Labor Day weekend became the time for the Muscular Dystrophy Association Telethon.[3]

CHARITY IMAGERY

Begging versus Fund-Raising

The images used in early disability charity fund-raising were similar to those employed in begging

cards. Both featured real people, individuals to whom potential donors could relate. Many charity campaigns employed pity as their major draw. Some were heavily laced with religious themes.

The similarities can be seen in the 1909 fund-raising postcard shown in illustration 4.2, produced and distributed by the Good Shepherd's Home in Allentown, Pennsylvania, as part of its campaign to support a residential facility for "crippled orphans." It features two well-dressed boys using crutches. The message on the card emphasizes that the crippled children served are the neediest, yet they are the very ones other orphanages turn away. They are "too much trouble" for other facilities "to take care of and exercise." The text makes its appeal by evoking the Lord and using phrases from the Bible.

As America moved into the twentieth century, crucial and deliberate differences emerged between begging cards and disability charity pictures with regard to who was pictured, how they were depicted, and the nature of the appeal. I address most of these differences later in the chapter, but two overriding distinctions should be clarified up front. With begging cards, the person pictured was the same individual who directly received the donation. In charity campaigns, the people depicted, sometimes in groups and other times alone, were soliciting for the organization's clients in general or a particular category of people with disabilities—"crippled children," for example. In other words, the people pictured stood for the charity; they were symbols or icons. Crucial for the designers of charity campaigns was choosing the right people to feature. The ones they chose were quite different from the individuals who appeared in begging cards. Also, children as opposed to adults were most often featured in charity drives, whereas adults dominated begging cards.

Begging cards had limited distribution; charity solicitation pictorials found a larger audience. Although the latter did sometimes appear on postcards and other handouts, they more commonly appeared on posters, on collecting cans, in

2. The United Way had its beginnings in 1887 in Denver, Colorado, where church leaders began the Charity Organization Society, which coordinated services and fund-raising for twenty-two agencies. The first Community Chest was founded in 1913 in Cleveland, Ohio, and that organization served as a model for "federated giving." The number of Community Chest organizations in the United States increased from 39 to 353 between 1919 and 1929 and had surpassed 1,000 by 1948. By 1963, the name "United Way" was adopted, but not everyone chose to use it. In 1970, the organization was renamed the United Way of America. In 2007, United Way of America was the largest charity in the United States, with 1,285 local branches reporting more than $4.2 billion in contributions, a 2.2 percent increase over 2006.

3. The Muscular Dystrophy Association campaign originated in the 1950s, but it did not become a national phenomenon until 1966.

DEAR FRIEND :—

If we cannot heal the crippled Orphans, and give them new limbs in answer to our prayers, we can at least give evidence of our heavenly birth, and in His name, provide a home for them If we do not help them where we can, we would not heal them if we could. Did you ever think of the fact that all our Orphanages are closed for the most needy, the crippled Orphans. The reason for this we are told is because they make too much trouble. care and expense. Is the fact that they are so needy any proof why they should not be taken? What is your answer? We answer ten thousand times no. The Lord's blessing is often in proportion to our sacrifice. our faith and our willingness to do His will.

Anniversary on Donation Day. Saturday. October 2nd. 1909.

Post Card

The MASTER'S CARE.

4.2. Fund-raising postcard for orphanage for "crippled children," Allentown, Pennsylvania, 1909. Printed postcard.

magazines and newspapers, and in privately published booklets as well as on other forms of ephemera (see Hevey 1992; Garland-Thomson 2009). Charity images were more prolific than any other genre of disability representation.

New charity imagery emerged starting in the 1930s. Relying on the rapidly evolving Madison Avenue advertising techniques, one image, the poster child, came to dominate.

The Poster Child

The most popular approach to charity fund-raising after 1940 was the poster child.[4] The phrase *poster child* refers to a child with a disease or disability whose picture was used on posters and other media in the campaign for a particular charity to encourage people to give.[5] Adults, with the exception of veterans, were underrepresented as charity

symbols. The use of children was pervasive even when the specific condition the funds were being raised for was predominately an adult impairment—for instance, in blindness and even arthritis campaigns (Scott 1969). Although the United Way represented organizations that serve people of all ages, the most common images in its fund-raising were of the child with a disability. Using children in their appeals, charity promoters believed, would be a most effective money-raising strategy.

Illustration 4.1 is the personification of the poster child approach. The lovely girl on the card leaves her crutches behind as she walks on her own after being treated at an Elizabeth Kenny Foundation clinic in Minneapolis, Minnesota.[6] The

4. Although the poster child approach to fund-raising is still popular today, it does not dominate as it once did.

5. The original meaning of the term *poster child* has expanded to include informal and sarcastic use in referring to any person who is an exaggerated personification of a partic-

ular role, activity, or category of person (e.g., Angelina Jolie is the poster child for celebrity adoption).

6. The treatment for polio espoused by the Kenny Foundation was one that Elizabeth Kenny, an Australian nurse, introduced around the world in the 1930s and 1940s. It involved more active intervention, physical therapy, for patients rather than immobilization. She came to the United States in 1940, where she demonstrated her approach; some people embraced it, and others mocked it. Although Kenny

Kenny Foundation established a number of clinics in different parts of the country to treat infantile paralysis—or polio, as it was popularly called—a condition often resulting in paralysis of the legs.

The Kenny Foundation poster child and other poster children were chosen to pull on potential donors' heart strings. Particular children were singled out because they were photogenic: attractive, cute, and perfect in every way (in other words, lived up to the mass-media representation of the typical person) except for their disability. The children featured were almost exclusively middle class, well groomed, white, and attractively attired—and thus children to whom potential donors could relate.

Poster children's visibility was not limited to their images on posters and other ephemera. The children themselves often appeared at fund-raising events to which the press was invited. Newspaper photographers brought their cameras, resulting in illustrations for widely distributed stories. In illustration 4.3, we see the popular movie and television star Robert Young (of *Father Knows Best* and later *Marcus Welby*) passing out handbills at a March of Dimes charity drive sponsored by the New York City Junior Chamber of Commerce in 1955. Appearing with him is poster child Terry Landsburger. The event was held at the *New York Daily News* building. Extensive press coverage was guaranteed in this location.

Nine-year-old John Fitzpatrick became a poster child in 1958. The photograph of him shown in illustration 4.4 was taken for a local newspaper in a Meet the Press Luncheon that was part of an Easter Seals fund-raising campaign. John, wearing a bow tie and a pleasant smile, sits in his wheelchair and holds artist-drawn "Help Crippled Children" posters that were part of the campaign.

Fund-raisers banked on the assumption that potential donors would see a child with a disability

4.3. Robert Young with a poster child at fund-raising march to fight polio, 1955. Press photo.

as a greater tragedy yet more likely to benefit from services than an adult. Although children evoked pity, they also, if photographed in a particular way, expressed hope. Pictures could be constructed in ways that promoted the idea that children could best benefit from rehabilitation and even be "cured" by means of contributions to a charity organization (Garland-Thomson 2004, 86; Siebers 2010, 21–23).

Various Easter Seals affiliates used postcard mailings to remind potential donors to give. The 1963 card in illustration 4.5, sent by the Dade County Society for Crippled Children, confronted would-be donors with a picture of a toddler holding a sign saying, "You Can Help." He is surrounded by Easter Seals stamps and posters urging patrons to "Help Crippled Children." The text to the right of the picture promotes the idea that through donors "this child and hundreds of local children will learn to walk, talk and use their hands."

---

was initially financed by the National Foundation for Infantile Paralysis, this foundation later withdrew its support, prompting her backers to start their own foundation.

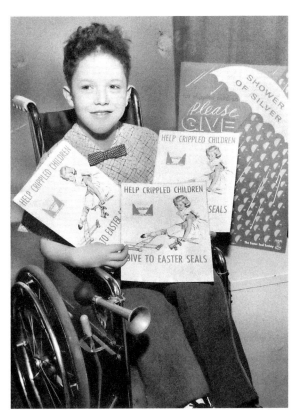

4.4. Easter Seals poster child at appearance at newspaper reporter and photographer luncheon, 1958. Press photo.

In 1946, Donald Anderson became the first March of Dimes national poster child.[7] In a 1949 Join the March of Dimes campaign, the organization produced a folded heavy postcard to distribute to patrons. The inside featured twenty slots into which contributors could insert dimes. A larger space, the width of a dollar, was provided to insert bills, checks, or money orders. The outside featured a picture of a five-year-old poster child, Linda Brown, a pretty girl dressed in a frilly dress (illus. 4.6). She is shown pushing herself out of the wheelchair into a standing position. The message above her, set off in quotation marks, reads, "Look! I can walk again," suggesting that donations would produce cures.

This approach continued to be used. The widely distributed Easter Seals promotional "Set a child free this Easter" from around 1971 is another example of a charity promising cures for contributions (illus. 4.7). The image consists of a series of five superimposed photographs of the same attractive child, wearing the braces, moving across the page from right to left, gradually dropping her crutches, and finally standing unassisted.

Beyond those poster child ads promising donors that their contributions would set children free, some ads asserted that the poster child's disability could be eliminated altogether. A contribution could save future generations of children from suffering. Some even suggested that donors could create a miracle.

I am not suggesting that organizations making such campaign promises did not deliver. Many organizations were successful in rehabilitation, and some supported research that diminished the symptoms of disease and even helped to prevent them. For example, the March of Dimes was central in funding development of a potent vaccine for polio. I am not saying, either, that organization ads were not effective. As stereotypic and demeaning as these Madison Avenue images are, they worked, and the results helped millions of people.

Most poster children were local notables, but many represented national organizations and were countrywide celebrities. The National Foundation for Infantile Paralysis, later called the March of Dimes, was launched in 1938 by President Franklin D. Roosevelt. Established to support the care of people with polio and carry on research for prevention and treatment, it became the most successful and well-known foundation in the country. Its success came in part from its innovative fundraising strategies. The March of Dimes approach was to get millions of people to give small amounts of money—hence, the organization's name (Rose 2003, 43). It relied extensively on the poster child for fund-raising.[8] As the illustrations suggest,

7. This information comes from the website http://americanhistory.si.edu/polio/howpolio/march.htm.

8. Donald Anderson in 1946 was the first in a long line of March of Dimes poster children. Anderson is currently a

Did You Forget?

CRIPPLED AND CEREBRAL PALSIED CHILDREN NEED **YOUR EASTER SEAL DONATION NOW!!**

It's through people like **YOU** that this child and hundreds of local children will learn to walk, talk and use their hands.

Dade County Society for
Crippled Children
159 N. E. 51st Street
Miami 37, Florida

"The Easter Seal Society"

4.5. "Did you forget?" Easter Seals fund-raising postcard, 1963.

4.6. "Look! I can walk again." March of Dimes poster child appearing on solicitation handouts, 1949. Printed picture on fund-raising card.

Set a child free this Easter.

Our therapists teach kids to walk when they can't learn by themselves. And when their parents can't teach them. We teach kids to talk. We teach kids to hear. To control arms, and fingers. To move legs. Toes. We take little kids that are imprisoned inside themselves and help set them free. It takes money. Give to Easter Seals.

Easter Seals: c/o Your Local Postmaster

4.7. Easter Seals poster child, ca. 1971. Magazine advertisement.

most poster children were photographed wearing braces, using wheelchairs, or in some way making their disability evident. Most were cheerful if not jubilant. The organization was so successful in its fund-raising that after it had reached its initial goal, the eradication of polio (an effective vaccine became available in 1955), it continued its campaigns and in 1958 changed its focus to the prevention of "birth defects."[9]

Perhaps the most widely viewed poster children were those who appeared in the Jerry Lewis/Muscular Dystrophy Association campaigns capped off by the marathon Labor Day weekend telethon (B. Haller 2010). The telethon became a fund-raising spectacular in which some of the nation's most popular entertainers assisted Lewis in getting citizens to pledge millions of dollars to help those whom the organization came to refer to as "Jerry's Kids."

Lewis and his partner Dean Martin began hosting the telethons to benefit the Muscular Dystrophy Association in 1956, but at that time the telethons were only local television events seen exclusively in the New York City area. In 1966, at the urging of association officials, the Lewis marathon was parlayed into a national event.

Paul Carker Hawkins was the first Muscular Dystrophy Association poster child to appear on the national telethon. He was there with Lewis on the 1966 Labor Day Telethon, and because this telethon was the first to raise more than one million dollars, Lewis referred to him as "our million-dollar baby."[10] In illustration 4.8, Hawkins is pictured with Jerry Lewis; Lewis's arm is around the boy, one cheek on the boy's forehead, and, with his head down, he looks off into space, making no

"The race of mankind would perish did they cease to aid each other. We cannot exist without mutual help. All therefore that need aid have a right to ask it from their fellow-men; and no one who has the power of granting can refuse it without guilt . . ."
— Walter Scott

JERRY LEWIS, *National Chairman*
PAUL HAWKINS, *National Poster Child*
Muscular Dystrophy Associations of America, Inc.
288

4.8. Jerry Lewis with Muscular Dystrophy Association national poster child, ca. 1966. Printed postcard.

eye contact with Hawkins and apparently enveloped by his own sadness.

Using theme songs such as "Smile" and "You'll Never Walk Alone" and an array of appealing poster children, the show became a national event. Lewis's maudlin approach was extremely successful. By 1999, the total amount of money raised by the Labor Day Telethon reached more than one billion dollars.

The postcard in illustration 4.9 was sent to potential Muscular Dystrophy Association donors in conjunction with an early 1970s Jerry Lewis fund-raiser. In this graphic, Lewis solicits donations with the help of four poster children. The

retired postal worker living in Seattle (from http://american history.si.edu/polio/howpolio/march.htm).

9. The March of Dimes has more recently turned its attention to the prevention of premature births. See Rose 2003 for a pictorial review of the organization's accomplishments.

10. See the Muscular Dystrophy Association's website at http://www.mda.org/JerryLewis/JLBodyOfWork.htm.

approach here reverts back to some of the rhetoric of begging cards—language to evoke pity—but there is an important difference. Here the emphasis is on finding a scientific cure for the disease. As the text on the "YOUR HELP IS THEIR HOPE" card reads, "There are no cures or even effective treatments for muscular dystrophy and related neuromuscular disorders, the tragic diseases that afflict these beautiful children and hundreds of thousands like them. MDAA supports more than 130 research projects in a massive international effort to unravel the mysteries of these cripplers before

There are no cures or even effective treatments for muscular dystrophy and related neuromuscular disorders, the tragic diseases that afflict these beautiful children and hundreds of thousands like them. MDAA supports more than 130 research projects in a massive international effort to unravel the mysteries of these cripplers before it's too late. The future of these children depends on that research — and on your support.

YOUR HELP IS THEIR HOPE

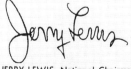

JERRY LEWIS, National Chairman

ⲘUSCULAR DYSTROPHY ASSOCIATIONS OF AMERICA, INC. ⟨⟨⟨ 288

4.9. "Your Help Is Their Hope" Muscular Dystrophy Association campaign card featuring "Jerry's Kids," ca. 1970. Printed postcard.

it's too late. The future of these children depends on that research—and on your support."

Starting in the early 1990s, however, disability activists took Lewis and his telethon to task for the way he depicted disabled people in his fund-raiser marathons (B. Haller 2010, chap. 7). The same poster child images that had been used to raise money were reinterpreted to criticize the negative depiction. The activists referred to the use of Jerry's Kids as "pity mongering," and they picketed the telethon with signs reading, "Exploitation is not entertaining."

CELEBRITIES

Jerry Lewis and the other film and television stars who assisted him in his muscular dystrophy campaigns were part of a long line of celebrities who gave their time and names to disability charities' fund-raising. From its beginnings, the March of Dimes built a close association with the entertainment industry. Eddie Cantor, a popular movie and radio star in the 1930s, was an early supporter and is credited with coining the organization's name.[11] March of Dimes volunteers, in conjunction with movie house owners, raised money by regularly stopping films in the middle, turning up the lights, and passing out collection canisters bedecked with pictures of poster children.[12]

During the era covered in this book, movie, theater, and radio stars from Mary Pickford to Marilyn Monroe made regular public appearances with March of Dimes poster children. Campaign publicity included the most popular stars of the day: Mickey Rooney, Judy Garland, Shirley Temple, Louie Armstrong, Liberace, Duke Ellington, Frank Sinatra, Jane Powell, Lucille Ball, and Robert Young to name a few.

11. The name "March of Dimes" was at first applied just to the organization's fund-raiser campaign, but was later adopted to designate the organization itself.

12. The same cans were placed on store counters.

The outrageously popular Elvis Presley made multiple appearances for the organization. In illustration 4.10, Elvis holds an oversize lollipop emblazoned with the fund-raising slogan "JOIN MARCH OF DIMES" in 1957. The poster girl, wearing braces and standing with the aid of crutches, gazes into Elvis's eyes.

Marilyn Monroe was a March of Dimes regular, making appearances at various fund-raising events, including the fourteenth annual March of Dimes New York City fashion show with poster children Sandra and Linda Solomon (illus. 4.11).

Celebrity-conscious Americans responded to stars, who drew crowds and press coverage. Photographers came to get images to publish in newspapers and other news sources. Entertainment personalities at events increased a charity's visibility and importance. Celebrities provided fund-raising campaigns with a better chance for publicity and added legitimization to the charity as well. The commonsense logic was that if people of national prominence backed a campaign, the cause must be just and deserving. The celebrities' benefited, too. They got publicity, and their personal profile was enhanced by their presentation as caring citizens.

Politicians were ahead of movie stars in being photographed with people with disabilities. From early in the twentieth century, officials from presidents to local officeholders maximized their visibility and appeal by being photographed with people with disabilities. As was the case for movie stars, their appearances were beneficial to both the politicians themselves and the charities.

4.10. Elvis Presley with March of Dimes poster child, in publicity photograph supporting the organization, 1957. News release. March of Dimes Foundation.

4.11. March of Dimes fund-raiser with Marilyn Monroe, 1958. News release. March of Dimes Foundation.

A long line of presidents and their spouses were regularly photographed for fund-raising campaigns. Early presidential fund-raising photos, however, were *not* taken with poster children, but instead with disabled veterans. Mrs. Grace Coolidge, wife of thirtieth president Calvin Coolidge (1923–29), regularly appeared with disabled World War I veterans. A regular at Walter Reed Hospital, she was often photographed promoting the sale of crafts veterans produced. In a 1923 press photo, she appeared with L. B. Clark, a blind and disabled member of the Disabled American Veterans organization. He is presenting her with a flower to wear on Forget-Me-Not Day, an annual fund drive for disabled veterans (illus. 4.12).

The White House was often the site where presidents were photographed with war veterans with disabilities. Illustration 4.13 shows President Coolidge on the White House lawn in an awkward pose. He apparently is confused about whether to offer to shake hands with a World War I veteran who appears to be a quadriplegic.

President Franklin Delano Roosevelt, the thirty-second president of the United States (1933–45), was involved in disability-related fund-raising far beyond starting the March of Dimes. In illustration 4.14, he and his wife, Eleanor, appear at another Walter Reed charity campaign for veterans with disabilities on the lawn at the White House.

As the poster child came to dominate fund-raising, presidents began regularly appearing in photographs with that symbol of charity. Richard Nixon, the thirty-seventh president (1969–74), was actively involved in March of Dimes campaigns throughout his political career. In illustration 4.15, we see him participating in a national campaign

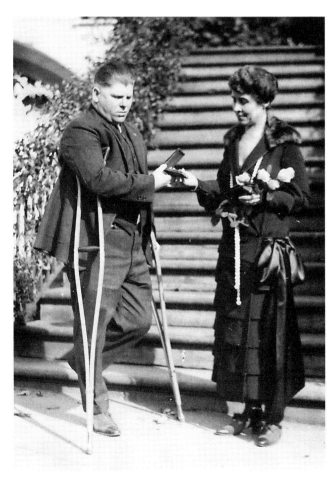

4.12. Mrs. Calvin Coolidge being presented with an artificial flower by a disabled World War I veteran for a Forget-Me-Not Day fund-raising drive, 1923. News photo.

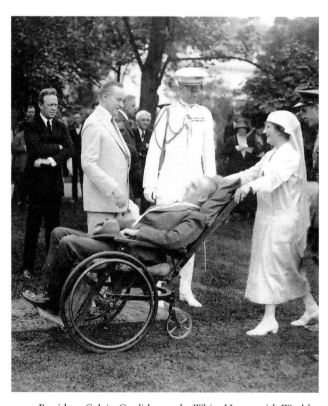

4.13. President Calvin Coolidge at the White House with World War I disabled veteran, 1923. News photo by Harris and Ewing.

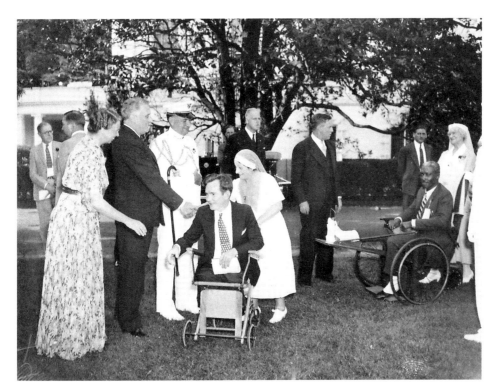

4.14. President and Mrs. Franklin D. Roosevelt receiving veterans from Walter Reed Hospital on the White House lawn, 1936. Mrs. Roosevelt is about to shake hands with Guy Pendelton, an amputee. News photo.

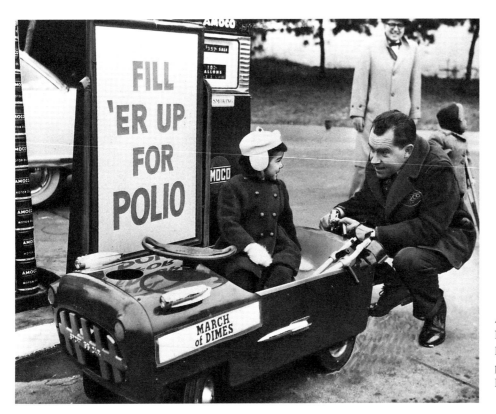

4.15. Vice President Richard Nixon participating in March of Dimes campaign, ca. 1954. News photograph. March of Dimes Foundation.

where customers at gas stations could donate to the organization when buying gas. This photo is one of many news photos that show Nixon actively participating in March of Dimes campaigning.

THE POSTER CHILD THANKS YOU

The charity ephemera in my collection include pictures of children with disabilities juxtaposed with "thank you" messages. The first illustration in this chapter is an example. Rather than asking for contributions, this type of advertisement expressed appreciation for those who gave. These messages were designed to make donors feel that their contribution was worthwhile and appreciated. Their purpose was not only to express gratitude, but also to lay the groundwork for future contributions. In order to be more personal, these ads featured a picture of a child with a disability and included a message directly from him or her. The caption under the picture of Gary in illustration 4.16 reads: "Two-year-old Gary says, 'T'ank you.' Gary who was too young to walk when he had Polio is now at the Capper Center being taught to walk with crutches."

Some "thank you" messages were produced to give the impression that the message was actually handwritten by the child who is pictured and had benefited from the organization's services. A series of postcards sent by the Philadelphia Society for Crippled Children and Adults, an affiliate of the national Easter Seals, thanked donors for contributing to Camp Daddy Allen, a summer camp for children with disabilities. (The camp was named after the founder of the Easter Seals, Edgar Allen.) The society produced postcard images of many different groups of campers, but all the messages were written by the same cursive hand.

Illustration 4.17 shows the front and back side of one of these cards. The picture side shows the campers with braces and crutches. On the extreme left of the picture, one girl's head is circled by a dark line. To the right of the circle is the word *me*. The idea was to single out a child in the crowd to suggest that she wrote the message that appears on the back of the card. The fact that the cursive handwriting on different cards is the same suggests that an organization staff member or publicity designer wrote it.

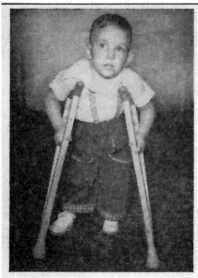

Two-year-old Gary says, "T'ank you." Gary who was too young to walk when he had Polio is now at the Capper Center being taught to walk with crutches.

Dear Friend:

Thank you for your contribution to the crippled children fund.

Your gift added to the gifts of others will make it possible for many boys and girls handicapped as Gary was to know the joy of walking again.

If you know of a crippled child in need of the type of care we can give, write us or have the parents do so. We shall accept eligible children so long as funds and facilities are available.

THE CAPPER FOUNDATION
FOR CRIPPLED CHILDREN

J. M. Parks, Secretary

4.16. "T'ank you" from Gary, Capper Foundation for Crippled Children, 1965. Printed postcard.

PHILADELPHIA SOCIETY FOR
CRIPPLED CHILDREN AND ADULTS
CAMP DADDY ALLEN
HICKORY RUN, WHITE HAVEN, PA.

Thanks for helping
to send me to
Camp by buying Easter
Seals.
Having a swell
time
Your friend
Jeannie

ADDRESS

Mr. Edward L. Line
816 Woodland Drive
Havertown, Pa.

4.17. Front and back of
Camp Daddy Allen "thank
you" postcard, 1947.
Printed postcard.

BEFORE AND AFTER

Fund-raisers for organizations that lay claim to helping the people with disabilities often used the visual convention of "before and after" in their appeals.[13]

13. The before-and-after visual cliché is common in medical photography.

I have already addressed a modified version of the approach in my discussion of poster children where the pictures show how the children were cured through the organization's efforts (they leave their crutches or leave their wheelchairs). In a purer use of the before-and-after visual, the presentation juxtaposes two pictures of the same person, one taken before the intervention, the other after he or she has been under treatment. The idea is to show the changes in that person's condition brought about by the charity.[14]

"Before-and-after" charity photography has a long history.[15] One organization that used this approach extensively in its fund-raising was the Shriners, a national Masonic group. In 1920, members of the organization voted to focus their philanthropy on building and supporting hospitals for "crippled children." That designation included those afflicted with orthopedic disabilities such as scoliosis, limb discrepancies, clubfoot, juvenile arthritis, cerebral palsy, and spina bifida, to name only a few. The goal was "to rehabilitate children, who, were it not for the Shriners' Hospitals, would never receive the necessary treatment to relieve deformities."[16]

How did the Shriners pay for the hospitals that they eventually established and maintained? Membership dues provided some support, but the organization launched a campaign to raise additional funds not only from members, but from business organizations and the general public. Its main organ for fund-raising was what became an annual yearbook titled *Real House of Magic*. Every temple was given a large supply of these booklets to dis-

tribute to potential donors. As the booklet states, "Many people, after reading about the Hospitals and studying the cases shown therein, have become so interested that they have mentioned Hospitals in their wills and many liberal contributions have resulted."

By 1937, with the help of this booklet, the Shriners were funding fifteen hospitals around the country. The heavily illustrated booklet includes pictures of buildings and staged photos of happy people actively engaged in recreational or therapeutic activities. The building and group images do not dominate the booklet, however. The featured graphics, fifteen pages of them, consist of a series of before-and-after photographs of children served by the different Shriners hospitals.[17] The first is of the Shreveport Louisiana Hospital patient "Glenn," a boy then approximately ten years old (illus. 4.18).

In the first picture, Glenn is shown helpless, seminude, and held in a standing position by a staff member. In the second picture, the after portrait, he stands fully clothed under his own power and sporting a smile. The accompanying text states that his handicapping condition was the result of "creeping paralysis" and points to his transformation as resulting from his treatment at the Shriners facility so that now he can use "his limbs and be able to walk like the other boys."

CONCLUSION

Those who produced and selected charity campaign images were pragmatic. People I interviewed in the early 1970s who were attached to disability organizations knew that their imagery was inaccurate or only one part of the story of the people they served. Some even acknowledged that the imagery presented an impression of their clients that was demeaning and harmful to public perception of

14. Some organizations that used this approach skipped the before shot and showed the person only after intervention, restored to being a healthy, happy human being. As a substitute for the before picture, a statement describes the person's prior condition.

15. Dr. Thomas Barnardo, an English doctor, provided the most famous examples of such photos. In the early 1870s, he commissioned a series of before-and-after photographs of children who were residents of his street shelter, Home for Working and Destitute Lads, as part of a fund-raising campaign for that charity. His fame among photo historians stems from the fact that his portraits were fraudulent. He was brought to court and found guilty of fabricating and manipulating the pictures; he dressed the before shot children in rags, posing them as disheveled and blank faced, then posed the same children on the same day cleaned up and engaged in productive activities (Goldberg 1991, 163).

16. From a 1937 Shriners pamphlet I found.

17. Twelve hospitals and three mobile units attached to host hospitals were featured.

Glenn came to us quite a handicapped little lad as a result of creeping paralysis. See the transformation. He now has the use of his limbs and is able to walk like the other boys

4.18. Shriner before-and-after photographs, 1937. Pamphlet image.

them. But the images worked. People dug into their pockets to get the dimes and dollars that the organizations depended on. The organizations' clients were dependent on their services. The fund-raisers were concerned with clients' immediate needs and cures, not with long-term abstract issues connected to negative imagery.

5 Asylums
Postcards, Public Relations, and Muckraking

ADMINISTRATION BLDG.
STATE ASYLUM
164
FERGUS FALLS MINN.

5.1. Administration building, Minnesota State Asylum, Fergus Falls, ca. 1914. Photo postcard.

In this chapter, I diverge slightly from my focus on photographic images of people with disabilities. Here I spotlight pictures taken of one type of facility that housed people with disabilities—asylums, large residential settings that dominated some rural landscapes in the later part of the nineteenth century and the first sixty years of the twentieth century. Some of the images I examine include people with disabilities, but many, such as illustration 5.1, do not.

I scrutinize three types of photographs. First are picture postcards of asylums created by businessmen to sell to the public as souvenirs or vehicles for correspondence. Illustration 5.1 is an example. Next I look at public-relations photographs taken by or for institutional administrators for placement in reports, brochures, and newspapers for the purposes of promoting their facilities. Finally, I look at muckraking images taken by people who wanted to make institutional abuse public with the purpose of rousing citizens and officials to action in order to alleviate the terrible conditions. Absent from this review of asylum images are clinical photographs—photos taken in institutions for patient records and to be used as illustrations in textbooks and professional articles. Martin Elks takes up this type of photo in chapter 6.

5.2. Main building, Northern Illinois Insane Asylum, Elgin, 1911. Photo postcard.

Looking at these three categories of pictures taken by people with different agendas reveals how photographs of similar locations can vary radically depending on different picture takers' intentions. In the case of asylums, the picture makers ranged from local and regional postcard photographers who produced images for profit to administrators who sought to promote their own institutions to those outside the system who wanted to expose the abuse of inmates.

WISH YOU WERE HERE:
POSTCARDS OF INSTITUTIONS

On October 11, 1911, Mrs. Herman Miller walked to her roadside rural mail box in Iowa to see what the postman had delivered.[1] A picture postcard from her cousins Clara and Frank greeted her. She flipped it over to look at the view. It was of a large ornate building in attractive, landscaped surroundings. The caption read "MAIN BUILDING

— NORTHERN ILL. INSANE ASYLUM, ELGIN" (illus. 5.2).

Although the idea of receiving a postcard with a picture of an "insane asylum" seems odd today, Mrs. Miller most likely thought nothing of it. In fact, views of that subject matter were so common at the time that it was not even referred to in the message on the opposite side. It was just another card to add to Mrs. Miller's growing postcard collection.

By 1911, picture postcards were outrageously popular, and those with asylums on them were a common, taken-for-granted genre of the medium. They sparked my curiosity as well as my collecting zeal. Mrs. Miller's card is part of my collection of more than sixteen hundred US picture postcards with scenes of institutions for the so-called mentally ill, feebleminded, defective, and epileptic that I put together over fifteen years. I draw on these cultural artifacts in this chapter.

ASYLUMS IN THE EARLY PART
OF THE TWENTIETH CENTURY

In the mid–nineteenth century, Americans launched a campaign to erect publicly funded asylums to

1. The information in this section on asylum postcards is based on an article I wrote with Ann Marshall (Bogdan and Marshall 1997). I thank her for her contribution.

house people they defined as having mental and other disorders. The vision for these institutions was originally as much about cure or training as about confinement. Although historians differ as to when or if cure was abandoned by the time postcards had become popular, 1905, detention and custodial care were to become the asylums' chief functions (Grob 1983; Rothman 2002).

By 1912, a massive network of institutions had been established, with more than 350 asylums in the forty-eight states housing hundreds of thousands of inmates. Every state had at least one. New York State had more than twenty-five. Although asylums could be found in cities, most were located in rural areas. Early institutions were usually small, with only hundreds of patients, but during the golden age of asylum postcards, from 1905 to 1935, many expanded to immense proportions. The largest institutions housed thousands. Many were self-sufficient enclaves that isolated their inmates from surrounding communities, producing their own food, power, heat, clothing, and other essentials.

Conditions for residents varied from institution to institution and from ward to ward within the same institution, but life at all of them was at best restrictive and barren (Dwyer 1987). The ratio of staff to patients was low, which meant that therapy was impractical if not impossible. Custodial care was accomplished by using the labor of inmates for cleaning, patient care, and other basic maintenance. The grounds and the building facades provided a serene front that hid the crowded and inhumane conditions that existed inside many of the buildings. Thick metal screening on windows and locked doors kept many patients on their crowded wards. Physical, chemical, and surgical restraints as well as forced sterilization were common. Physical abuse, lack of privacy, corporal punishment, regimentation, and forced labor were routine as well. Restricted communications, poor food, unsanitary water and living conditions, parasites, disease, and boredom were also normal parts of life in the facilities pictured on asylum cards.

EARLY TWENTIETH-CENTURY ASYLUM POSTCARDS

The asylum postcard is one variation of the picture postcard. With the onset of rural delivery and changes in postal regulations early in the twentieth century, the exchange of letters and other material transmitted by the US Postal Service momentously accelerated. By 1907, picture postcards had become a preferred way of keeping in touch as well as a collecting fad for millions (Miller and Miller 1976). They were sold in a range of stores as well as at tourist stops.[2] Travelers bought and sent postcards, and those who stayed at home consumed them as well. Relatives and friends used them to correspond and traded them. The zeal to accumulate postcards produced an incredibly rich visual archive of American social history and popular culture that is as yet almost untapped.[3]

The View Side of the Asylum Postcards

By 1905, there were separate institutions specifically designated for people labeled "insane," "feebleminded," and "epileptic."[4] In my collec-

2. In the years of picture postcards' greatest popularity, from 1905 to 1920, up to one billion were mailed annually (Dotterrer and Cranz 1982, 44), more than ten times the US population. And the number mailed represents only a fraction of those bought. People passed on cards by hand, enclosed them in envelopes with letters, and purchased them for their own collections.

3. Because I compiled my collection in a haphazard way, I cannot make definitive statements about the representativeness of what I have compared to the universe of what exists. But there is no reason to believe that my collection is significantly different from what was produced in general. I report frequency counts and percentages in this discussion. Although these data may be of use in substantiating my findings, they must be read cautiously and in light of the way the collection was compiled.

4. Those institutions that served the mentally ill were referred to by such names as "insane asylum," "state lunatic hospital," "hospital for the insane," "state hospital," and just "asylum." Those for the mentally retarded went by such names

tion, approximately 10 percent of the cards show institutions designated as serving the intellectually impaired; 5 percent feature institutions that served people with epilepsy; and the remaining 85 percent show institutions for the mentally ill.

The picture side of the card is what grabs the viewer's attention. Captions identifying the type, name, and location of the institution appear either superimposed on the images or on the white border that surrounds some cards. The caption also typically includes specific information about where on the grounds the picture was taken or the name of the building that is pictured. Most captions are purely informational, but a few are boastful. A card from Bryce State Hospital in Tuscaloosa, Alabama, for example, declares itself "One of the Finest in the US." Table 5.1 provides a summary of the aspects of asylums pictured on these cards, indicating the percentage of cards in each category in my collection.

As was the case with the card Mrs. Miller received from Clara and Frank, 56 percent of the pictures show a particular building. In more than half of this group, the building pictured is the one that housed the administration (illus. 5.3). Other structures commonly pictured include the superintendent's residence, inmate dormitories, employee quarters, the hospital, the laundry, and other buildings where employees and patients worked (illus. 5.4).

The buildings pictured are large, imposing, and architecturally ornate, and they are usually located in well-landscaped surroundings with manicured lawns, trees, and shrubs. The administration building and other buildings pictured were usually the first constructed and had the most ornate facades and massive presence. Although on some cards the scene looks stark, cold, and dreary—like

---

Table 5.1

Aspects of Asylums Featured in Asylum Photographs

Featured Aspect	% of Author's Asylum Cards That Feature This Aspect
Buildings	56
Institution from a Distance	27
Grounds	7
Gate or Entrance	3
Multiviews (collage)	3
Interiors	2
Other	2

---

something out of a horror movie (illus. 5.5)—these institutions most often look pleasant, more like a college campus than a prison.

The great majority of the cards featuring asylum structures does not include people. In the 13 percent that do, the people are shown at a distance, as minor accessories to the main subject, the buildings (see how the buildings dwarf the people in illustration 5.4). It is difficult to discern whether the people pictured are staff, inmates, or visitors.

About one-quarter of the cards show the institution from a distance and are referred to as a "bird's eye view" or some similar phrase in the caption. These shots were taken from atop a hill or from a tall building on the edge of the grounds and provide an expansive view of a significant portion of the institution, the buildings as well as the grounds. The size of some of the campuses is striking. The hand-written comment on the picture side of the card in illustration 5.6 states: "There are fifteen hundred Insane patients in This Hospital." In another, a bird's eye view of the Hospital for the Insane in Weston, West Virginia, the institution is spread over the valley floor (illus. 5.7).

Seven percent of the cards feature the grounds. Well-tended lawns, flowers, lakes, and water fountains are on display. These scenes are almost idyllic, with babbling brooks, calm lakes, lush vegetation, and blooming flowers. A few show golf courses. The viewer might have the impression that she or he is looking at a millionaire's estate or a

---

as "state home for the feeble-minded," "state school," "idiot asylum," and "state training school" (Ferguson 1994; Trent 1994). Those designated for epileptics were called "epileptic village," "state hospital for epileptics," and "epileptic colony."

5.3. Administration building, Kansas State Hospital for the Insane, Osawatomie, ca. 1910. Photo postcard.

5.4. Typical cottage, Illinois General Hospital for the Insane, ca. 1910. Printed postcard.

well-maintained park. Illustration 5.8 is of decorative water fountain on the grounds of the State Insane Asylum in Salem, Oregon, with the statue of a nymph on top and water spraying into the surrounding pool.

Only 3 percent of the cards show the gate or entrance to the campus. A favorite view of this

type is of the elaborate iron and masonry entrance, with the name of the institution displayed on the arch entryway (illus. 5.9).

Most activity took place inside the buildings, but only 2 percent of the pictures on postcards are interior shots. They show a sanitary orderly setting and, although sparsely furnished, a pleasant,

Main Building of the New York State Custodial for Feeble-minded Women. Newark, N. Y.

*Now is mamas dear little Boy will I hope
mama sends her love & a kiss to her Darling
good Boy*

5.5. Main building of the New York State Custodial Asylum for Feeble-Minded Women, Newark, New York, ca. 1906. Printed postcard.

*There are fifteen hundred Insane
patients in This Hospital*

5.6. View of an asylum from a distance, North Warren, Pennsylvania, ca. 1908. Photo postcard.

almost hotel-like living environment. We see hardly a hint of the unhealthy and inhumane conditions so prevalent in these institutions at the time.

The interior-view cards are more likely to include people than the outside-view cards. In illustration 5.10, patients and staff are lining the long corridor on Ward 3 in Gowanda State Mental Hospital in Collins, New York. This interior-view card and others show wards adorned with Christmas, Fourth of July, or other holiday decorations. On such occasions, an institution's staff spiffed up the facility for visitors.

Birds-eye view Hospital for the Insane, Weston, W. Va.

5.7. Bird's eye view, Hospital for the Insane, Weston, West Virginia, ca. 1909. Printed postcard.

FOUNTAIN IN PARK AT INSANE ASYLUM. SALEM, ORE.

5.8. Fountain in the park at the insane asylum in Salem, Oregon, ca. 1907. Photo postcard.

Illustration 5.11 was taken inside Gowanda at the same time as illustration 5.10. The staff is neatly dressed; some patients are sitting in the background, and others are occupying beds. The ward is exceptionally clean and orderly, as are the patients.

The Gowanda cards are real photo postcards rather than machine-printed ones. Real photo postcards were printed directly from a negative onto photo postcard stock and were produced by local photographers in smaller numbers than printed cards. Photographers who shot real photo postcards were locals, and because of personal ties to the people who worked in these institutions they could gain access to their interior spaces. They of course did not have free entry to all parts of the buildings at any time and operated under constraints. If they did not take images that showed the facilities in a positive way, they suffered the institution officials' wrath. Staff sanctions were not the only constraint. There were economic incentives for positive views. People who bought postcards wanted to see images that showed off the institution, not exposed its faults.

People at the time the pictures of Gowanda's interior were produced probably accepted the

5.9. Gate at the entrance of the West Virginia Hospital for the Insane, Weston, ca. 1910. Printed postcard.

5.10. Ward 3, Gowanda State Hospital for the Insane, Collins, New York, ca. 1909. Photo postcard.

images as positive, even complimentary to the people who ran the facilities, but through the critical eyes of present-day observers, the scenes in illustrations 5.10 and 5.11 show overcrowding and forced idleness. In the hall scene, the male patients who line the walls are slumped over; one is even lying down on a bench, doing nothing. The Christmas decorations in both gloomy scenes are ironic. Despite the order and cleanliness of the hospital ward image in illustration 5.11, the room is so jam-packed with beds that the image documents excessive overcrowding rather than orderly cheer.

5.11. Holiday season on the hospital ward of Gowanda State Hospital for the Insane, Collins, New York, ca. 1909. Photo postcard.

Choosing What to Depict

Whether the pictures were taken by local crafts-people or by company agents, there were standard views to shoot and conventions in taking these shots. Any notable landmark on a card had sales potential. It does not appear that asylums were purposely sought out more than any other place. In some rural areas, finding something distinctive to photograph could be a challenge. In towns with mental hospitals or other asylums, these venues provided the most impressive and unique architectural structures and landscapes available. In small towns, asylum postcards contributed to rendering the institution's main buildings into local icons.

Photographic technique was not sophisticated for asylum cards. In shooting buildings, be they of an asylum or other facility, photographers chose angles that made the buildings attractive by exaggerating their size and emphasizing their architectural splendor. Buildings that were the subject of the picture dominated the card and were often the only object in view.

It was not just on asylum cards that the roads and grounds around buildings were barren of people and activity. This was common in cards of noninstitutional settings as well. The photographer typically took the pictures in the early morning or on Sunday when people were not around. It was easier that way, and it was known that the presence of people or automobiles in a picture dated the card, decreasing its shelf life. Thus, leaving people out of most of the images used for asylum cards was not done out of respect for the inmates or for their protection; it was for commercial reasons.

That the conventions used in photographing asylums were the same as those used to photograph other local buildings and scenes is well illustrated by the difficulty in distinguishing asylums from other major constellations of buildings without reading the captions. This difficulty was made vivid when I looked for cards under the name of a town that included both an asylum and a college. Poughkeepsie, New York, was the home of both the Hudson River State Hospital, a large institution for the mentally ill, and Vassar College, an elite women's college. In looking at postcard images of buildings in Poughkeepsie, I often mistook the insane asylum for the college.

In addition to purposely shooting attractive asylum images, artisans embellished the images during the process of converting photographs into postcards. Although they approached their image-making as realists, there was room for innovation and creativity. Real photos might be tampered with—an American flag added to the top of a building or people removed—but it was with printed cards that most manipulation took place, especially with color. The postcard manufacturers received black-and-white photographs, but they produced colored postcards.[5] The colors were decided upon by the producers and were a figment of their assumptions and imaginations. For example, the grass is typically greener in the pictures than in real life. The color of buildings on cards does not necessarily match their true appearance. On cards, facades look brighter, and their color is more uniform. Postcard producers added, subtracted, and in other ways altered the original image in ways other than just the color. A day scene could be changed to a night view by darkening the hue and adding a moon. Even the seasons could be changed by removing trees and adding snow. Roads were eliminated or added in the transformation of the photograph to a postcard. People and automobiles were removed from the scene.

Both printed and real-photo asylum postcards were produced for commercial purposes to be sold to visitors as well as to townspeople. I found no evidence that any of the cards were fashioned by, for, or under the direction of government employees, institutional staff, or other officials associated with the asylums. Nevertheless, the cards depict the institution in an unrealistically positive light, a view that the administration would favor. Although the photographers did not produce cards to please the administration, they did want to attract potential buyers.

At first, I was incredulous when I discovered asylum postcards. To me, they were morbid—cruel. The senders, receivers, and producers had clearly not shared my disquietude. They looked at asylums and asylum postcards through a very different lens. The sheer number of early-twentieth-century postcards with pictures of institutions for people with mental disorders and the fact that so many messages on the cards did not even refer to the asylum pictured suggest that such cards were taken for granted. For some, they were perhaps even a display of pride. Asylums, like schools, post offices, main streets, and other local sites, were just part of the local landscape, symbols of place.

INSTITUTIONAL PROPAGANDA

For one group of stakeholders, administrators and other institution-affiliated officials, including boards of visitors, the visual championing of their facilities was a conscious, strategic part of their public-relations arsenal. The officials of virtually every institution either hired local photographers or employed staff to take pictures to promote their institution's amenities. Some of the images were released to the press for wide public distribution; others were used in annual reports and pamphlets produced for state bureaucrats and legislators and distributed to other citizens.

Although the use of photographs in institutional propaganda goes back to the nineteenth century, it was not until the early twentieth century that they were widely employed. The surge in their use was a function of advances in printing technology. By the start of the twentieth century, copies of photographs could be easily and inexpensively included in newspapers, magazines, brochures, and other printed materials.[6] Most annual institution reports, commissioners' reports, and other official

---

5. Many of the illustrations in this chapter were colored postcards. They are shown in black and white here because the cost of including color images was prohibitive.

6. Half-tone and other ways of transforming photographs into plates that could be incorporated with text and run off on printing presses were used.

5.12. "First Public Building Erected in America to Care for the Feeble-Minded." Syracuse State School for Mental Defectives, 1922. From the institution's annual report.

printed materials soon contained illustrations that were originally photos.[7]

In the late 1910s and early 1920s, the director of the Syracuse State Institution for Feeble-Minded Children (in the 1920s its name was changed to "Syracuse State School for Mental Defectives"), like other administrators of the time, engaged a photographer, William Allen, to take pictures of the institution.[8] In exchange for room and board and a modest stipend, Allen, a Syracuse University student, took not only the mug shot that appeared in each inmate's official record, but also public-relations pictures of the institutional grounds. Although he was only starting his career as a photographer, he produced images that were well executed, nicely composed, and professional looking. That professional touch was typical of visual institutional propaganda. By virtue of his and other institutional picture takers' competence in producing pictures that had the aura of authority, these images came to dominate how people thought about these places.

7. See Baynton, Gannon, and Bergey 2007 for many examples of institution photography.

8. Although I am not certain, all evidence I have been able to collect suggests that the photographer was William Allen.

Illustration 5.12 is an example of the Syracuse photographer's work. It was the lead illustration in the 1922 annual report produced by the Syracuse State School's Board of Visitors as required by the New York State Legislature. Reminiscent of postcard photography, it shows the asylum's imposing main building. The caption under the picture proudly hails the structure as "The First Public Building Erected in America to Care for the Feeble-Minded."

In the second Syracuse asylum photograph included here (illus. 5.13), the institutional residents are diligently engaged in what the caption labels as "Morning Colors," the morning institutional ritual of raising the large American flag up the imposing pole in front of the main building. Four boys form a straight line to the right of the flag, three of them holding bugles and apparently playing the National Anthem. Another boy is posed next to the pole to the left about to pull the rope that will hoist the flag. Some of the boys wear knickers and ties; all are the picture of well-behaved youngsters. Even though the photographer's intent was to make the picture look natural, the arrangement of the boys and their posture suggest that he carefully posed the shot. The way the boys holding the flag are facing the camera and the symmetry with the boys holding the bugles indicate that the picture

5.13. "Morning Colors." Raising the flag, Syracuse State School for Mental Defectives, 1921. From the institution's annual report.

was set up. In addition to the subject matter itself, the well-organized composition of the image gives the viewer confidence that all is well and orderly at the asylum.

One photo from the Syracuse State asylum appeared in the 1922 annual report with the caption "Canning factory at work" (illus. 5.14). A more telling and appropriate caption might have read "Residents at Work at the Canning Factory." This carefully constructed picture shows a dozen female residents outside a building preparing bushels of tomatoes for processing. The canning facility is in the rear, and other female residents are most likely canning in that building. All are wearing the same white, institutionally issued work outfits, including a cotton hat. As in the previous photograph, this image is carefully posed, its purpose to create the sense of industrious, orderly workers.

MARGARET BOURKE-WHITE
AT LETCHWORTH VILLAGE

I leave the Syracuse State School photographs in order to take up another set of photographs from this genre, a collection of images taken by one of the most heralded and well-known photographers

5.14. "Canning Factory at Work." Syracuse State School for Mental Defectives, 1922. From the institution's annual report.

of the twentieth century, Margaret Bourke-White. In 1932, the wealthy philanthropist and eugenicist Mary Averell Harriman,[9] engaged Margaret Bourke-White to take pictures of Letchworth Village, an asylum for children and adolescents with intellectual disabilities that was located in the country north of New York City.[10] Harriman had been a trustee of Letchworth since its opening in 1911 and was a close associate of Charles Little, the institution's superintendent. Little embraced Bourke-White's willingness to assist the institution (Trent 1994, 225). When Bourke-White took the pictures, the United States was in the depths of the Depression, and funding for government services for people with mental disabilities was contracting. Letchworth had undergone an extensive building program, but it was becoming overcrowded and underfunded. Harriman and institutional officials were eager to show that their facility was contributing to the general welfare and living up to its official goal, which was to segregate mentally disabled inmates from the general population and make them productive.

Like the Syracuse State Institution photographer and other picture takers engaged by institutions, Bourke-White was assigned to document Letchworth's success—to present idealized visual documents for public relations. She embraced the task with her considerable photographic skill and talent.

The superintendent and other officials were pleased with what Bourke-White produced—the pictures were what they had hoped for. Her photos of Letchworth appeared in three annual reports that were, like other such reports, distributed to New York legislators and to the public.[11] They also appeared in other official public-relations documents and were displayed in the halls around the administrative offices at the institution.

Several of Bourke-White's images of Letchworth Village bring to mind the asylum postcards discussed so far. She took commanding pictures of the most substantial buildings and the loveliest spots on the grounds. Illustration 5.15 shows a memorable formal photograph of the impressive administration building. Of all her images, this one was used most often in the institution's publications and pamphlets. It was the only photograph in a 1933 New York State invitation sent to dignitaries for the opening ceremonies to lay the cornerstones for buildings at the facility. It was also the lead photograph in the twenty-sixth annual report.

Letchworth Village was located in a beautiful spot high in the hills overlooking the Hudson River. Bourke-White's views of the grounds took advantage of the scenic location, and these photos became part of her Letchworth portfolio. They, too, were included in institutional public documents.

Given Bourke-White's exceptional photographic eye and her mechanical expertise, her pictures are both technically and aesthetically far superior to the postcard images reviewed earlier. Nevertheless, she used the same conventions that supported the legitimacy of the institution by highlighting the splendor of the architecture and the grounds.

Unlike the great majority of the postcard images, however, most of Bourke-White's photos feature inmates. Some even show close-ups. Although, as in the Gowanda photos discussed earlier, local postcard photographers occasionally had access to the interior of institutions, thereby

9. The eugenics movement is discussed in chapter 6.

10. Margaret Bourke-White became a *Life* magazine photographer in 1936. One of her photographs was featured on the cover of *Life*'s first issue.

11. Ten of Bourke-White's photographs of Letchworth appeared in that institution's twenty-fourth annual report

published in 1933 for the year 1932. Seven more were in the twenty-sixth annual report, and four others were in the thirtieth annual report. The reports can be found in the New York Library in Albany, New York.

ADMINISTRATION BUILDING

5.15. Administration building, Letchworth Village, 1935. From the institution's annual report. Photograph by Margaret Bourke-White.

allowing them to include inmates in their photos, most did not. Photographers hired by an institution were free to go about the grounds and interiors, but being given access did not mean that whatever they photographed would be published. Institution officials chose which pictures would be used for publicity purposes and which would not.

In the institutional pictures Bourke-White produced, the residents are actively engaged in productive activities, working in the laundry room, on the Letchworth Village farm, and in school learning occupational skills. Illustration 5.16 shows the young female residents of Letchworth lined up in class, each posed in the same position and wearing institutional uniforms. In illustration 5.17, young residents are busy working at looms producing handwoven cloth that was sold to visitors and through outside outlets. At Letchworth and other institutions, such craft industries were widely publicized. Photographers showed that residents could be productive even if working in a closely supervised institutional setting.

In an effort at being self-sufficient, asylums established farms where residents labored as a way of providing income to the institution as well as rehabilitation for the inmates. Illustration 5.18 shows Bourke-White's photograph of young male

5.16. "School Work." Girls in class reading, Letchworth Village, 1935. From the institution's annual report. Photograph by Margaret Bourke-White.

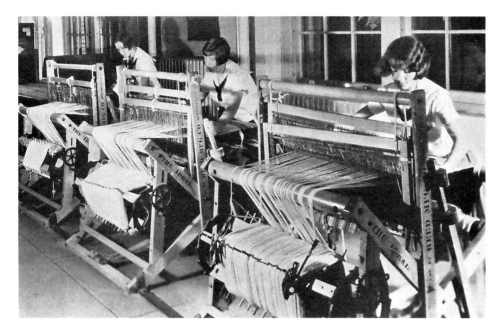

5.17. "At the Looms." Letchworth Village, 1933. From the institution's annual report. Photograph by Margaret Bourke-White.

5.18. "End of the Day." Letchworth Village, 1937. From the institution's annual report. Photograph by Margaret Bourke-White.

residents of Letchworth Village, picks and shovels in hand, working on the farm.

The pictures that Bourke-White and other institutional photographers took show clean, well-dressed inmates happily engaged in labor. As illustration 5.18 reveals, their clothing and clean appearance are quite incongruous with the tasks in which they are engaged.

The major focus of institutional photography was to produce depictions of the inmates as potentially productive, useful citizens. Bourke-White's images were an extension of the tradition of institutional photography that promoted the message that if institutionalized, possibly dangerous and certainly incapable people with disabilities could be tamed, even trained, they might eventually live more useful lives. Institutional images of people with mental disabilities presented them in a more positive light, but in that endeavor they hid the overcrowded, understaffed conditions that actually existed. In addition, they showed only those inmates who were the most attractive, those in programs, those who lived in the best sections of the facility.

As Bourke-White's and the Syracuse State Institution photographer's pictures suggest, institutional photographers were typically skilled picture takers who produced images that were technically excellent. Their pictures were usually posed rather than action shots. Their excellent professional quality was part and parcel of the impression the institution was striving to project.

MUCKRAKING PHOTOGRAPHY

Other photographic views of institutions are radically different from those I have presented thus far. Muckraking photographers showed asylums as appalling hellholes. They purposely featured the negative—the terrible conditions, the crowding, the inhumanity, the failure of these forms of residential living to serve their clientele. The same institution presented in institutional photography as the epitome of care was revealed as appalling by muckraking images.[12]

The attempt to bring the injustice of such institutions to the public eye using photography has a history similar to that of administration-generated institutional photography.[13] As print technology improved, the mass distribution of pictures of institutional abuse appeared in newspapers as well as in brochures and investigative reports. The earliest use of photos to document abuse I have come across was in the Illinois General Assembly's

Investigation of Illinois Institutions in 1908 (Trent 1994, illus. 19). Conscientious objectors who were assigned to an institution for alternative service during World War II produced a visual portfolio of institutional atrocities.[14] More recently, in the early 1970s, the journalist Geraldo Rivera brought photographers into what was to become the symbol of abuse, Willowbrook State School for the intellectually disabled on Staten Island, New York. Rivera wanted to bring to the attention of a national audience the atrocities behind the walls of that institution.

In 1965, Burton Blatt, a professor of special education at Boston University[15] and an advocate for people with mental disabilities, recruited a neighbor, Fred Kaplan—a skilled professional photographer—to accompany him on visits to four state schools for the intellectually disabled in the eastern United States.[16] During his career, Blatt had visited many institutions and knew their directors as well as the squalid conditions that existed inside. His purpose was to document the horror within. He and Kaplan asked cooperative officials to show them the wards they were most ashamed of, those places where the most difficult residents resided—the ambulatory and most aggressive young adults. These wards were usually the most despicable, where brutality and filth were most obvious. Not wanting to change the staff's behavior, Kaplan concealed his camera under his jacket.[17] Blatt distracted the staff so that Kaplan could shoot from his hip. Their photographic sojourn

14. Steven Taylor (2009) gives an account of various muckraking magazine articles published in the 1940s through the 1960s.

15. Blatt was a professor at Boston University at the time of the visits, but in the early 1970s he moved to Syracuse University, where he was the chair of the Special Education Department and later the dean of the School of Education.

16. Blatt and Kaplan visited a fifth institution that they chose because of its progressive practices.

17. The officials had given them permission and even led them to the wards with the worst conditions. Concealing the camera allowed Blatt and Kaplan to hide their picture taking

12. We do not know what the exact conditions at Letchworth Village were when Margaret Bourke-White took her photographs, but Letchworth Village was later part of Geraldo Rivera's documentary showing the horrors inside state institutions.

13. There is a long history of people trying to bring the terrible conditions in these institutions to the public's attention. In the 1840s, Dorothea Dix visited various asylums and exposed institutional abuse.

resulted in the heavily illustrated book *Christmas in Purgatory* (Blatt and Kaplan 1966). The introductory sentence of that book set the scene for the visual dreadfulness that was to come: "There is hell on earth, and in America there is a special inferno. We visited there during Christmas, 1965."

Blatt and Kaplan widely distributed the book to prominent legislators, commissioners of mental health, leaders of professional organizations, and various voluntary associations. *Look* magazine later picked up the story and published an article featuring Kaplan's photographs and Blatt's observations.

In arranging his visits, Blatt promised the unusually cooperative officials who gave him entry that he would not disclose the names of the institutions he and Kaplan visited. He made this promise for two reasons. First, it was to protect the officials. As was typically the case in the aftermath of exposés, rather than bringing about meaningful change, officials at the state level fired directors and others below them to please the public. Second, Blatt and Kaplan's concerns were not just with specific institutions, but with the system as a whole. Their logic was that if the asylums were identified specifically by name, it would be easy to shrug off the problems shown in the photos as the product of individual, poorly run facilities—a few bad apples. Interestingly, many people who saw the pictures falsely thought that the pictures were taken in institutions they worked at or were in their own communities. Unlike most photographic exposés that cause only a local stir and are quickly forgotten, Blatt and Kaplan's efforts are credited with helping to launch the national deinstitutionalization movement.

Unlike the asylum postcards, only one of the pictures in *Christmas in Purgatory* shows buildings. The book contains no distant shots, no scenes of the ground or the gates. These missing views

can be in part attributed to Blatt's promise of anonymity. Muckraking photographs, in contrast to such views, are almost always pictures of dark interiors. Rather than showing beautiful spots on the grounds, fountains, and flags, they feature the crowded living areas, as in illustration 5.19, which shows the sleeping arrangements on one huge, overcrowded ward.

Muckraking images such as Blatt and Kaplan's do not emphasize the order and the structured activity, the facilities' uniform dress and cleanliness. Instead, in them the viewer is confronted by bedlam, filth, and runaway chaos. In illustrations 5.20 and 5.21, taken from *Christmas in Purgatory*, the men on the ward are barefoot, some are naked; the ward is disorganized and completely out of control. The subjects of Blatt and Kaplan's images are shown up close, slightly out of focus, with photographer-added blackouts over their eyes and genitals.

Muckraking photographs reveal a different form of photographic rhetoric. Rather than being

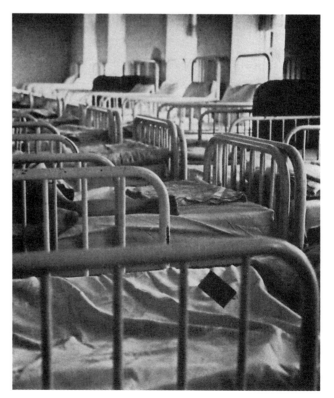

5.19. Ward interior, unidentified institution, 1965. Center on Human Policy at Syracuse University.

from ward staff, who might have altered their behavior and in other ways covered up the conditions.

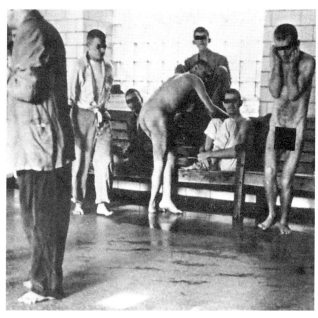

5.20. Ward interior, unidentified institution, 1965. Center on Human Policy at Syracuse University.

5.21. Ward interior, unidentified institution, 1965. Center on Human Policy at Syracuse University.

neat and orderly, the people in them are shown as filthy and out of control. Rather than being clearly focused and carefully composed, the photos are chaotic, with people scattered helter-skelter within the frame. The snapping from the hip with a concealed camera produced pictures that were blurred, candid, and disordered. The pictures were both characteristic of the approach and in line with what the photographers hoped to produce, a view of institutions that revealed their chaos and abuse.

CONCLUSION

Institutional photographers produced images of people with disabilities who were well dressed and orderly; muckraking photographers, in contrast, created images of people who were naked and frenzied. Photographers presented the facilities that people with disabilities lived in as either therapeutic centers or snake pits. Many institutions could be photographed both ways at the same moment. All, even the most heralded, were cheered at one point and exposed at another, despite the fact that actual conditions did not change radically. Letchworth Village, the setting of Margaret Bourke-White's

photographic documentation, was later featured in a national exposé on the *Dick Cavett Show*. Asylum photography best illustrates how the pictures taken of disability are more a reflection of the perspective of those who take the images than of the people and institutions in the photographs.

6 Clinical Photographs

"Feeblemindedness" in Eugenics Texts

MARTIN ELKS

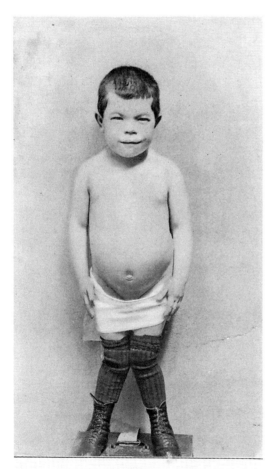

CASE C.

CRETINOID.

6.1. "Case C. Cretinoid." From Barr 1904, plate XXXVIII.

This chapter is based on an extensive study of photographs that appeared in eugenicists' writings in the period from 1900 to 1930 (Elks 1992). The sources cited show that some

pictures come from texts published in Great Britain. Eugenicists abroad shared both US eugenicists' perspectives and their clinical texts. The sources in this chapter do not include annual reports and other forms of institutional propaganda like those noted in chapter 5 on asylums. A more complete analysis and discussion of the research reviewed in this chapter can be found in Elks 1992.

The eugenics era, a period covering approximately the last decade of the nineteenth century and the first three decades of the twentieth century, was a time when many medical and other professionals focused their attention on describing, explaining, photographing, and controlling classes of people they thought were responsible for most social problems. One such group of major concern encompassed those people labeled "feebleminded."[1] Roughly speaking, *feeblemindedness* was the general term used in the United States to describe conditions later referred to as "mental deficiency," "mental retardation," "intellectual disabilities," and "developmental disabilities."[2] In the eugenics

1. The terminology used in this chapter reflects the clinical vocabulary used during the period. The term *feeble-minded* was spelled two ways, with or without a hyphen after *feeble*. For histories of mental retardation in the United States, see Ferguson 1994, Trent 1994, Noll and Trent 2004.

2. The term *feeblemindedness* was used inconsistently. Although most professionals used it the way I am using it, others used it to refer only to people who were "higher-functioning mental defectives."

era, it was widely believed that feeblemindedness was one of the root causes of crime, pauperism, dependency, alcoholism, prostitution, and other social ills.[3]

Eugenics was "the science of the improvement of the human race by better breeding" (Davenport 1911, 1). Eugenicists believed that the major cause of intellectual disability was biological—heredity as well as inbreeding and disease, so they considered the best solution to the problem was to control who bred. They believed that feeblemindedness unchecked would reproduce so prolifically that society as a whole would degenerate. They advocated such practices as regulating the marriage of "undesirables," strict immigration laws that would keep mentally deficient people out of the country, confinement of the feebleminded in institutions, and sterilization. Even euthanasia was suggested as a possible remedy (Hollander 1989; Elks 1993).

Many of these ideas were widely held not only by professionals, but by the general public. By 1914, eugenics was taught at major universities such as Harvard, Columbia, Cornell, and Brown (Chorover 1979). Exhibits extolling eugenics principles were common at state fairs, where families would be examined and trophies given to the "fittest families" in order to promote positive eugenics. Numerous books, journals, and associations were devoted to the public dissemination of eugenics' ideas and policies. Prominent eugenics associations that flourished included the Eugenics Education Society, the American Breeder's Association, and the Race Betterment Foundation.

The destructive influence of the eugenics era on the lives of persons with intellectual disability then and now cannot be downplayed (see M. Haller 1963; Ludmerer 1972; Kevles 1985; Ferguson 1994; Carlson 2001). And photography played an important role in promoting eugenics ideas and policies. The photos in this chapter appeared in eugenics texts and articles written by experts in mental deficiency and represent the embodiment of their beliefs about the cause and clinical dimensions of feeblemindedness. I refer to these images as "clinical photographs" in that they were produced by clinicians to describe various aspects of the clinical condition they referred to as "feeblemindedness."

Armed with theories of degeneracy, genetic inheritance, intellectual disability, and intelligence testing, eugenicists led the crusade to seek out the feebleminded in order to control them and their reproduction (Davies 1930). Disability professionals took on the mandate of studying them as well as popularizing theories about the dangers of feeblemindedness. Photography was one of their most important tools (Fernald 1912, 91–97).[4]

THE CAMERA IN THE HANDS
OF EUGENICISTS

During the eugenics era, it was widely believed that a person's physical features, the shape of his or her body, and facial appearance revealed basic information about his or her moral character and mental abilities. They believed that the trained eye could tell whether a person was feebleminded just by looking at that person.[5] In addition, they believed that the environment in which the feeble-

3. One eugenicist who was the leader in the field of intellectual disability, the psychologist Henry Goddard, showed his contempt for people with feeblemindedness when he stated: "The feebleminded person is not desirable, he is a social encumbrance, often a burden to himself. In short it were better both for him and for society had he never been born" (1914, 558; for another statement like this one, see Barr 1904, 102).

4. Intelligence testing—which was at a rudimentary state of development in the eugenics era—was also ranked high as a diagnostic tool. I have not included it in my discussion.

5. Earliest clinical textbooks described the links between mental disorders, on the one hand, and body types, facial features, and expressions, on the other (e.g., Morel 1857). Early pioneers in the field of mental disorders advocated the use of pictures, even photography, in identifying and diagnosing mental patients (Diamond [1856] 1976, 18–21).

minded lived, their homes and surrounding area, could be documented as proof of their degeneracy.

Early-twentieth-century technical advances in photography and the increasing ease with which photographic images could be reproduced in books and journals proved to be a boon to professionals in the field of mental deficiency; they helped to promote these professionals' theories. Eugenicists trusted the camera to record the facts accurately and rapidly. Photography became a diagnostic tool, a method of developing classification systems, and a way of providing empirical proof of the link between the physical body and psychological disorders and deficiencies (Gilman 1982).

Eugenics textbooks that emphasized feeblemindedness followed the popularity of theories and writings of Italian criminal anthropologist Cesare Lombroso. Lombroso's theories of the born criminal and the stigmata (bodily indicators) of criminals were widely accepted in the United States at the turn of the twentieth century (Reilly 1991). His classic text *L'homme criminal* (1876), published in English as *Criminal Man* in 1911 (Lombroso [1911] 2006), provided a format for textbooks on feeblemindedness. In addition to graphs and drawings, Lombroso freely used pictures derived from photographs to illustrate and prove his ideas.[6]

Most eugenics texts were extensively illustrated with photographs of people with mental disabilities. Like others, Martin Barr used many photographs in two influential texts, *Mental Defectives* (Barr 1904) and *Types of Mental Defectives* (Barr and Maloney 1920). Barr was one of the advocates of photography as a useful tool in eugenics and described the camera's utility in detail. He encouraged students and professionals to study photographs carefully so that they could gain knowledge of the types of feeblemindedness and use that

information to diagnose defective children and adults (Barr and Maloney 1920, 177).

The power of the belief in photography to achieve the goals of recognizing the feebleminded can be seen in the abundance of illustrations in the books and journals of this era. For example, Henry Goddard's 1914 text *Feeblemindedness: Its Causes and Consequences* contains thirty-eight plates, each with multiple photographs. Martin Barr and A. B. Maloney's *Types of Mental Defectives* (1920) contains thirty-one plates of up to nine photographs each, and Alfred Tredgold's 1908 work *A Textbook of Mental Deficiency (Amentia)* has thirty-two such plates. Eugene Talbot's text *Degeneracy: Its Causes, Signs, and Results* (1901) contains 120 illustrations, many of which are photographs. In the *Journal of Heredity*, the premier eugenics journal of the period, there was scarcely a page without a photograph or some other graphic image.

Eugenics textbook photographic illustrations can be sorted into three major categories. In the first group, the most numerous, were photographs of people who were supposedly feebleminded. The second included pictures of parts of their bodies—mainly ears, tongues, hands, and brains. The third offered social documentary views of feebleminded people living in what was described as their "natural habitat," their homes and surrounding environments. I concentrate on the first two categories and only touch on social documentary toward the end of the chapter.

PORTRAITS

The vast majority of the photographs found in the texts are portraits of people who were allegedly feebleminded. The illustration at the start of this chapter (6.1), showing a person designated as a "cretinoid" in the caption, is a good example. Although most illustrations are of a single subject taken full body or from the waist up or of the shoulders and the head, group shots were also common. Rather than being photographed as individual

6. For examples, see the format used in Tredgold's 1908 text on mental deficiency and Goddard's 1914 text on feeblemindedness.

AMENTIA WITH ACHONDROPLASIA.

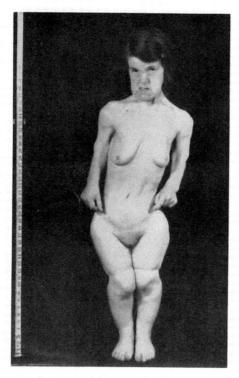

Age 55 years. Sixth of a family of seventeen. Feeble-minded. Usefully employed in needlework and is a good crochet worker.

(Photograph by courtesy of Dr. J. K. C. Laing.)

6.2. "Sixth of a family of seventeen. Feeble-minded." From Tredgold and Soddy 1956, 305.

persons, the subjects were depicted as specimens, examples of types of mental defectives, or carriers of particular diseases or conditions. Although their first names are sometimes given or their full name in rare instances, in the great majority of the captions their diagnosis is used as their designation—for example, "cretinoid" (cretin)—or they are referred to by such phrases as "case 3" and the "mongol type." Clinical photographs of this era are the only genre of disability imagery where subjects are regularly shown nude or only partly clad (illus. 6.2).

The composition of the photos is straightforward and simple. As in the photos of criminals in Lombroso's work and of "the types" of tribal peoples in physical anthropologists' texts, the subject of a photo illustrating feeblemindedness was placed in the center of the frame, facing the camera or in full profile. As in illustration 6.3, it was common for textbook portraits to include the subject in two views, fully facing the camera and in profile.

In portraits taken indoors, there are no decorative backdrops. The backdrop is typically monocolored—black, white, or gray—and it often looks as if a bed sheet were used. Although most of the

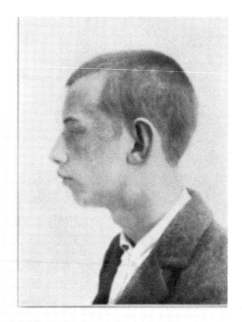

CASE F.

6.3. "Case F . . . ," "Moral Imbecile—Low Grade." From Barr 1904, plate XXII.

portraits were taken indoors, many, especially those of higher-functioning institutionalized people and those of small groups, were taken outside with either buildings or trees in the background. Many of the outdoor shots have a snapshot quality—they are not formally posed, and the composition is not well organized—as if these pictures were taken by amateurs, albeit competent ones (the focus and the contrast are good). Although in some pictures the subjects are nude, they are most often dressed, some in normal and even dressy clothes, others in institutional garb. Instead of subjects being posed in the way most people might be in a normal picture-taking scenario, they were photographed to emphasize their abnormalities and their status as clinical subjects.

Illustration 6.4, a photograph of a man with microcephaly, is a prime example of posing a subject in order to emphasize his abnormalities. Subjects were often chosen to be featured in texts because they displayed some extreme physical characteristic that could be linked to feeblemindedness. In this illustration, the man's head is exceptionally small and abnormally shaped even for someone classified as microcephalic. His head is also shaved, a feature of the picture that visually dramatizes the size of his head and contributes to his strange appearance. We do not know whether his hair was removed for purposes of the photo or not. Institutional staff usually shaved inmates' heads to simplify maintenance and to control parasites.

Most clinical portraits were taken inside buildings or on the grounds of institutions or hospitals where subjects were either confined or under observation. As institutional officials began including mug shots of "patients" in their records and producing institutional visual propaganda, some of them established photographic studios on the

 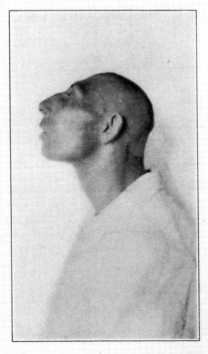

Front view of low-grade micro-cephalic imbecile, chronological age 25, mental age 3. Reproduced by permission from photograph supplied by Dr. Charles S. Bernstein

Profile view of same micro-cephalic imbecile. Reproduced by permission from photograph supplied by Dr. Charles S. Bernstein

6.4. Front and profile view of a "low-grade microcephalic imbecile, chronological age 25, mental age 3." From Paterson 1930, 82.

premises. Institutions with research centers often had their own photographic facilities. Many of the photographs were likely taken by mental health professionals, some even by the authors of the studies where they were used as illustration. Others were taken by professional staff photographers. The photographs have a straightforward, clinical, utilitarian quality; the modes of presenting are repetitive to the point of being boring. No attention is paid to the aesthetics of the picture. In this regard, they are the opposite of art photography.

In addition to the general characteristics of eugenics photography just discussed, other special features define the genre, such as measurement of body parts, the presence of a "helping hand" in the photo, and documentation of brains and other body parts.

MEASUREMENT

Aside from the portrait genre of disability photographs, eugenic clinical photographs often show the subjects next to rulers, calipers, and other measuring devices. These devices' obvious function is to show the reader the dimensions of the subject's body, typically his or her overall size or the magnitude of his or her head. Although in some photos the measuring device's practical function is obvious, in others, such as illustration 6.5, it is not. (Also see illustration 6.2, left side.) In this illustration, it is difficult to decipher what the ruler is measuring, and no information is provided in the text describing what the reader is to learn from viewing it.

In illustration 6.6, a boy is posed with a man holding a large caliper. The purpose of the instrument is made clear by the caption: "Making head measurements during a mental examination. The shape of the head is often important."

These measuring devices not only gauged the physical characteristics of subjects but provided a symbol of the alleged science behind the study of feeblemindedness. After all, precise measurement is the trademark of science.

HELPING HAND

By "helping hand," I mean that in addition to the person who is judged feebleminded in the photo, part of the body of a staff person, usually his or her hand, is visible. The helping hand is most often an attempt to guide or control the subject being

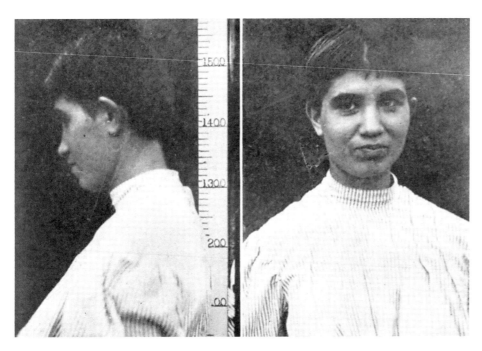

6.5. "Case 324. Hattie, Age 23. Mentally 3." From Goddard 1914, 20.

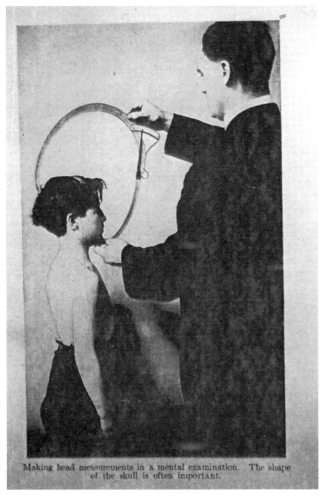

Making head measurements in a mental examination. The shape
of the skull is often important.

6.6. "Making head measurements in a mental examination. The
shape of the skull is often important." From Holmes 1912, 82.

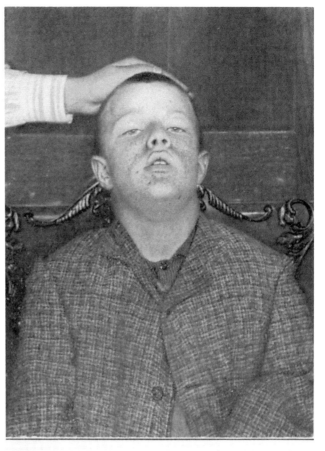

CASE D.

6.7. "Case D," "Ademona Sebaceum." From Barr 1904, plate III.

photographed. The helping hand usually comes
from an anonymous person who is outside the
frame. Although it is present in many pictures, it is
primarily associated with pictures of lower-func-
tioning intellectually disabled persons, those who
were called "idiots" and "imbeciles" (illus. 6.7). It
is seldom present in portraits of "morons," which
was what higher-functioning persons with intellectual disabilities were called at the time.

The presence of the helping hand in the images
varies from minimal—barely visible—to demon-
strably intrusive. In a few examples, two people are
present (illus. 6.8). The helping hand can be holding
the subject in a standing position or manipulating
him or her into a favorable pose or even keeping
him or her from leaving the frame. The force of the

contact of the helping hand varies from barely a
touch to a strong grab.

What does the helping hand tell us about picture taking and the relationship between the photographer and the subject? For the most part, it is
there because the person taking the picture could
not rely on the subject to pose as desired. The helping hand tells us that the positioning of the body
was largely involuntary and that the composition
was largely in the picture taker's hands.

Although the presence of the helping hand in
some photos can be construed as a symbol of the
subject's rebellion—that the subject was resist-
ing the photo opportunity—that interpretation
is farfetched. In the great majority of the photos,
the helping hand is an indicator of the subject's
dependency and is a powerful communicator of

of people labeled feebleminded and the brains of anyone in the general public. Nevertheless, some brains taken from some dead people diagnosed as feebleminded did exhibit abnormal patterns. These brains were featured in the texts. The inference was that it was only a matter of time before other brain anomalies in feebleminded people would be recognizable by scientists.

Pictures of brains concretized feeblemindedness—reified it as a physical, objective condition with clear visible causes. The captions of photographic illustrations of brains focused on their relative size, shape, convolutions, and special diseased-related abnormalities. Seeing is believing, and the more people saw pictures of abnormal

6.8. "Case B," "Profound, Excitable Idiot." From Barr and Maloney 1920, 13.

the feebleminded person's incompetence (Fernald 1912).

BRAINS

Pictures of the diseased and deformed brain extracted from the sculls of dead feebleminded persons are in most eugenicists' texts on so-called mental defectives. Some illustrations even include profiles of the subject alive juxtaposed with pictures of his or her postmortem brain. Photographs of the brain represent physical evidence of eugenicists' belief that the most common cause of feeblemindedness was defective brains. In fact, with the exception of some severely disabled people, a viewer cannot really tell the difference between the brains

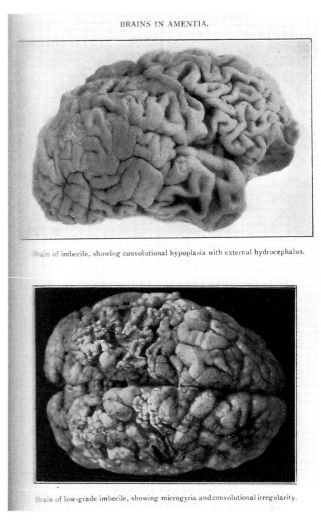

BRAINS IN AMENTIA.

Brain of imbecile, showing convolutional hypoplasia with external hydrocephalus.

Brain of low-grade imbecile, showing microgyria and convolutional irregularity.

6.9. "Brain of imbecile" and "brain of low-grade imbecile." From Tredgold 1947, 104.

brains, the more they believed that such brains were the source of mental deficiency (illus. 6.9).

LIVE BODY PARTS

Eugenicists thought that external parts of the body, in addition to brains, revealed feeblemindedness or mental deficiency as well. These abnormalities were called the "stigmata of degeneracy." A typical list included "facial asymmetry, harelip, protruding or malformed ears, facial grimaces, strabismus or other eye difficulty, high, cleft, or missing palate, deformities of the nose, irregular impacted teeth," as well as peculiarities in the shape of the head, malproportioning in general physique (such as unduly long arms or legs), gigantism or dwarfism, extreme awkwardness, and so on (Pressey and Pressey 1926, 40).

The list was endless, but certain body parts were singled out for documentation, photographed, and featured in texts. The mouth was one. Reference to the mouth may be found frequently in case descriptions of idiots and imbeciles.[7] Alfred Tredgold described the mouth of the feebleminded person this way: "The lips are often thick, coarse, prominent, and unequal in size. The mouth is heavy and flabby-looking, generally open, and devoid of either refinement or firmness" (1908, 84). Photos showing close-ups of the mouth and captions making reference to the mouth's position, shape, or size were common.

One type of mouth associated with feeblemindedness was what eugenicists called "the gape" (illus. 6.10). The term referred to a mouth that was open beyond that which was considered consistent with a normal relaxed mouth. The gape could be caused by an abnormally large tongue—common

6.10. "A mischievous, excitable imbecile; usually grimacing as shown." From Tredgold 1916, plate VI.

in syndromes referred to as "mongolism" and "cretinism"—or just be a characteristic of the way a person held his or her mouth.

Particular-shaped mouths and tongues were used in eugenics texts as the personification of feeblemindedness. When being photographed, subjects were posed so that their mouths or tongues were highlighted and thus so that the abnormality the picture takers wanted to illustrate was emphasized (illus. 6.11).

Ears were another body part given attention. Like brains, ears were examined for their shape, size, and various abnormalities. In addition, their position on the head was noted. Asymmetrical ears, where one ear was not the exact duplicate of the other, was a sign of mental deficiency, as were various irregular-shaped ears. Illustration 6.12 is from a page devoted to "ear anomalies" in Tredgold's 1929 book *Mental Retardation*. The two pictures on the top are from the same person and show asymmetry. The ear on the lower left was described as "deformed and elongated," whereas

7. Elizabeth Kite, Goddard's fieldworker, made the following observation on one of her field trips: "Three children, scantily clad and with shoes that would barely hold together, stood about with drooping jaws and the unmistakable look of the feeble-minded" (quoted in Goddard 1914, 77).

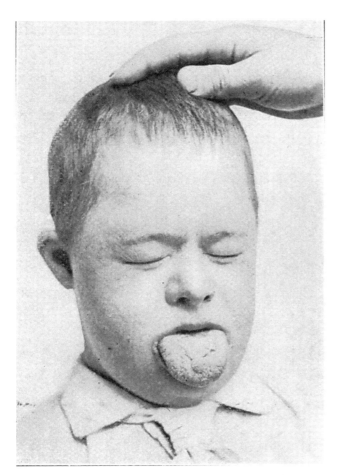

6.11. "Case C," "Mongolian Type." From Barr 1904, plate XXXIII.

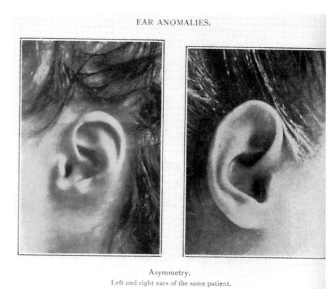

EAR ANOMALIES.

Asymmetry.
Left and right ears of the same patient.

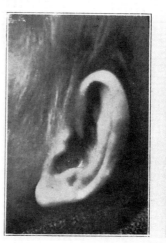
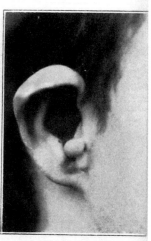

Deformed and elongated.   Deformed with supernumerary
                                           auricle.

6.12. "Ear Anomalies." From Tredgold 1947, 121.

the one on the lower right was distinguished by having a "supernumerary auricle."

The forlorn fellow in illustration 6.13 is labeled in the caption as possessing "constitutional inferiority." The caption makes special mention of his "jug handle ears."

Hands and arms were also frequently featured. The hand irregularities found in people with Down syndrome are commonly shown (illus. 6.14).

In addition to abnormalities in specific body parts, eugenicists believed a person's body type and posture could reveal feeblemindedness. Thus, many textbooks had full-body illustrations of subjects in which they pointed out characteristic stances of particular categories of mental deficiency (illus. 6.15).

SHOWCASED SYNDROMES

Professionals documented and described specific major syndromes associated with feeblemindedness. These syndromes included microcephaly, "mongolism," and "cretinism," all of which were considered to have demonstrable physical manifestations.

Although the eugenicists' views were reprehensible, their observations did lead them to occasional correct inferences. People who are classified as microcephalic have small craniums and other

Fig. 30.—Constitutional inferiority. Note jug handle ears.

6.13. "Constitutional inferiority. Note jug handle ears." From Gulick 1918, 106.

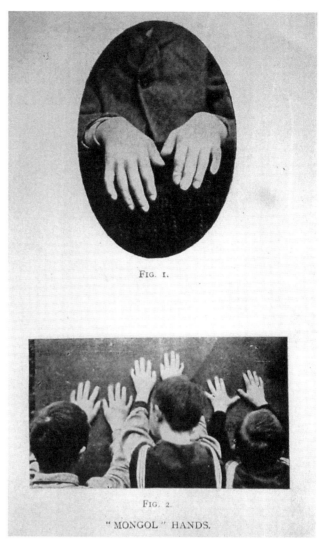

Fig. 1.

Fig. 2.

" MONGOL " HANDS.

6.14. "Mongol hands." From Shuttleworth and Potts 1916, figs. 1 and 2.

body abnormalities that make the condition obviously visible. In addition, the condition is clearly linked with intellectual disability and has a hereditary component. The eugenicists, however, carried these conclusions a large step further. For them, it was in many respects the paradigmatic case of feeblemindedness; it embodied all of their beliefs about mental deficiency.

Pictures of people with microcephaly abound in eugenics writings. Most are individual profile portraits, a pose that best showed the individuals'

small, unusually shaped skulls (see illus. 6.4). In addition, many photos show people with the condition juxtaposed with individuals with hydrocephaly, a condition in which there is an abnormal amount of fluid accumulation in the cavities of the brain. This fluid can cause pressure inside the skull, which brings on a progressive enlargement of the head and mental disability. Photographs that juxtapose an abnormally large head with an abnormally small head exaggerate the appearance of the abnormalities in both subjects—the small head looks even smaller, and the large head looks even

CASE D.   CASE E.   CASE F.

IDIOTS—SUPERFICIAL APATHETIC.

6.15. "Idiots—Superficial Apathetic." From Barr 1904, plate VII.

6.16. Hydrocephalic individuals juxtaposed with microcephalic individual. From Barr 1904, plate XLII.

larger. The juxtaposing of extremes in general, not just of people with unusually large or small heads, but of abnormally tall and abnormally short people, and so on, is used extensively in eugenics illustrations (illus. 6.16).

Another extensively displayed syndrome was what mental health professionals called "mongolism." Today such people are diagnosed as having Down syndrome. Believing that people with this syndrome were genetic throwbacks to what were considered inferior races and that they resembled

certain Asian peoples, Mongolians, eugenic scientists coined the name "mongolism." Although the resemblance between people with Down syndrome and Mongolians was fanciful, texts juxtaposed pictures of people with the syndrome with pictures of Asian Mongols in an attempt to concretize the theory (illus. 6.17).

As I pointed out in earlier illustrations, people with Down syndrome, like those with microcephaly, have facial and body characteristics that are easy to recognize. People with the syndrome were

Fig. 1. AN "ASYLUM MONGOL."
(Dr. Shuttleworth's Case.)

Fig. 2. A KIRGHIZ MAN (RACIAL MONGOL.)

6.17. "Asylum Mongol" and "Racial Mongol." From Crookshank 1924, plate III.

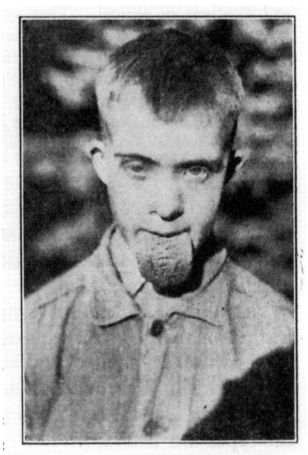

FIG. 24.

A mongolian showing fissures of the tongue.

6.18. "A Mongolian showing fissures of the tongue." From Morgan 1928, 321.

photographed and included in texts at various ages from birth to old age. The large "mongol tongue" was a favorite photograph (illus. 6.18).

Aspects of Down syndrome shown in photographs also included forehead furrows, eyes, profile, posture, hands, ears, and feet. People with Down syndrome were regularly displayed in group photographs, too (illus. 6.19). Notice that the man in the center front is pulling at the mouth of the person to his left. Is he imitating a doctor who would pull the tongue down?

One easy way to exaggerate an abnormality, stigmata, or peculiarity was to multiply it by grouping people with the same deviancy together. The exaggeration was even further enhanced if they were wearing similar clothing. This approach can be seen in illustration 6.20, showing children with Down Syndrome and captioned "a group of Mongols." Note the helping hand on the upper left.

"Mongols" were also juxtaposed with other categories presumably to document their similarities and differences and to add validity to "mongolism" as a distinct type. One such other category was "cretins" (see illus. 6.1 at the beginning of the chapter). Like "Mongols" and microcephalics, cretins—in reality, people with hypothyroidism—were photographed in ways that would emphasize

A GROUP OF MONGOLIAN IMBECILES

6.19. "A Group of Mongolian Imbeciles."
From Popenoe and Johnson 1918, 144.

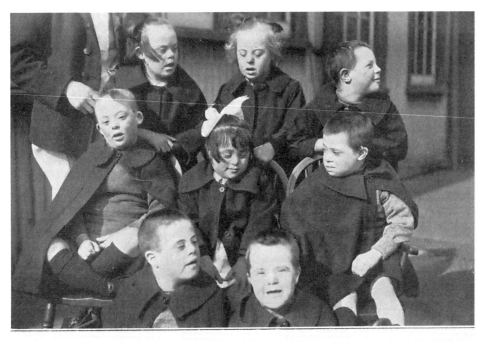

A group of Mongols.

6.20. "A group of Mongols." From
Tredgold 1947, plate xiv.

6.21. "A cretin imbecile, Age, 39 years." From Tredgold 1916, plate XXI.

the physiology of their condition. Cretins were more often photographed naked to show their underdeveloped bodies. For similar purposes, they were regularly photographed next to people of normal size (illus. 6.21).

CLASSIFICATION SYSTEMS

Eugenicists' believed that inferior persons would affect later generations by passing undesirable traits to them. As they saw the situation, this detrimental cycle needed to be stopped.[8] Thus, as part of their arsenal of intervention, they developed classification systems to sort out the various types and grades of feeblemindedness. Classification

schemes provided experts with a guide they could use to implement their genetic-control policies—for instance, in determining who should be institutionalized or sterilized.

The search for a classification system that was comprehensive, definitive, and easy to use was of the utmost importance (Barr 1904, 78). Barr and Maloney's widely adopted classification system laid out in *Types of Mental Defectives* (1920) listed five major types of mental deficiency: "idiot," "idio-imbecile," "imbecile," "moral imbecile," and "backward or mentally feeble." In addition, each of these major categories had up to four subcategories, yielding a total of twelve classifications or "grades." The scheme took into account physical and behavioral characteristics as well as intellectual functioning. It was widely endorsed by professionals, including doctors.[9]

Barr and Maloney's text contains twelve plates of photographs corresponding to the twelve categories of feeblemindedness, each plate with up to eight photographs. For example, seven photographs on one page are labeled "Idiots: Profound Apathe [*sic*]" (illus. 6.22). On the next page are eight photographs of people labeled "Idiots: Superficial Excitable" (illus. 6.23).

To the eugenicists, "superficial excitable idiots" apparently looked different from "superficial apathetic idiots," who in turn looked different from those considered representative of the other categories, such as "idio-imbeciles," "middle-grade imbeciles" and so on. As the illustrations show, they do look different, but not because of any physical anomalies. The individuals pictured in the collection labeled "Idiots: Profound Apathe" appear to be younger, more often in chairs, and less dressed up than those in the collection "Idiots: Superficial Excitable." In addition, the illustrations

8. The Eugenics Record Office outlined ten such dangerous "varieties of the human race" (Laughlin 1914, 16).

9. The system was first published by Martin Barr (1904), who was chief physician at the Pennsylvania Training School for Feeble-Minded Children and an early president of the American Association on Mental Deficiency.

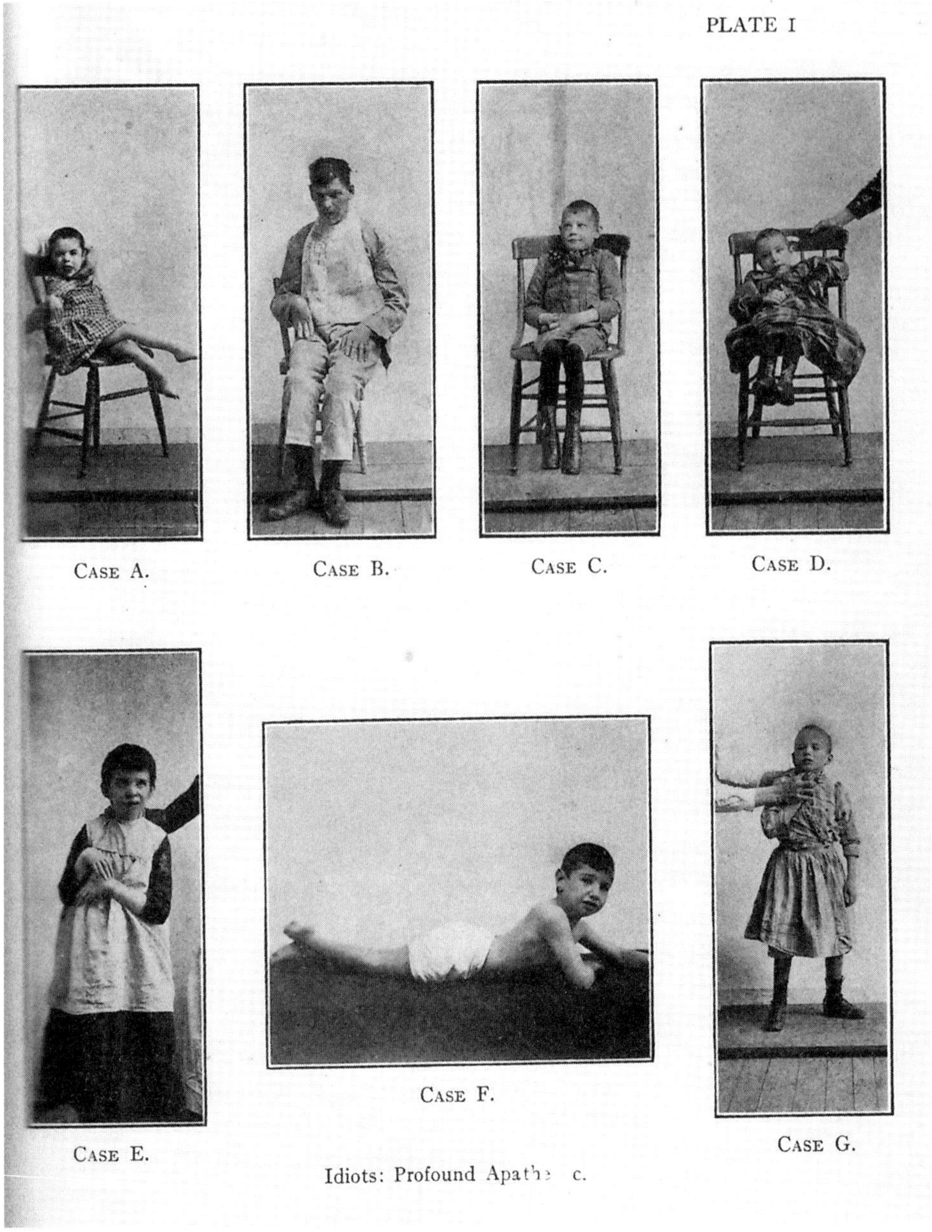

PLATE I

CASE A. CASE B. CASE C. CASE D.

CASE E.

CASE F.

Idiots: Profound Apathe c.

CASE G.

6.22. "Idiots: Profound Apathe [*sic*]." From Barr and Maloney 1920, plate I.

do not match the written descriptions of the characteristics. Nevertheless, the text, accompanied by the photographs, asserted that each type and grade had a characteristic appearance and that it was possible on the basis of inspection to recognize it.

Barr and Maloney claimed that by arranging the photographs side by side from the lowest grade, "idiots," to the highest, "high-grade imbeciles," it was possible to grasp visually the range of mental defect (Barr and Maloney 1920, 50). When the pictures are carefully examined next to one another,

however, they do not accomplish this aim. The best indicators of the types of feeblemindedness in the photographs are not the physiological identifiers named in the classification system, but rather the format and composition of the photographs: the choice of subjects' age, the presence or absence of the helping hand, how the subjects are dressed, their posture and facial expression. "High-grade imbeciles" could be identified because their portraits were often taken only from the waist up, the subjects are wearing stylish clothes, and the picture

PLATE IV

CASE A.　　　　　CASE B.　　　　　CASE C.　　　　　CASE D.

CASE E.　　　　　CASE F.　　　　　CASE G.　　　　　CASE H.

Idiots: Superficial Excitable.

6.23. "Idiots: Superficial Excitable." From Barr and Maloney 1920, 23.

was taken in a studio (illus. 6.24). All these aspects of the photos could be manipulated by the photographer or by others involved in the picture taking.

Further, it is not clear from the images how "high-grade imbeciles" differ in appearance from people not diagnosed with a mental disability. If the individuals shown did not look feebleminded, as the eugenicists defined it, how did they illustrate "feeblemindedness"?

It would appear that the "ascending scale of mental defect" coincided with an ascending scale of socially valued characteristics. The bottom of the scale carried images of abnormality, disability, and dependence (e.g., plain clothing and helping hands), whereas the upper parts of the scale carried images of independence and achievement (studio portraits, stylish clothing, books, and jewelry). There was no neurological reason why studio portraits and good clothes should not have been as valid for "idiots" as for "high-grade imbeciles."

In 1930, a leading eugenicist, Paul Popenoe, pointed out the wooliness of associating mental

PLATE XI

CASE A.

CASE B.   CASE C.

CASE D.

CASE F.

CASE E.

CASE G.

CASE H.

Imbeciles: High-Grade.

6.24. "Imbeciles: High Grade."
From Barr and Maloney 1920, 65.

competence with appearance in an article based on a study he did focusing on photographs of boys of similar age and dress in similar poses and positioned in front of the same backgrounds and in the same settings (see Popenoe 1930). Some had been diagnosed as feebleminded, others as highly intelligent. Popenoe asked test participants to look at the photos and guess the boys' intelligence quotients (illus. 6.25). Their judgments were inaccurate, no better than chance. Except for three or four photographs showing people of the very lowest intelligence, the participants could not predict intelligence by appearance in any reliable way. (See also Popenoe 1929.)

The inappropriate and inaccurate use of photographs by eugenicists as scientific proof is obvious when one reviews the thousands of pictures used as illustrations in eugenics texts. Some assertions about the photographs are just plain absurd. Many photographs were taken of conditions that are

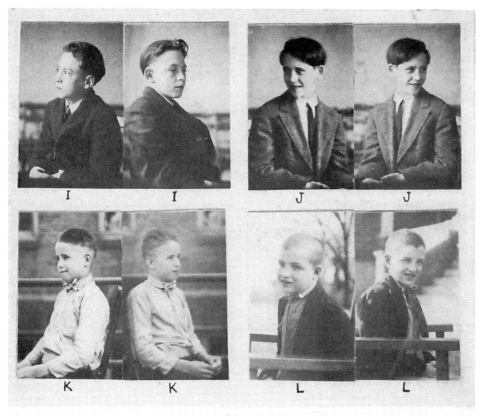

THE STUPID AND THE BRILLIANT—CAN YOU TELL THEM APART?

6.25. "The stupid and the brilliant—Can you tell them apart?" From Popenoe 1930, 225.

impossible to be captured in photos—for example, the picture of a person with "echolalia" in Barr and Maloney's text (1920, 157) (illus. 6.26). Barr and Maloney defined echolalia as a "parrot-like repetition of words and sentences which may or may not be fully comprehended by the speaker" (157). Echolalia, however, has no visible photographic features. People do not look "echolalic." The caption in the picture is the only element in the photo that would lead to the interpretation that the subject has echolalia. The belief in the validity of photography in general and of this specific photograph led the viewer to see *in* the photograph the condition identified in the caption.

Illustration 6.27, showing a so-called idiot savant, demonstrates this same issue. An idiot savant was defined as a person who was feebleminded but had an unusual skill. For example, he or she might be incompetent in basic life skills but

ECHOLALIA.

6.26. "Echolalia." From Barr 1904, plate I.

be able to accurately add large numerals in his or her head. Other savants could tell the day of the week that any given date occurred on. Although there is no visible sign of this condition that can be photographed, the simple act of placing a caption labeling the person pictured as an idiot savant in a eugenics text made him or her "look" as if he or she were indeed an idiot savant.

Why include in eugenics texts so many illustrations of people who had no outward signs of feeblemindedness? As I have already suggested, eugenicists believed that feeblemindedness was a threat. Although they held that the cause of feeblemindedness was mainly biological, they worried that in many cases feeblemindedness was difficult for the untrained person to recognize. They

CASE D.
Idiot Savant.

6.27. "Case D. Idiot Savant." From Barr and Maloney 1920, 129.

wanted to warn the world that higher-functioning mental defectives, "morons," were out there and dangerous. This picturing of people who did not look feebleminded alerted the general public to the unrecognizable danger that surrounded them.

THE HOVEL AND THE
NOTORIOUS FEEBLEMINDED

Although illustrations in eugenics texts were mostly of feebleminded people taken in institutions and hospitals, some emphasized what was considered to be feebleminded persons' "natural" environment. These photographs are found in case studies of families published by eugenicists.

In the case study of the Hickories, the caption of one photo (illus. 6.28) reads: "A HOME THAT SHOULD BE BROKEN UP: In this cabin live two of the Hickories (second cousins) and their two young children. Both husband and wife are decidedly feebleminded, and it is certain that all their children will be. It is sometimes a crime for society to break up a family: but it is unquestionably a crime for society not to break up this one, segregating the members for life" (Sessions 1917, 297).

The "natural habitat" of the feebleminded was most often labeled a "hovel." Dilapidated and poorly constructed, maintained, and furnished, the hovel was substandard housing where, according to the eugenicists, people lived a disorganized and depraved lifestyle. The hovel became a symbol of those feebleminded people. In photographs, the housing conditions of "degenerate families" were portrayed as dismal: roofs sloping in the wrong direction, construction from scraps of building materials, holes in the roofs and sides, crumbling structures. Such housing was often located in rural settings, with animals either cohabiting with the family or housed nearby.

Feebleminded people who lived outside the boundaries of institutions were feared for what was considered their criminal and excessive reproductive tendencies. Pictures of hovels in eugenics literature went along with eugenicists' interest

6.28. "A home that should be broken up." From Sessions 1917, 297.

in seeking out and documenting the heritage of feebleminded families who became notorious for their "debauchery." Their real names usually did not appear in the texts, but such names as "Kallikak," "Juke," "Nam," "Hickory," and "Piney" became the stereotype of feebleminded families in their habitat.

Many photos include family members in front of their hovel. These illustrations shared some of the same qualities of the muckraking photos discussed in chapter 5 on asylum photography. Rather than being carefully posed and well focused, the photos are often blurry and off kilter, techniques that compounded the impression of disorganization yet gave the feeling of candid authenticity. They were produced to serve the same purpose as institutional muckraking images—to expose the people's horrible living conditions. But here the location is not the institution, but the horror of community living. The irony here is that the institutional muckraking photographs were directed at the evils stemming from the practices that the eugenicists were promoting, but the eugenicists used the same photographic techniques as the muckrakers.

Illustrations 6.29 and 6.30 are taken from Henry Goddard's famous study of a branch of the Kallikak family, a line that allegedly produced generations of decadent feebleminded relatives. Many

years later biologist Steven J. Gould asserted that the Kallikak photos in these illustrations, which appeared in Goddard's book *The Kallikak Family* (1912), were retouched to make the eyes and mouths look sinister (see Gould 1981). The director of photographic services at the Smithsonian, James H. Wallace Jr., agreed with Gould's judgment that the eyes, eyebrows, mouth, nose, and hair in the photos had been retouched to give the impression of evilness. The assertion that Goddard was engaged in conscious skullduggery in his photographic touchups and that the modifications of the pictures cast the subjects as evil has nevertheless been debated (Francher 1987; Elks 2005). The details of the argument aside, whether a conscious intent in the zealous pursuit of eugenics ideology or an attempt to improve the pictures' visual quality, the Kallikak photo modifications remind us to be skeptical about the claims eugenicists made about these photographic images.

The image of the hovel is one of poverty, squalor, and an animal-like, unhealthy, and disease-ridden lifestyle. It is a particularly powerful image because eugenicists believed that the feebleminded created their own environment. The hovel and the accompanying notorious family studies were the eugenics movement's "central, conformational image: that of the degenerate hillbilly family, dwelling in filthy shacks and spawning endless

6.29. Children of Guss Saunders, with their grandmother. From Goddard 1912, 88.

6.30. The great-grandchildren of "Old Sal." From Goddard 1912, 88.

generations of paupers, criminals, and imbeciles" (Rafter 1988, 2).

DEBORAH KALLIKAK

Eugenicists believed that a feebleminded person could be saved from a life of debauchery through training and careful supervision in segregated institutions. The threat that person posed could be minimized by locking up him or her. Like charity organizations focused on physical disabilities, eugenicists had their own version of before-and-after photography of the feebleminded that illustrated how custodial care could improve lives and save society. The institutional propaganda photos included in chapter 5 showed how orderly and productive the feebleminded could be behind institution walls.

A single person would occasionally be showcased as the "poster child" of what proper care and supervision could accomplish. Deborah Kallikak was one such person. H. T. Reeves called her "the World's Best Known Moron" (1938, 199). Deborah was a member of the infamous Kallikak family that Goddard featured in his widely read book. The study on which the book was based falsely documented the feebleminded line of the Kallikak family tree for a purpose: to show how the progeny on the "bad side" of the kin were prostitutes, criminals, and prolific producers of their degenerate kind (Smith 1988). Illustration 6.31 is a portrait of Deborah that appeared in Goddard's book. It was taken at the Vineland Training School for Feeble-Minded Boys and Girls in Vineland, New Jersey, where she was an inmate. She is pictured as an attractive, well-dressed young lady. Note the fine dress, the bow in her hair, and the book she is holding.

The juxtaposition of complimentary pictures of Deborah with the touched-up pictures of her relatives in front of their hovel was meant to illustrate how she had been saved by eugenicists'

intervention. The degenerate children on the porch (illus. 6.30) represented how she was before that intervention, and the young lady sitting in a refined manner (illus. 6.31) showed her as she was after it was accomplished.

Deborah was institutionalized at Vineland for eighty-one of her eighty-nine years, in spite of the fact that she demonstrated competence in a number of ways, including serving as the nanny for the children of institutional staff and housemaid for the institution's director (Smith 1988, 29). Until his own death in 1957, Goddard continued to refer to her as feebleminded and as a potential threat to society if set free. She died in 1978 at the Vineland Training School.

CONCLUSION

Eugenicists were for the most part wrong about the correlation between appearance and feeblemindedness and in almost all other aspects of their doctrine (Gould 1981). Their ideas and classification systems are laughed at today. However, for the people labeled feebleminded, the eugenicists'

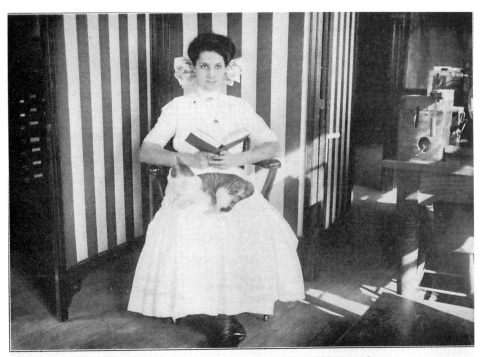

DEBORAH KALLIKAK, AS SHE APPEARS TO-DAY AT THE TRAINING SCHOOL.

6.31. "Deborah Kallikak, as she appears to-day at the Training School." From Goddard 1912, first illustration.

mistakes were costly. These mistakes fueled a big-
oted ideology and its subsequent abuses (e.g., Black
2003). We can only imagine how many ordinary
lives were disrupted and changed forever when
individuals were labeled feebleminded.

The "objectivity" of clinical photographs was
an illusion. Through photography, eugenicists
created an imaginary disease, feeblemindedness
(Smith 1988; Trent 1994). Their textbook and
journal illustrations are better described, however,
as rhetoric rather than science. Nevertheless, the
belief in the truth of photographs helped to elevate
eugenics to scientific social policy.

7 Advertising Photographs
People with Disabilities Selling Products

Dear:
We just saw these little Sunshine Bakers at the Loose Wiles Biscuit Co. Exhibit at the New York World's Fair! They're the cutest little midgets you ever saw and they put on a grand show!

Sincerely,

7.1. Sunshine dwarf bakers, 1939. Printed postcard.

In an earlier chapter, we saw how disabled beggars finessed solicitation by offering begging cards and other petty items to would-be donors. In most cases, the goods were insignificant and provided merely the illusion of a real exchange. But in some transactions, such as those involving magazine subscriptions, what was transferred had real worth. Although the beggars were in one sense merchants, they exploited their disability to provoke sales via sympathy and were aided by photos that presented them as pitiful.

In this chapter, I explore another dimension of people with disabilities as merchants. In the late nineteenth and early twentieth centuries, national and regional manufacturing companies proliferated, and aggressive advertising flourished. Businesses sent salespeople on the road to cities, towns, and villages to push their products. Some efforts involved advertising gimmicks. In addition, the forerunners of present print advertising campaigns, company ad departments, and later advertising agencies created graphic designs, slogans, trademarks, and other symbols to facilitate product identification. With the development of half-tone printing, photographs were transformed into printed images that could be widely distributed in brochures, newspapers, and magazines. In addition, photo postcards were distributed locally as part of advertising campaigns.

I look at how companies employed photographs of people with disabilities to publicize and sell products. In some cases, the person with a disability made public appearances to lure the curious to venues where the product was sold. In others, the person with the disability was used as a product symbol, sometimes even as a trademark. I also look at images in which people with impairments are featured in ads selling products (i.e., prosthetic devices) or services (treatment or healing) designed specifically for people with disabilities.

It has not been common to use people with disabilities to sell products, but I have included this genre here because it demonstrates yet another dimension of picturing disability that needs further exploration.

PEOPLE WITH DISABILITIES AS RETAILERS

The people featured in this section are people of short stature—also known as little people or dwarfs (illus. 7.1). All were self-sufficient and even prosperous. As in their work as sideshow attractions, they parlayed their difference into careers. According to official definitions, those people featured here would currently be considered to have a disability.[1]

Buster Brown Shoes is an interesting case of the merging of advertising and disability. The Brown Shoe Company was started in 1878 by George Brown in St. Louis, Missouri, long before the popular cartoon character Buster Brown was featured in newspapers. The company became a leading shoe manufacturer and presently has a global clientele.

The newspaper cartoon character Buster Brown was created by pioneer cartoonist Richard Outcault and was popular during the first third of the twentieth century. Outcault's most famous character, five-year-old Buster, his friends, and his dog, Tiger, delighted newspaper readers with their mischievous adventures. Until 1904, the Brown Shoe Company and Buster Brown had nothing to do with one another. In that year, a Brown Shoe executive purchased the use of the cartoon character Buster Brown for advertising purposes. The company launched the Buster Brown brand of shoes with a Buster Brown logo, a trademark that is still used today.

What does all this have to do with disability? In addition to featuring Buster Brown and Tiger in its printed advertisements, the company made marketing history by launching a wildly popular advertising campaign. It sent troupes of actors, all dressed like Buster and his friends, on tour visiting towns across the country, and these actors were dwarfs, or midgets,[2] as they were called then. Those who portrayed Buster wore short pants, a wide-brimmed child's hat, and fancy shoes; they were accompanied by dogs resembling the one in the comic strip. These entourages toured the country from about 1904 until 1930 selling Buster Brown shoes. At the height of their activity, they visited more than three hundred communities a year. They performed skits, told jokes, and in other ways entertained the public in venues such as department stores, shoe stores, and local theaters.

The company did not produce its own line of photographs documenting Buster's appearances. Photographers in the towns where they performed caught the occasions on photo postcards and sold them to spectators as mementos. A talented local photographer, H. Montgomery, snapped the action in Hartford, Wisconsin, when Buster came to town and sold postcard images to local people. In illustration 7.2, Buster is riding in the back of a touring car advertising his appearance at a local clothing store. The person acting the part of Buster Brown

1. The generally accepted definition of the term *dwarf* is an adult who is less than four feet ten inches tall. Some might dispute the inclusion of little people in the disabled category. *Disabled, handicapped,* and other such designations are not objective categories that exist outside of human definitions and political wrangling. What conditions led someone to be labeled "disabled" vary from time to time and location to location. The use of the word *disability* to describe certain conditions is contentious. The American with Disabilities Act of 1990 states that dwarfism is a disability.

2. Although *midget* was a widely used term, people of short stature have rejected it as offensive. In the show world, it referred to dwarfs whose condition was the result of hormone imbalance and whose body parts were in the same proportion as typical adults.

7.2. Buster Brown appearance in Hartford, Wisconsin, ca. 1914. Photo postcard. Joel Wayne, Pop's Postcards.

7.3. Dwarf playing Buster Brown, Cherokee, Iowa, ca. 1914. Photo postcard. Joel Wayne, Pop's Postcards.

was William "Major" Ray." Ray, who was purportedly forty-four inches tall, is shown riding through the town in a banner-strewn open car accompanied by a proud merchant and Tiger, Buster's dog.

Another local photographer in Cherokee, Iowa, produced the studio portrait close-up of William Ray playing Buster Brown in illustration 7.3. Buster Brown is shown in full costume perched on an ornate chair lecturing "Tige," who is standing attentively on his hind legs looking directly into his master's face.

Notice how the caption states that this Buster is "THE ORIGINAL." As the story goes, prior to his employment by the shoe company, William "Major" Ray owned a clothing store that sold

Buster Brown shoes. It was Ray who had brought the idea of using midgets to the company. At the beginning of the campaign, the company had used children as Buster Brown look-a-likes, but it had become difficult to recruit kids to go on the road. Ray was the first dwarf to play the role. Interestingly, the employment of dwarfs started as a matter of convenience rather than as a ploy to use their drawing power as what were considered human oddities, which they soon became.

Although it was not the photographers' or company's intention, adult people of small stature playing Buster, a mischievous child, reinforced the dismissive, stereotype of dwarfs as childlike and silly people to be laughed at. The photographs capture the advertising ploy as well as how promoting a product could exacerbate stereotypes that are now considered degrading.[3]

The little people who played Buster Brown were stand-ins for or facsimiles of the trademark that appeared on labels and other graphics produced by the company. In other cases, the dwarfs became the actual trademark. A prominent and early example was Johnny Roventine, a dwarf who became "Johnny," the symbol for Philip Morris, a major manufacturer of tobacco products. The company advertised extensively in national magazines and newspapers, on the radio, and later on television. Wearing a red bellboy uniform, Johnny Roventine was featured in all the company ads for forty years. He became one of the best known figures in American advertising.

How Roventine became the symbol of the Philip Morris company is one of the advertising world's legends. In 1933, at age twenty-two, he was working as a hotel bellboy in New York City. He was a regular employee at the New Yorker hotel, but the management also played up his small statue, featuring him as the "World's Smallest Bellboy." An advertising man from the Phillip Morris Company went to the hotel to observe Johnny in action. In addition to his small, neat appearance, he had a distinctive paging voice. He was offered a position with the company, and that voice was used in the famous announcement, "Call for Phillip Morris." He became a living trademark. Illustration 7.4 is one of hundreds of ads that featured him during his career. Unlike the Buster Brown dwarfs playing a comic-strip child, the Philip Morris Johnny was a more dignified adult, albeit deferential and of low status. He became a real-life celebrity using

7.4. Johnny of the "Call for Philip Morris" advertisement campaign, ca. 1940. Magazine advertisement.

his personal and photo charm to launch a lucrative career.

Although none was as respected and central to an advertising campaign as Johnny, many other dwarfs played a role in company advertising. At the 1939 New York World's Fair, a team of eight "midget" bakers promoted Sunshine Biscuits (illus. 7.1). A specially contrived exhibit included giant Crispy Cracker boxes and oversize crackers postcards that were distributed to visitors. The printed caption, written as if on a postcard sent to the exhibit by a visitor, stated: "We just saw the little Sunshine Bakers at the Loose Wiles Biscuit Co. Exhibit at the New York World's Fair! They're the cutest little midgets you ever saw, and they put on a grand show."

Around the same time that the Sunshine Bakers appeared in ads, Meinhardt Raabe, a dwarf,

3. Ray was the first of more than twenty "midgets" hired by the shoe company over the years to portray the five-year-old comics character. A number of those who played Buster went on to be Munchkins in the film *The Wizard of Oz,* including William Ansley, who worked as Buster Brown for twenty-seven years. Buster Brown dwarfs went on to work for other companies as well.

launched his thirty-year career representing Oscar Mayer as "Little Oscar, the World's Smallest Chef." He was one of the dwarfs who traveled around the country in the "Wienermobile," a hot dog on a bun-shaped novelty vehicle that the company used for advertising. They distributed advertising ephemera showing them dressed as butchers on their cross-country journeys. Unlike Johnny, the Little Oscars and the Sunshine Bakers played the rather demeaning role of cute little folks, much like those who played the Munchkins in the popular *Wizard of Oz* movie that opened in 1939, the same year that the Sunshine exhibit opened at the World's Fair.

It was not just nationally known companies that used dwarfs to promote their products. A regional candy company in Council Bluffs, Iowa, Woodward's Candy Company, had a longtime relationship with a dwarf couple, Mr. and Mrs. Bregant. Labeled the "Candy Kids," they became icons for the company, traveling around Iowa and to neighboring states. The Bregants were pictured with Woodward Candy products and promoted as the "Lightest Weight and Best Proportioned Little Couple in the World." Jean Bregant, the husband, was promoted as being forty-six inches tall, and his wife, Inez, as forty-two inches. Both had been vaudeville performers before working for the company. They retired to Council Bluffs and a home built to their proportions in 1912. The company produced an elaborately illustrated brochure featuring the couple and an advertising postcard that the couple gave out while making appearances (illus. 7.5).

The extensive use of little people in advertising photography was for the most part the result of companies' embracing novelty to get a foot up in what was becoming the highly competitive world of marketing. They wanted product symbols that grabbed the attention of potential buyers. Unlike in the freak show, where a wide range of nonconforming bodies were featured, in advertising dwarfs were a singular attraction. And not just any dwarf would do. Those chosen were "midgets," people whose dwarfism was the result of a

7.5. Mr. and Mrs. Bregant selling Woodward's candy, ca. 1908. Printed advertising card.

pituitary dysfunction and who thus had well-proportioned bodies and were "cute," not offensive, a pleasant novelty. They were perfect little ladies and gentlemen. Although some such as the Bregants and Johnny Roventine were treated with respect and photographed in enhanced poses, for the most part the dwarfs used for advertising were cast in roles that were either childlike as in the Buster Brown campaign or made a mockery of as in Little Oscar and the little Sunshine Bakers.

Although little people dominated the ranks of people with disability in advertising, not all promotional celebrities were of small statue. A few people were extremely tall—giants. Robert Wadlow is perhaps the most widely known. His unusual stature was the result of a hyperactive pituitary gland, which resulted in a man who by the age of twenty had reached the height of eight feet eleven inches and weighed 490 pounds (illus. 7.6).

Wadlow's shoes were size 37. He had to special-order them from the International Shoe Company and thereby became personally known to the company executives. Their relationship was cordial, and the company eventually provided the shoes free of charge. When Robert turned twenty, he traveled for the company as a paid employee, visiting more than eight hundred towns in forty-one states to promote its products. He once appeared as the main attraction in the Ringling Bros. and Barnum & Bailey Circus, but he was a shy man and turned down lucrative offers to be in the circus sideshow. He preferred the lower-paid but, in his eyes, more respectful role of advertiser.

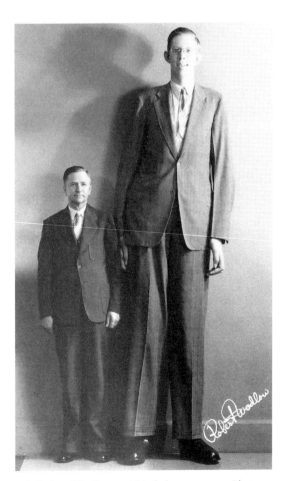

7.6. Robert Wadlow and his father, ca. 1939. Photo postcard.

The traveling was hard on Wadlow. To make room for his long legs in the family car, his father removed the passenger side of the front seat so Robert could sit in the back seat and stretch out. His father drove his son more than three hundred thousand miles on their sales tours. In his biography, written by his father, Robert's affiliation with the shoe company is not explained as being the result of his unusually physiology (Fadner 1944). He preferred to think of himself as a businessman rather than a spectacle. Wadlow died in 1939, the victim of a foot infection; he was in his early twenties.

With the exception of people of small stature and unusually tall people, people with other types of disabilities have until recently been missing from advertisements produced for the general public. Advertisers developed the image of the average American to promote their products, and people with disabilities did not fit that prototype. With the urging of disability advocacy groups, however, this situation has significantly changed over the past few decades.

SELLING DISABILITY PRODUCTS

Another area of advertising where photographic images of people with disabilities turned up in my research was in advertisements for products for this particular group. Such merchandise as prosthetic devises, wheelchairs, patent medicines, and other forms of cure or aid began being widely marketed toward the end of the nineteenth century and the beginning of the twentieth.

Of all the products that were marketed to people with disabilities, artificial limbs and other prosthetic devices were the ones I found to be advertised the most. In the United States, the first large-scale manufacturers of artificial limbs were established in the middle of the nineteenth century. Prior to the 1850s, most devices were fashioned by local craftspersons whose products were often primitive—peg legs and the like. A. A. Marks, a New York firm established in 1853, was one of the leaders in producing a wide range of artificial limbs for both amputees and people with congenital deformities. Although the firm produced in quantity, it, like other manufacturers, maintained a tradition of craftsmanship in its work.

Before the Civil War, the loss of limbs was largely the result of work-related accidents. Many US patents for leg and foot designs were awarded immediately following the war. Starting in 1862, the US government was required by law to provide funds to veterans who lost limbs in war service so that they could purchase artificial ones (Marks 1906).[4] That requirement led to more manufacturers getting into the business and thus to more advertising for the products produced (Mihm 2002). By 1918, there were approximately two hundred artificial limb manufacturers in the United States (Linker 2011, 98). The range and complexity of devices increased as companies began producing and marketing wood, metal, and leather artificial devices.

Illustration 7.7 is an advertising cabinet card from around 1891 for A. Niehans, a Chicago firm that specialized in the production of artificial limbs. The image was taken by a talented photographer who had both technical skills and an eye for composition. In the caption, the company brags of producing an artificial leg with "rubber feet" and an "ankle joint." The advertisement features a photograph of a happy, young, middle-class man who appears pleased with his purchase. By 1891, although Civil War veterans were still eligible for new artificial limb replacements, marketing seemed directed to a younger audience.[5]

7.7. Artificial leg advertisement, ca. 1891. Cabinet photo.

Illustration 7.8 is a photo postcard advertising Forester Artificial Limb Company of Pittsburg, Pennsylvania. Although this photo was taken twenty years after the A. Niehans photo, the presentation is similar—two satisfied, relatively young, middle-class costumers displaying their purchases. The caption reads: "The above is an actual photograph of two of our patrons for whom we have recently constructed Artificial Limbs." The declaration that the advertising image is an

4. For discussion of the manufacturing of artificial limbs and US government involvement in the industry, see Linker 2011, chap. 5. Also see McDaid 2002 for a discussion of James Hanger, a Confederate Civil War soldier who lost a leg in the war and went on to become a successful manufacturer of artificial limbs. For other writings on the development of prosthetic devices, see Ott, Serlin, and Mihum 2002.

5. In 1891, Congress enacted a change in the artificial-limb law. The old law was amended so that veterans could receive a replacement for a prosthetic device every three years. Prior to the amendment, the schedule allowed replacement every five years.

The above is an actual photograph of two of our patrons
for whom we have recently constructed Artificial Limbs.
    All our artificial devices are constructed by practical work-
men of long experience, the materials used are the best obtain-
able, consequently our productions are the most durable and
perfect fitting yet produced.
    If you contemplate getting an Artificial Limb, it will be to
your advantage to call on us before placing your order.

FORSTER ARTIFICIAL LIMB CO.
113 Smithfield Street,   PITTSBURG, PA.

7.8. Advertisement for Forster Artificial Limbs, ca. 1907.
Joel Wayne, Pop's Postcards.

"actual photograph" is interesting in that photographs were at the time believed to tell the truth. There was a growing confidence in scientific fact and the ability of photographs to convey it. In this photo, as in earlier examples, the people with disabilities are posed as respectably dressed, discerning consumers, a depiction that does not stray from how a nondisabled consumer of different products would be portrayed.

The "before-and-after" visual trope discussed in the chapter on charity was used in advertising campaigns for prostatic devices and other disability products. As in the charity campaigns, there were typically two photographs, the first showing the person before the intervention or treatment and the second showing the same person after it. On the left side of the picture in illustration 7.9, an unnamed man sits in a fancy studio chair displaying the stump that once was his leg. Beside him is a mechanical device supplied by the manufacturer. In the image on the right, the same man has installed his artificial leg and is standing straight and tall.

The image in illustration 7.10 does not follow the pattern of the other images I have discussed. Rather than showing a dressed, middle-class person, the before image displays a scantily dressed young man. He is legless, and only the frame of a prosthetic is shown. In the photo on the right, however, he is still almost nude but has put on his appliances. The use of his seminude appearance in both shots resembles the approach taken in medical photography rather than the usual approach of photography advertising disability products directly to the consumer. The subject's appearance leads me to believe that this before-and-after sequence was directed at medical professionals who might prescribe the artificial legs pictured rather than at persons with this same disability.

The man holding the miniature demonstration model of a prosthetic leg in illustration 7.11 was clearly a sales representative for a supplier of medical products. He most likely used the photo postcard to announce his visiting schedule to medical personnel and retailers or to leave as a calling card when he visited new clients.

By the turn of the twentieth century, national firms were marketing medical supplies to physicians and hospitals. They had their own sales forces that traveled extensively. The man in illustration 7.11 was one such salesperson. The companies also produced elaborate catalogs that their sales staff used to take orders and to leave with customers for future reference. These catalogs typically devoted pages to products directed at people with disabilities. In 1904, one firm, the Chicago-based Truax-Greene and Company, produced an 894-page, elaborately illustrated catalog of medical supplies,

7.9. Before-and-after photos for prosthetic device advertisement, ca. 1900. Cabinet cards.

with 50 of these pages devoted to products for people with disabilities, including prosthetic devices. In addition to drawings of the various products, the catalog included before-and-after pictures of satisfied customers. Testimonials were also offered.[6] The endorsement from Andrew McIlquham, who was fitted with a pair of artificial legs, is shown in illustration 7.12. Mr. McIlquham is shown in printed pictures derived from photographs without his artificial legs, sitting in a chair and showing

6. Although some pictures in the catalog were drawn by hand, those like the one in illustration 7.12 were derived from photographs. Note the statement in the caption. Those derived from photos were not half-tones, images directly generated from photographs, but instead were created by an earlier method of converting photographic images into printed pictures.

his stumps. The next two images show him selling newspapers and riding a bicycle. The caption at the bottom of the ad tells us that since getting his legs, he has worked as a newsboy on the railroad and presently holds a position as a salesman for a chemical company. He testified that he can now ride a bicycle, dance, skate, and, as he expressed it, do "anything anyone else can."

With the US entry into World War I, the Council of National Defense and the Army Office of the Surgeon General established the Artificial Limb Laboratory. This agency pushed for the standardization and mass production of artificial limbs. Most companies resisted government pressure to modernize their manufacturing techniques and their products. One firm, E-Z-Leg, did cooperate, however, and so became the main provider of government-issued artificial limbs to wounded soldiers

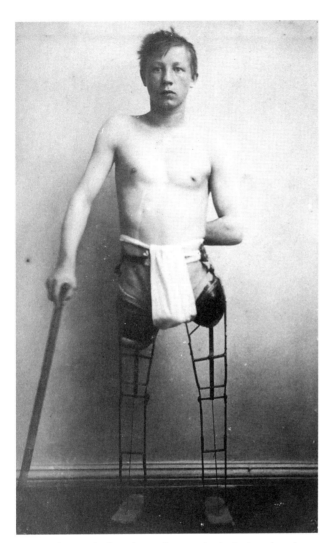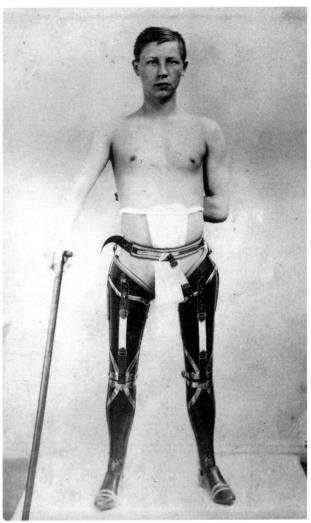

7.10. Before-and-after photos for prosthetic device advertisement, ca. 1919. Cabinet card. Matthews Collection.

(Linker 2011, chap. 5).[7] Veterans of World War I were not provided with a limb allowance; rather, their prosthetic device was given to them before they were discharged. Because of government involvement in providing and influencing artificial limb development during the war and after, design, fitting, and manufacturing of prosthetic devices fell under the control of the medical profession.[8]

Artificial limbs were not the only disability-directed merchandise sold with the help of photographs. As with prosthetic devices, the first large-scale commercial production of wheelchairs in the United States occurred during the later part of the nineteenth century. In 1869, a patent was granted for a wheelchair with rear push wheels that had small casters in front. The 1870s saw the addition of rubber, bicyclelike wheels on metal rims. In 1881, push rims were added.

Competition among manufacturers led to innovation and produced many styles of wheelchairs. Illustration 7.13 is a photographic postcard advertisement from 1904 for a model with a cane chair,

7. E-Z-Leg's product was known as the "Liberty Leg."

8. For a discussion of the development of prosthetic devices during and after World War II, see Serlin 2004.

hand-crank wheels, rubber tires, and a mostly metal frame. The pleasant person sitting in the chair is the epitome of the well-dressed, middle-class young man.

In the late nineteenth and early twentieth centuries, people were more trusting of photographic information than they were as the twentieth century moved on. A photograph was seen to convey a real truth. After all, if it could be shown in a photograph, it had to be true. The happy customer was the mantra of advertising for all products, not just products for the disabled. And those pushing fraudulent products to disabled consumers took advantage of this approach.

PRODUCTS OF DUBIOUS VALUE

Although prosthetic devices, wheelchairs, and other products designed for people with disabilities were functional and did aid people, I also came across a number of ads for products that appeared to be ill conceived or even outright fraudulent. One of the earliest photo advertisements (1878) of this kind that I found was for Dr. Clark's Spinal Apparatus (illus. 7.14). The picture shows a well-dressed girl with no apparent disability using the unwieldy and

7.11. Prosthetic device salesperson displaying a sample of his wares, ca. 1909. Photo postcard. Joel Wayne, Pop's Postcards.

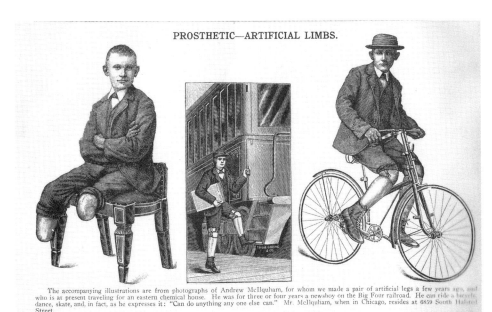

PROSTHETIC—ARTIFICIAL LIMBS.

The accompanying illustrations are from photographs of Andrew McIlquham, for whom we made a pair of artificial legs a few years ago, and who is at present traveling for an eastern chemical house. He was for three or four years a newsboy on the Big Four railroad. He can ride a bicycle, dance, skate, and, in fact, as he expresses it: "Can do anything any one else can." Mr. McIlquham, when in Chicago, resides at 6859 South Halsted Street.

7.12. Prosthetic limbs advertisement, 1904. Catalog illustration.

7.13. Wheelchair advertisement, ca. 1910. Photo postcard.

7.14. Dr. Clark's Spinal Apparatus, 1878. Printed advertisement.

complex equipment. The paraphernalia consists of a heavy, wheeled, wooden frame and a heavy metal spring hanging above the user. Attached to the spring is a set of supports, one for the chin, the others for under the arms. On the back of the card, Dr. Clark declares that the apparatus can be used in the house and out of doors, for sitting, standing, or walking for a few minutes or hours at a time.

The script on the back states that the device is intended for use by people with a wide variety of conditions, including "curvature of the spine," "weakness and paralysis of the legs," and the "inability to walk, or to control the use of the limbs." It goes on to assert that in addition to allowing mobility, Clark's Spinal Apparatus will

lead to "better circulation and purification of the blood, resulting in renewed appetite, improved digestion and increased strength." In addition, "it makes braces unnecessary and applies mechanical treatment directly to the seat of the difficulty without burdening, binding, bruising[,] [c]ompressing, or in any way hampering any portion of the body, but inviting it rather to healthful activity in every part." These are only a few of the claims. Upon inspection of the photo, one can see how unlikely it is that the apparatus lived up to the manufacturer's claims.

Another photo advertisement that appears to be pushing a fraudulent intervention for people with

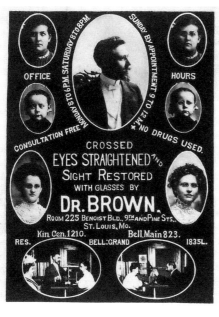

7.15. Advertisement for Dr. Brown's eye treatments, St. Louis, Missouri, 1909. Collection. of Leonard A. Lauder.

disabilities offers a treatment of eye dysfunctions (illus. 7.15). We do not know whether Dr. Brown was a legitimate doctor or a quack, but he used a photo postcard to claim to be able to straighten crossed eyes and restore sight without using eyeglasses. The advertisement includes not only photos and text, but a calendar for the year 1909 to make the advertisement a gift, an object that might be useful to the recipient. Examining the inserted pictures, we can see that the largest is a portrait of Dr. Brown himself. The two on the bottom show Brown with patients. The left and right sides of the advertisement show patients who had been treated by Brown—the before treatment portrait on the left and the after treatment portrait on the right.

HEALERS

At the turn of the nineteenth century, the distinction between quack and legitimate medical practitioner was even less clear than it is today. Some healers we would now consider hucksters were famous and highly respected among their patients, at least those who considered themselves to have been successfully treated. Some practitioners claimed to cure disabling conditions and used photographs to promote their products and services.

In an ad in the widely read progressive monthly family magazine *Review of Reviews*, a healthy girl standing on her own is described as one of the success stories of the L. C. McLain Sanatarium in St. Louis, Missouri (illus. 7.16). In addition to the picture, there is a statement allegedly from her father testifying that the sanitarium cured her. The ad harkens back to the charity fund-raising images shown in chapter 4, but here McLain is not soliciting donations; he is advertising for patients.

One healer whose practice was extensively documented in photographs and who was an out-and-out fraud was John Till, "the Famous Plaster Healer" of northern Wisconsin. Photographers from his region came to his clinic, snapped pictures, and sold photo cards to Till's clients and neighbors. Till also ordered a series that he used as advertisements. Both types were sent through the mail to promote Till and his practice.

In illustration 7.17, an example of one such photo postcard, the healer's portrait is in the center of a montage, with three other pictures showing his home, the town he practiced in, and the carriages waiting at the railroad station to take patients arriving by train out to Till's home, where he practiced his trade. And illustration 7.18 shows some of Till's patients outside one of the hotels they

This Little Girl Had Infantile Paralysis

Both legs were paralyzed as a result of Brain Fever. Her father brought her here for treatment. Read what he says:

Gentlemen: Edith is well, she uses her limbs splendidly and this is hard to realize when we remember that when we took her to you, five years ago, she could not walk at all. We recently had her picture taken and send you one to show you how well she is, but unfortunately the picture does not tell the entire story, for one must see her run around to appreciate her present condition. We have referred many to your place and hope some of them have seen you.

Yours truly,
George W. Funderburk,
Springfield, Ill.

Write us regarding any case of

Club Feet, Spinal Deformities, Deformed Limbs and Joints, Infantile Paralysis, etc.

—will be pleased to advise you and send descriptive literature. Ex-patients everywhere, our references.

L. C. McLain Sanitarium,

969 Aubert Ave., St. Louis, Mo.

7.16. Magazine advertisement for cure for infantile paralysis, 1910.

inhabited while waiting their turn to go to Till's residence/clinic for the cure. Note their crutches and canes.

John Till was an Austrian immigrant. In the early part of the twentieth century, his healing powers became known in the logging camps of northern Wisconsin. As word spread, Till left the woods to devote full time to being the "Wonder Healer." Hundreds of patients were soon arriving each day. He was so popular that the economy of the area depended on him.

Patients who stood in crowds outside the clinic were called in twelve at a time. Till quickly diagnosed each by momentarily placing his fingers on their jugular veins. From that, he claimed, he could spot the problem and prescribe a treatment. The list of diseases and disabilities that Till claimed to be able to cure was as long as the lines of sufferers who came to see him. Till's assistants applied one of two magic formulas, his home-made healing "plaster salves," to their bare backs and wrapped their torso with cloth. One of the ointments contained an ingredient Till called "4X." It was reserved for the most difficult cases. Most got the rub with what was called "burning plaster." It was made with Croton oil and kerosene, a mixture

7.17. John Till advertising card, ca. 1910. Photo postcard.

7.18. John Till's patients, ca. 1909. Photo postcard.

7.19. Patients outside the clinic waiting to be seen by John Till, Almena, Wisconsin, ca. 1909. Photo postcard.

that caused chemical burns and left lesions. During Till's first year in business, his manager deposited eighty thousand dollars in the near-by bank. Needless to say, Till became rich.

Illustration 7.19 shows the crowd outside of Till's practice in 1909. Such photo postcards were widely distributed to document and advertise the popularity of his treatment and to promote his clinic.

Till's personal appearance, hygiene, and strange behaviors—he did not wear shoes; his clothes were caked with salve and dirt; he seldom washed or brushed his teeth; he wore small gold earrings and talked to himself during treatment—did not keep visitors away, nor apparently did the burns caused by the treatment or the fact that it was not effective. People came from all over the Midwest. Hotels in the area expanded and were always filled. Sixteen carriages owned by Till's transport company, each one carrying six passengers, transported people to and from the farmhouse and railroad station.

Till was arrested several times and charged with practicing medicine without a license. At first, no jury would convict him, and he would return after the trial to the farm, where hoards of patients and well-wishers would celebrate. In 1916, after a number of people had sued him on various counts, he was found guilty of practicing without a license. He served ten months before protests and lobbying on the part of supporters resulted in a pardon. In return for his freedom, he agreed to return to Austria. Twenty-four years after his departure, in 1946, he returned to Wisconsin, where he died.

CONCLUSION

Although it is asserted today that people with disabilities were absent from advertising photography until recently, this chapter demonstrates that they were very much in evidence. Of course, the way they were presented in some ads was not in line with current sensibilities. As in early advertising that included women and blacks, stereotypic portrayals dominated. Rather than normalizing people with disabilities into the mainstream of American life, advertisers exploited period ideas about disability to capitalize on the novelty of disability. However, whereas advertisements to sell products to the general public used people with disabilities as attention getters—freaks of sorts—advertisements designed to sell products to people with disabilities did not stray far from typical product advertisements.

8 Movie Stills
Monsters, Revenge, and Pity

8.1. *The Hunchback of Notre Dame*, starring Lon Chaney as Quasimodo, 1923. Universal Pictures.

I was discussing this book with a colleague and mentioned that I was writing a chapter that included horror and gangster movies. He was taken aback. He wanted to know: "What do these movies have to do with disability?" As I show, people with both feigned and actual disabilities are central to horror and gangster genres as well as to other types of films featuring murderers and other perpetrators of violence. In this chapter, I focus on disabilities and film. Killers and other evildoers are the main topics of discussion, but

I end with a brief look at other movie images of disability (Bogdan et al. 1982).[1]

From their beginnings, the movie industry's studios produced photographs to publicize their films. Some were posed portraits of the star actors, but most were taken on the sets of the production

1. For an extensive and comprehensive look at cinema depictions of people with disabilities, see Norden 1994. Also see Chivers and Markotic 2010.

itself or were printed from actual frames of the film. They were referred to as "stills." These photos, usually eight by ten inches, were sent with press releases to newspapers, given to theaters to use in advertising, and incorporated into the designs of printed posters. Their most common use was as come-ons set into display cases outside movie houses designed to lure moviegoers into the show. Stills emphasized the most striking aspects of the production and showed leading actors in the most compelling poses. Photographic images from the stills were used to manufacture half-tone printed posters that were also displayed outside movie theaters.

The still shown in illustration 8.1 was produced in conjunction with the release of *The Hunchback of Notre Dame*. This 1923 film was the most popular pre-Disney adaptation of Victor Hugo's novel. It was Universal Studio's jewel of that season, its most successful silent film. The still shows Lon Chaney in the role of Quasimodo, a stooped-over, half-blind, barely verbal, deaf, persecuted bell ringer of the famous Notre Dame Cathedral. With him is Esmeralda, a beautiful Gypsy. Quasimodo had kidnapped Esmeralda earlier in the film and is being whipped for that transgression. In the still picture, Esmeralda, showing pity for Quasimodo, is bringing him water. The film presents a sympathetic portrait of the leading character, but his daunting disability nevertheless estranges him from others and eventually results in his death.

Moviemakers produced stills and posters for the same reason they created movies: for monetary gain. The movie industry was first and foremost a business, and its publicity favored hype and misrepresentation over accuracy. Hundreds of thousands of studio stills were produced, and although they are not as collectible as other forms of photography, some movie fans bought and kept them. They provide a source to examine visual depictions of people with disabilities in movie promotion and correspondingly in the movies. In this chapter, I concentrate on stills from the early years of the movie industry.

HORROR FILMS

The term *monster* is most commonly used today to refer to strange and frightening creatures that injure and kill. In scientific terminology, it means an animal with a congenital deformity. In the language of medicine, it designates a fetus or infant with a severe disability. These different definitions overlap in stills as well as in movies; the dangerous characters commit appalling and ghastly acts, but they are also scarred, deformed, maimed, and mentally impaired and have other physical and mental disabilities. Movies link physical and mental differences with murder, terror, and violence. Nowhere is this more evident than in horror films.

Horror films—movies that strive to stimulate fear, terror, shock, and disgust in viewers by featuring ugly, dangerous creatures who kill and maim people—appeared in the late 1800s at the start of the film industry. The earliest examples were short-subject scary movies shown at dime museums and on the midway at expositions and fairs (Dennett 1997). The midway varieties were organized in much the same way freak shows were: an outside talker and ticket seller lured patrons into the show tent.

From the first horror films to modern-day renderings, physical and mental disabilities signify murder, violence, and danger.[2] The connection is vividly shown in transformation scenes during

2. The association of disability with violence in images did not start with movies. Age-old folktales contained such portrayals and were illustrated with graphic depictions when they appeared in written form. In the late nineteenth and early twentieth centuries, scientists embraced theories linking physiology and mental defects with crime. In the late 1800s, the influential Italian scientist Cesare Lombroso embraced and popularized such theories. Greatly influenced by Darwin, he and his followers saw criminals as a lower species of human being. He concentrated on discovering criminals through physical examination. His writing contains illustrations showing examples of criminals with asymmetrical skulls, flattened noses, large ears, enormous jaws, high cheekbones, and narrow eyes.

which a triggering event such as a full moon or a secret potion provokes a dramatic change in the actor; before our eyes, he or she transforms from a harmless, respected, good citizen to a killer monster (Gifford 1973, 32–45). This conversion is central to all vampire movies, but the one that occurs in *Dr. Jekyll and Mr. Hyde* epitomizes the type. There are many versions of *Dr. Jekyll and Mr. Hyde*. The first American film version appeared in 1908, and remakes continue today. Before viewers' eyes, the gentleman scholar and mild-mannered Dr. Jekyll ingests the potion and changes into the ferocious, ugly, stooped maniac Mr. Hyde. In the 1931 version of the film, Fredric March plays the lead, a role that won him an Academy Award. Publicity stills for this and other versions of the movie feature either a series of pictures showing the step-by-step transformation or Jekyll juxtaposed with Hyde (illus. 8.2).

Although horror films were sometimes censored for their excesses, they have always enjoyed a strong following. For a long time, actors became stars by playing evil, ugly perpetrators of violence. Lon Chaney (1883–1930), the "Man of a Thousand Faces," is a prime example (Mallory 2009). He is never discussed in disability studies circles but is an important figure in the history of disability. Both of Chaney's parents were deaf and did not communicate orally. His empathy for outsiders, his pantomime skills, and his closeness to people with disabilities are attributed to his early family life. This experience translated to incredible dramatic and scary but sympathetic depictions of movie monsters.

Chaney played in more than 150 films but is probably best known for his roles in *The Hunchback of Notre Dame* (illus. 8.1) and *The Phantom of the Opera*. He won fame by playing physically deformed, depraved brutes in both. Known for his ability to distort his body, he spent hours accomplishing his metamorphosis using pounds of makeup and other appearance-altering devices (illus. 8.3). His makeup artistry has been heralded as a pioneer contribution to film production.

In his role as Quasimodo, the frightful, crooked, bug-eyed, and in other ways deformed bell ringer in *The Hunchback of Notre Dame*,

8.2. Fredrick March in his Oscar-winning role in *Dr. Jekyll and Mr. Hyde*, 1931. Paramount Pictures.

8.3. Lon Chaney showing his makeup chest, ca. 1928. Universal Pictures.

Chaney was the classic disabled victim of others' violence who himself turns to violence. For that film, he wore a hump that weighed more than fifty pounds, twisted his torso, and caused him great pain, which he said he endured so he might empathize with Quasimodo.

In the 1925 version of *Phantom of the Opera*, the facially deformed protagonist tells his beautiful woman captive, "Feast your eyes, gloat your soul on my accursed ugliness." The makeup Chaney fashioned for that performance created a deformed face that is an icon of the horror film genre (illus. 8.4).

It is a common plot in horror films for beauty, an attractive young woman, to be the victim of the monster's rage. The erotic overtones behind the monster-meets-beautiful-woman theme imply an association between certain disabilities and a propensity for sexual assault. At the same time, victims such as the Phantom's heroine are often people who befriend the murderer (illus. 8.5). We are told in one movie, for example, "The werewolf instinctively kills the thing it loves the best" (*The Wolf Man*, 1941).

8.5. Lon Chaney in *Phantom of the Opera* with the imprisoned object of the Phantom's desire, 1925. Universal Pictures.

Although Chaney's son, Lon Chaney Jr. (1906–73), lacked his transforming skills, he followed his father's example by appearing in many horror films and is probably best known for his performance in *The Wolf Man*.[3]

Boris Karloff (1887–1969) had one of the longest acting careers as a movie monster. He played a variety of roles, but his most famous was Frankenstein's monster. Like Chaney, Karloff spent hours in makeup preparation. He played the role first in 1931. In illustration 8.6, the monster is shown being tormented by Fritz, a hunchbacked dwarf who steals bodies from cemeteries to supply parts for Dr. Frankenstein's creations.

The pairing of a monster and a person with a disability appears in most of Karloff's films. In the 1935 *Bride of Frankenstein*, the monster teams up with a blind hermit. Karloff continued the series with *Son of Frankenstein* (1939), in which Bela Lugosi plays a crazed, deformed shepherd gravedigger, Igor, who orders the monster to kill. In the

8.4. Lon Chaney in *Phantom of the Opera*, 1925. Universal Pictures.

3. Chaney's and his son's contributions to the history of film was acknowledged with US postage stamps in 1991 and 1997.

8.6. Frankenstein's monster with Fritz in *Frankenstein*, 1931. Universal Pictures.

1945 film *The House of Frankenstein,* Karloff is a doctor killed by Daniel, a psychopathic, hunchbacked killer.

Most of the themes in the movies Karloff did in his fifty-year career were common ones in horror movies. In 1932, he portrayed Morgan, the scar-faced, hulking butler who becomes homicidal when drunk. Karloff also often played a mad scientist. In the 1940 film *Dr. Adrian and the Ape,* Frances, a paralyzed woman, becomes the object of Dr. Adrian's concern. In searching for a cure for polio, he seeks the spinal fluid of apes. Linking lower primates with handicap and violence picks up on the Darwinian theme present in earlier pictures.

In 1945, Karloff played the grave robber in *The Body Snatcher,* the movie adaption of Robert Louis Stevenson's short story. In that role, he supplies dead bodies for doctors' experiments. After an unsuccessful attempt to cure a paralyzed child, they realize their failure and take up killing (illus. 8.7).

In *Dr. Adrian and the Ape,* the violence is not carried out by the person in the wheelchair, but for that person. But in 1965 Karloff did play a wheelchair-bound scientist who turns his family as well

as himself into monsters. As late as 1971, he played a famous blind sculptor who uses human bones for his work.

Horror films had their origins on the midways of the amusement industry, and as Dennis Gifford (1973), a historian of the horror film, notes, the association of horror and deformity was likely a product of the freak show. Many horror movies have a circus or carnival as their setting, and the sideshow provides their key characters. In *The Unknown* (1927), for instance, Lon Chaney plays an armless knife thrower. But no film is more transparent in linking disabled freak show performers with horror than MGM's 1932 film *Freaks.* Tod Browning, the creator of *Freaks,* employed Barnum & Bailey's sideshow attractions—including three people with microcephaly—for the film. It ends with the disabled actors creeping and crawling through the mud on a dark and rainy night to take revenge on the person who has done one of them wrong, turning her into a "freak" exhibit like themselves.

Horror films often provide psychological explanations for the frequent acts of violence committed

8.7. *The Body Snatcher* movie advertisement generated from stills, 1945. RKO Pictures.

8.8. Poster for *Freaks*, 1932. Excelsior Picture Corporation.

8.9. Lionel Atwill in *The House of Wax*, 1933. Warner Brothers.

8.10. Rondo Hatton in *The Pearl of Death,* ca. 1944. Universal Pictures.

by the people with disabilities in them. In the classic *Mystery of the Wax Museum* (1933), actor Lionel Atwill, shown in illustration 8.9, plays the mad, deformed, wheelchair-ridden sculptor who turns to making wax figures out of human bodies for his museum. Early in the movie, a fire leaves him paralyzed, so he seeks revenge. The message in this movie, as with others, is that people with disabilities hate themselves because of their circumstance and seek to get back at the world for their condition. The theme was so well received by the movie-going public that it was used again in the 1950s version titled *The House of Wax* and starring Vincent Price.

In most cases, the roles of people with disabilities in horror movies are played by people feigning disabilities. An exception is Rondo Hatton, who had acromegly, a rare body-altering disease that often manifests in adulthood. Hatton was cast in *The Pearl of Death* (1944) as the Hoxton Creeper, a mentally retarded, deformed madman. He was so well received in that role that he played other Creeper-like roles. A close-up of Hatton's face was usually featured in the stills for these movies (illus. 8.10).

Most of my examples of the relationship between disability and horror movies include the link between physical anomalies and violence. In many other movies, however, the villains are not physically impaired; they are mentally ill. In these films, mental illness goes hand and hand with murder, and mental hospitals are the dormitories of death. The examples are legion. Perhaps the most memorable, popular, and acclaimed film of the genre is Alfred Hitchcock's 1960 classic *Psycho*. The title itself screams out the link between mental illness and murder. The film received four Academy Award nominations and spawned two sequels. Interestingly, the stills and posters promoting the film do not feature the mentally deranged motel owner, Norman Bates, played by Anthony Perkins. It was more affecting to show the terror on the faces of Janet Leigh, the victim, and others rather than emphasize the deranged person's visage (illus. 8.11).

MURDER MYSTERIES AND OTHER FILMS WITH EVIL CHARACTERS

Beyond horror movies, other film genres link disability with evil, revenge, violence, torture, and murder. It is sometimes difficult to differentiate among horror films, murder mysteries, gangster and adventure movies, and other films with wicked and vicious characters. For example, *Psycho* has

8.11. Poster for *Psycho*, 1960. Universal/Paramount Pictures.

8.12. Lon Chaney inserting knees in leather cups in *The Penalty*, 1920. Goldwyn Pictures.

been characterized as a mystery, a thriller, and a horror movie.

Lon Chaney jumped from one genre to another to play evil killers. Perhaps his most famous gangster movie is *The Penalty* (1920). In it, he plays Blizzard, a notorious underworld figure. As in his horror film roles, he endured body-altering devices to capture Blizzard's disabled figure. Chaney bound his legs behind him, harnessing his feet to his thighs, and inserted his knees into leather cups that gave the appearance of missing legs (illus. 8.12).

The plot depicts Blizzard as a deranged amputee who lost his legs in an unnecessary childhood operation. He becomes obsessed with taking revenge on the rich and powerful, including the doctor who performed the operation (illus. 8.13). This obsession leads Blizzard to a career as a vicious criminal and mob leader. Tormented by his disability, he kidnaps the surgeon who amputated his legs as well as the physician's daughter's fiancé. In a morbidly grotesque turn, he has the fiancé's

legs grafted to his own stumps. In one scene, Blizzard poses for an artist who is doing a bust of the devil. The narrative is resolved with a bizarre twist when Blizzard undergoes brain surgery that cures him of his viciousness and criminal tendencies.

In the adventure film *West of Zanzibar* (1928), Chaney plays a similar role. Publicity for the film stated, "Fate made him a crawling thing, a crippled monster. So he took his revenge out on life" (illus.

8.13. Lon Chaney in *The Penalty*, 1920. Goldwyn Pictures.

8.14. Lon Chaney in *West of Zanzibar,* 1928. MGM.

8.15. Lon Chaney Jr. playing Lenny in *Of Mice and Men,* 1939. United Artist.

8.14). Chaney, however, did not have a monopoly on the role of the "crippled killer." Walter Huston played the part of a paralyzed tyrant, "Dead Legs" Flint, who rules his African kingdom from a wheelchair in *Kongo* (1932).

Many films take their plots from famous works of fiction. Lenny in John Steinbeck's *Of Mice and Men* is the archetypal mentally retarded, hulking brute. Unable to control his own strength, he first kills a puppy and then a young woman. In the end, Lenny's sidekick, a nondisabled man, shoots Lenny in the back of the head to protect Lenny from the painful death he is destined to face at the hands of the mob that pursues him. Lon Chaney Jr. is shown in illustration 8.15 playing the role of Lenny in the 1939 film adapted from the novella. This still captures the murder scene in the film.

Film renditions of Melville's *Moby Dick* depict Ahab, the obsessive one-legged captain of a whaling ship, seeking revenge on his crippler, the great white whale Moby Dick. In the 1956 version, the popular actor Gregory Peck plays Captain Ahab. One of the stills produced to advertise the film shows Ahab battling the mighty whale as he clings

to its side. The captain's wooden leg is prominent in the picture (illus. 8.16).

The limb-missing, patched-eyed pirates of *Treasure Island* are cloned again and again in film imitations of adventure stories. Following the plot of the classic tale by Robert Louis Stevenson, the villain, Long John Silver, played by Wallace Beery in the 1934 version of the film, displays his missing leg as a symbol of his wickedness (illus. 8.17).

MELODRAMA

Although horror and gangster films provide the most dramatic illustrations of the use of disability in films, filmmakers capitalized on disability in other ways. Melodramatic films used disability's ability to evoke sympathy.

The recipient of the sympathy is not always the person who has the disability. *Heidi,* a film about an eight-year-old orphan, was the number one box office hit in 1937. The title role was played by

8.16. Gregory Peck as Captain Ahab, straddling Moby Dick, 1956. Warner Brothers.

8.17. Wallace Beery playing Long John Silver in *Treasure Island*, 1934. MGM.

the most popular child actress of the time, Shirley Temple. At the beginning of the film, Heidi is living with her grandfather in his remote mountain cottage. But then she is taken from her idyllic life to live in the city as the working companion of Klara, a spoiled, physically disabled rich girl who gets around in a wheelchair. Heidi makes the best of her situation but is unhappy and longs for her grandfather. Because of Heidi's care and positive disposition, Klara becomes more cheerful and even begins to walk. The housekeeper, who wants to keep Klara dependant, sells Heidi to gypsies. Heidi is eventually reunited with her grandfather. Disabled Klara provides the perfect needy and unhappy person to make Heidi the sweet and loving star character that moviegoers loved. In illustration 8.18, we see Heidi (Temple) patiently teaching the disabled rich girl to walk.

Thousands of films used the same theme: disability in conjunction with sympathy and compassion. In countless film adaptations of *A Christmas Carol*, Tiny Tim, a physically impaired child, is the sweet innocent who is at first the object of Scrooge's meanness and later of his charity.

8.18. Shirley Temple playing Heidi, 1937. 20th Century Fox.

8.19. Edith Fellows as Winnie and Leo Carrillo as Uncle Joe in *City Streets*, 1938. Columbia Pictures.

Edith Fellows, a child star who appeared in the *Our Gang* comedy films, played a quite different role in the tear jerker *City Streets* (1938).[4] She wrings the audience's hearts as Winnie, a poor, crippled, wheelchair-bound orphan whose guardian is a kindly storekeeper, Uncle Joe (illus. 8.19). To pay for an operation that is supposed to cure the orphan girl, Joe sells his store, thereby becoming almost destitute, so that the state social workers take her away to an orphanage. Joe continues to rally to get her back but is so distraught by the situation he collapses in the street. Joe's illness can be overcome only if he has the will to live. Winnie, knowing this, walks to his bedside and sings his favorite song, "Santa Maria." She acquires the

full use of her legs, and Joe buys a catering truck. Although a box office success, the film was panned by critics as going well beyond the bounds of acceptable melodrama.

Another tearjerker with a wheelchair-bound central character but a different plot, one centered around unrequited love, is *Beware of Pity* (1946). The Austrian Lieutenant Marek befriends a beautiful baroness in a wheelchair, Edith, who is permanently disabled from a spinal injury she received from a fall from a horse. His attachment to her is out of pity, but she is in love with him. When she declares her love to him, Marek, guilt ridden, pretends to love her and agrees to marry her. When Edith hears about Marek's true feelings and that he has publicly denied their engagement, she becomes distraught. The movie ends with Edith wheeling herself to the edge of a rooftop terrace in her family's mountainside mansion and flinging herself to her death. In the still advertising

4. Fellows's role in Bing Crosby's *Pennies from Heaven* (1936) led to a series of leading roles such as the one in *City Streets*.

8.20. *Beware of Pity*, 1946. Universal Pictures.

photo, we see paraplegic Edith with the handsome lieutenant on the terrace at the family mansion (illus. 8.20).

COMEDY

Although not as prominent as in horror, gangster, adventure, and melodrama movies, disability was also used in some films to get a laugh. The earliest such films featured fraudulent beggars as a source of humor. In *Fake Beggar* (1898), a "legless" man begging on the street stands on newfound legs to retrieve a coin that misses his cup. Once discovered to be a fake, he is chased by the police (Norden 1994, 14).

Dwarfs have a long history of appearing in movies. Although a few have appeared in serious dramas, even horror movies (such as *Freaks*), most have been cast as comic figures who are the brunt of jokes. Little people have appeared in many films that people would classify as comedies or, more pointedly, where they are characters whom a viewer cannot take seriously. The epitome of this sort of typecasting is the Munchkins in the 1939 Academy Award–winning, blockbuster classic *The Wizard of Oz*. One hundred and twenty-two little

people—or midgets, as they were called then— were recruited from around the country to appear as the cute and laughable inhabitants of Munchkin Land. When Dorothy (Judy Garland) arrives in Munchkin Land, the timid Munchkins welcome her with song: "Ding-Dong! The Witch is dead" and "We're off to see the Wizard."

Two stills featuring Dorothy and the Munchkins were widely distributed to promote the film. One shows Dorothy with a delegation of Munchkins led by the mayor of Munchkin Land. Dressed in whimsical outfits consisting of oversize jackets with tails, extralarge bow ties, and tall, polka-dotted silk hats, they were great hits (illus. 8.21).

A 1938 film with an "all-midget" cast was the mock Western *Terror of Tiny Town*. Billy Curtis, the mayor of Munchkin City in the *Wizard of Oz*, starred as the good guy. It was a comedy that used a conventional cowboy/cowgirl story combined with little people to get laughs. The small-size cowboys gallop around on Shetland ponies and enter the local saloon by walking under the swinging doors. The film includes the convention that the good guy wears white, the bad guy black; the heroine is in danger, and the good guy and the bad guy engage in a fistfight.

Perhaps the most widely acclaimed comedy to feature disability is *Dr. Strangelove, or How I Learned to Stop Worrying and Love the Bomb* (1964). In this satirical dark comedy, physical disability was combined with a mental disorder to make for box office success. The film was nominated for four Academy Awards, including Best Picture and Best Actor for Peter Sellers.

Dr. Stangelove is a parody on America's Cold War fears of a doomsday nuclear war. The film's plot centers around a launched preemptive nuclear attack on the Soviet Union set in motion by an insane US Air Force general. In the Pentagon war room, politicians and generals frantically try to stop the bombing mission. Peter Sellers plays Dr. Strangelove, the mad, wheelchair-using, former Nazi, nuclear scientist, and presidential adviser who makes outrageous observations and suggestions

8.21. Dorothy with the Munchkins in *The Wizard of Oz*, 1939. MGM/Warner Brothers.

8.22. Peter Sellers playing Dr. Strangelove, 1964. Columbia Pictures.

about the crisis. (Sellers also plays two other roles in the film, a British captain and the US president.) In the widely distributed movie still reproduced in illustration 8.22, Strangelove lifts himself from his wheelchair while a barrage of nuclear explosions go off.

Although Dr. Strangelove was about a serious topic, it was a comedy and purposely used disability stereotypes. Joking or not, it can be listed along with the horror and other films discussed earlier that link disability with irrational acts of destruction.

CONCLUSION

The movie stills that highlight the role of people with or feigning disability are many. I have touched on just a few of the genres from which they come but have not mentioned others. One is children's films, both those using live performers and those using animation. Some of these children's films use similar disability-as-evil story lines. Disney has exploited disabilities as effectively as anyone else to create fear. The artificial lower arm of Peter Pan's Captain Hook comes to stand for the evil of the villain, who derives his name from his prosthetic devise. In *Snow White,* the beautiful queen must turn into a wart-nosed, hunched-over witch to accomplish her dirty deeds. Looney Tunes characters such as cartoon star Elmer Fudd continue to get laughs using a speech impediment.

Movie advertisements and other forms of movie imagery place images of disability before us every day that we do not register in our conscious minds as sending us messages about disability. They provide a hidden curriculum that informs people of all ages that people with disability are to be feared or pitied or laughed at.

9 Art for Art's Sake

People with Disabilities in Art Photography

J A M E S   A .   K N O L L

This chapter is based on an extensive study of art photographs found in various published books and exhibit catalogs. A more thorough analysis and discussion of the research in this chapter can be found in Knoll 1987.

Because of restrictions involved in obtaining permissions to publish some illustrations I had chosen for this chapter, I have been unable to include many of the images I hoped to. Those I have included are in the public domain, or the photographers or their agents have granted permission to reproduce them here. As a substitute for the images not included, I have provided the references to where the images can be found online or in hard-copy books. The limitations on publishing the images are a reflection on the degree to which the art world controls and defines certain photographic images as precious.

This book emphasizes the context in which photographs are created and displayed. When photographs get hung under designer spotlights on the white walls of an art gallery or displayed in expensive art books, they are transformed into art.[1]

Positioned in the art world,[2] pictures become images with *artistic* significance. Aesthetics soars above social content. A classic example of this transformation of a photograph of a person with a disability into art is the famous image "Tomoko and Mother in the Bath."[3] W. Eugene Smith took this photo in 1971 as part of his photographic essay on the effect of chemical pollution on the lives of Japanese fishermen and their families in the town of Minamata. In its original context, this powerful image was the culmination of a photo essay in *Life* magazine published on June 2, 1972. In the image, the mother is seated in a large Japanese bathtub washing her severely deformed daughter. A soft light illuminates the mother's loving gaze as she carefully observes her daughter's face.

Smith, a dedicated documentary photographer, spent years living in this village recording in

---

1. For example, Margret Bourke-White's public-relations photos of Letchworth Village (see chapter 5) might easily be resurrected into art if a curator framed them as such. Although Richard Sandell, Jocelyn Dodd, and Rosemarie Garland-Thomson do not focus on art museums in their discussion of disability and museums, their book *Re-presenting*

Disability (2010) raises interesting and important issues in regard to disability activism and agency in museums.

2. I use the term *art world* to refer of all the people and places involved in the production, commission, preservation, promotion, criticism, and sale of art (as in Becker 1982). The art world is held together by a belief in the concepts of "art" and "artist." Although it spans the globe, it is largely a Western institution that clusters in cities such as New York, London, and Berlin.

3. This image can be found online at http://www.christies.com/LotFinder/lot_details.aspx?intObjectID=5236759. It is also reproduced in Rosenblum 1984, 512.

photographs the progressive deterioration of many of the town residents. He was seriously injured and experienced an ongoing disability as a result of the beating he took at the hands of thugs hired by the chemical company in an effort to thwart his work (Smith and Smith 1975).

Why is this powerful image not reproduced here? In 2001, the heirs of Eugene Smith, who held the copyright to the image, publicly announced that they would no longer permit its reproduction and that they were transferring the copyright to Tomoko's family. It had come to the heirs' attention that Tomoko's family felt that their now deceased daughter was being exploited by the widespread reproduction of her image in art venues that had little to do with improving the conditions of the world. Transformed into art, the photo had lost its significance as the picture of a severely disabled child who was the victim of corporate greed.

You can still find reproductions of this picture in almost every history of photography published prior to 2001. And in spite of the family's wishes and the Smith heirs' actions, the image continues to be widely available on the Internet, particularly on the sites of art galleries, which have original prints available for sale for as much as $13,750 each (Christie's Auction House 2009).

As the transformation of "Tomoko and Mother in Bath" into an expensive art object illustrates, financial advantages can occur in framing a photo as art. Because many works of art are regarded as having intrinsic value, copyright holders limit the reproduction rights or require significant payment for permission to reproduce. Other genres of disability photographs displayed in this book—mostly from personal and institution collections—were distributed free of charge. Art photographers guard their work. For this reason, this chapter is bereft of illustrations that are important demonstrations of the points it makes.

Smith's muckraking image grabs the viewer and drives home the message that unfettered profiteering by corporations destroys both the environment and human lives. When the picture is removed from the essay and displayed on a gallery wall or in the pages of a history of art photography textbook, its artistic elements rather than its social message are front and center. Within the new context, the composition, the lighting, and the image's place within the history of art supersedes its original purpose as a piece of advocacy journalism. Art connoisseurs note how the composition of Smith's image echoes the classic pose of innumerable paintings of Jesus being removed from the cross and placed in his mother's arms. From the art critics' point of view, the picture is a Pietà for the twentieth century, not an image of disability caused by corporate gluttony.

PHOTOGRAPHY AS ART

Eugene Smith saw himself first and foremost as a photojournalist who used his work as a tool for social change. The balance of the discussion in this chapter focuses on famous photographers whose pictures include people with disabilities but who either saw themselves primarily as artists or were cast that way by the art world. *Artist* is a title of distinction reserved for people who are judged by connoisseurs to be especially gifted and whose art reveal the maker's essential exceptional talent (Becker 1982, 352–53). According to this tenet, artists by definition are creative, autonomous individuals who craft objects of beauty and depth that affect people who see their work.

The tension between the technology of photography and the concept of artist is as old as the medium. There have always been naysayers who deny the august title *art* to what they deem the photographer's mere technological products. These critics can usually be found echoing conservative values that hearken to the nineteenth-century art academy with its narrowly defined parameters. However, the avant-garde in art, in particular painters, connected with and were influenced by photography from the very dawn of the medium.

During the period 1900–1915, a time when the photograph was still marginal to the art world, a group of committed photographers known collectively as the "Photo Secession" and led primarily by Alfred Stieglitz and Edward Steichen laid the foundations for widespread recognition of photography as art. They closely associated their work with painting; they distanced themselves from both amateurs who pursued photography as a hobby and commercial photographers who had to worry about pleasing clients. This group's work, up to about 1915, was marked by a "pictorialist" style. Hallmarks of this approach include soft focus, "artistic" subject matter, and the use of technique and print manipulation to emulate the look of traditional painting. We see an example in illustration 9.1, the first photograph published in Alfred Stieglitz's quarterly journal *Camera Work*, a publication that served as the vehicle for advancing the agenda of photo secessionists' promotion of photography as art.

The pull of modernist painting—work that was more experimental and abstract than traditional art—drew leaders of the secessionist movement away from their conventional approach to photography (Hales 1984, 289). The transformation

of photography into modern art is captured well in Paul Strand's 1916 picture of a blind beggar entitled "Photograph—New York" (illus. 9.2). This image and others published in the last issue of *Camera Work* in 1917 set the stage for what was called "art photography" throughout the twentieth century (Metropolitan Museum of Art 2006).

To a person not schooled in art world aesthetics, Strand's picture may not seem to be a break from photographs such as "Dorothy." (illus. 9.1). To start, however, the title of the picture is abstract. Unlike "Dorothy," which focuses on the subject, "Photograph—New York" makes the medium central rather than the person. Unlike a photojournalist or documentary photographer, Strand did not engage with his subjects or comment on their circumstances. Instead, he used a modified lens so that his camera seemed to be pointed away from his subjects. They were thus unaware that they were being photographed (Metropolitan Museum of Art 2006). In "Photograph—New York," this lack of awareness can be seen in the way the subject

9.1. Gertrude Kasebier, "Dorothy," 1903. Published in *Camera Work* 1. Special Collections Research Center, Syracuse University Library.

9.2. Paul Strand, "Photograph—New York," 1916. Published in *Camera Work* 49–50. Special Collections Research Center, Syracuse University Library.

does not engage Strand; rather, her head and eyes are turned toward her left. The photograph is not softened or manipulated in ways to romanticize the figure. It is confrontational. No explanatory text accompanies the image. The emphasis is on composition, the pattern of lighting on the face, and the sign. Although the person in the picture is prominent, the picture is not about her; it is about the elements of art photography.

Strand was a student of Louis Hines, one of the leading documentary photographers of the early twentieth century whose work served as an impetus to efforts both to clean up the slums of New York and to pass child-labor laws. As Strand advanced his career as a photographer, however, he was drawn into Stieglitz's sphere of influence. He frequented Stieglitz's art gallery, where he was drawn to some of the first American exhibitions of modern European art (by Picasso, Braque, Cézanne, and others). Abstract art, expressionism, and Dadaism were some of the new styles that made pictorialism seem old-fashioned to him (Rosenblum 1984, 365).

Strand's image is regarded as seminal to that movement away from pictorialism. It marked the beginning of a different aesthetic in photography,

and, as related to our interest here, it set the agenda for future photographing of people with disabilities.

GARRY WINOGRAND

If we fast-forward fifty years to the 1960s, we see this vision brought to fruition in the works of a number of renowned photographic artists. I start with a photograph by Garry Winogrand, one of the major figures in the world of late-twentieth-century American photographic art: "American Legion Convention, Dallas, Texas, 1964" (illus. 9.3; reproduced in Marien 2006, 346).

This photo was taken on a busy downtown Dallas street corner. Seventeen people are visible in it as they walk, wait, chat, or just stand taking in the sights. Some wear conventioneer hats. In the center of the composition is a man with no legs crawling on the cement. From his position on the ground, he looks up with an exhausted expression and stares straight into the camera. All of the other human activity swirls around and away from him. The people's eyes look everywhere but at him. The only eyes that are watching this man are those behind the camera's viewfinder. The naive viewer, someone not schooled in the art world, usually

9.3. Garry Winogrand, "American Legion Convention, Dallas, Texas, 1964." © The Estate of Garry Winogrand, courtesy Fraenkel Gallery, San Francisco.

interprets the picture as pointing to the general indifference to a person with a disability.

But how is Winogrand's picture "American Legion Convention, Dallas, 1964" seen in the art world? Within that world, the primary spokespersons are the curators, the historians, and the critics. Statements by individuals from each of these groups put us in touch with the art world interpretation of Garry Winogrand's work. Be forewarned, though: people in the art world have their own vocabulary and way of talking that may seem foreign or incomprehensible to the uninitiated.

John Szarkowski, former director of the Department of Photography at the Museum of Modern Art and one of Winogrand's supporters, sees the artist as a pure formalist[4] who is concerned primarily with testing the limits of photography as an art medium (Stange 1978). In her history of photography, the eminent photography historian Naomi Rosenblum asserts that Winogrand's pictures are not statements about anything except "the uniquely prejudicial (intrinsic) qualities of photographic description" (1984, 523). The critic Bill Jay (1978) characterizes Winogrand as a naturalist[5] who is engaged in a value-free, detached cataloging of what he chooses to focus on.

One element in Winogrand's work that enchants the critics is his ability to transform an incredibly diverse array of human beings, caught in the act of daily life, into abstract visual components. They become the occupants of his picture's frame: "The scene does not illustrate any thesis but it does emblemize the stubborn pull that photographic exposure exerts upon us. We spectators see what those in the picture do not wish to see, and their reluctance becomes the subject of our look. The situation affords us a sharp pleasure made uneasy by the gaze of the crippled man" (Kozloff 1979, 38–39).

How does the artist himself describe what he is about in his photographs? In responding to a student's question about what makes a photograph "work," Winogrand said: "In the simplest sentence, I photograph to find out what something will look like photographed" (quoted in Malcolm 1980, 37).

Based on these descriptions, statements that likely are gobbledygook to those outside the art world and obscure even to some in that world, one might suspect that Winogrand belongs to a group of photographers who produce totally abstract work. It does not become clear until we actually look at the Winogrand's picture that he has produced an image of life on the street featuring a person with a disability.

Within the "art" frame, a picture that can be seen as a fascinating social document is effectively removed from the event as experienced by the people captured on film. A moment in time is frozen, analyzed, and interpreted on the basis of whether it "works" as an image. A picture that can be a symbol of the struggle of people with disabilities in American society becomes a visual metaphor for the aesthetics of looking at pictures and itself becomes an aesthetic experience for gallery-goers.

"American Legion Convention" is not the only Winogrand photograph that features people with disability. His pictures include dwarfs, people in wheelchairs, and people with various physical disabilities. They, too, were taken candidly on the streets and have a quality similar to the photo I have been discussing here.

DIANE ARBUS

Diane Arbus stands out as the central actor in the use of people with disabilities in art photography. More than any other photographer, she made people with disabilities central to her portfolio. Starting in the early 1970s, her photographs had a powerful effect on the art community (Bosworth 1984). The Museum of Modern Art launched a retrospective show of her work in 1972 (Arbus 1972). It had the largest attendance of any show

4. Formalism in art refers to the idea that aesthetic value is entirely determined by its form, not by its context and content.

5. The term *naturalist* refers to works of art that show subjects in the natural form in their natural environment.

in the museum's history to that date. Her suicide just prior to this exhibit created an Arbus mystique within the generation of photographers who credit her as a major influence on their work. Critical and biographical writings about her make her ideas about her work more accessible than those of most modern photographers.

Arbus stated her personal view of her subjects, people she saw as outsiders and referred to as "freaks,"[6] in a statement to a class she was teaching that one of her students taped. The statement was reprinted as the introduction to the monograph published in conjunction with the Museum of Modern Art's 1972 retrospective:

> Freaks was [sic] a thing I photographed a lot. It was one of the first things I photographed and it had a terrific kind of excitement for me. I just used to adore them. I still do adore some of them. I don't quite mean they're my best friends but they made me feel a mixture of shame and awe. There's a quality of legend about freaks. Like a person in a fairy tale who stops you and demands that you answer a riddle. Most people go through life dreading they'll have a traumatic experience. Freaks were born with their trauma. They've already passed their test in life. They're aristocrats. (Arbus 1972, 3)

There is consensus in the art world that the volume in which this quote is found is one of the most important and influential photographic publications of all time. By 2004, more than three hundred thousand copies of it had sold, and it has remained continuously in print in the forty-eight years since its original publication (Parr and Badger 2004).

As I page through the catalog of human faces that is Diane Arbus's legacy (Arbus 1972), I am overwhelmed by the sense that I am looking into a universe that exists out of synch with the "real world." Her pictures are populated by dwarfs, giants, transvestites, strippers, circus performers, nudists, old people, and, perhaps of most interest to readers of this book, the inmates of an institution for people with intellectual disabilities.

Her pictures simultaneously grasp an intimate quality about her subjects while also introducing as a counterpoint a sense of them as profoundly different. They mirror her own ambivalence about the people she was photographing. She knew many of them—some on an intimate basis—for many years and photographed them on multiple occasions. Yet her statements make it clear that she always regarded them as freaks from whom she got an almost narcoticlike rush (see the introduction to Arbus 1972 and Bosworth 1984). Referring to her relationship with her subjects, she spoke of "pursuing" them, which implies an aggressive hunt for the right image (Bosworth 1984, 246).

From all of the pictures she took of Eddie Carmel, the "Jewish Giant," she selected the one of him and his parents standing in their living room as the print to exhibit at the Museum of Modern Art (in Arbus 1972).[7] The key to this selection lay in the expression on Carmel's mother's face. As Arbus stated, "You know how every mother has a nightmare when she is pregnant that the baby will be born a monster? I think I got that in the mother's face as she glares up at Eddie, thinking, 'OH MY GOD, NO!'" (quoted in Bosworth 1984, 194).

Arbus's depiction of people with differences finds its fullest expression in the picture series she took of institutionalized people with intellectual disabilities ("Untitled" 1–7 [1970–71], in Arbus 1972; Arbus 1995).[8] These photographs seem to reflect her point of view that all of us are weird and live behind a veil of normalcy that we fight to maintain. However, when her subjects are the residents

---

6. In the 1960s, *freak* was a term associated with members of the hippy and beatnik movement. In that context, it was not necessarily as negative as it is today.

7. See Millet 2004 for a discussion of Carmel and the Arbus photograph of him. The image can be found online at http://dianearbus-photography.com and in Arbus 1972.

8. These images can be found online at http://diane-arbus -photography.com and in Arbus 1972.

of facilities for people with intellectual disabilities, the message the viewer gets is that for these people no veil exists. These inmates are set off as intrinsically different from the rest of humanity.

When Arbus's developmentally disabled subjects are viewed with some of the other elements at work in the picture, the overall effect is distressing (see, for example, "Untitled" 7, in Arbus 1972). The quality of light is eerie. As the sequence of pictures progresses, a storm cloud gradually envelopes the open field where these people gather, conveying a sense of deep foreboding, even doom. None of them is dressed in clothes that would be considered appropriate for the situation. One wears a bathing suit, another a hospital gown, and another a Halloween costume. The subjects may not have on social masks, but many are wearing real masks. Witches, death heads, devils, and strange knights abound on this dark landscape. The sequence of these images, with a picture of a lone figure in a flowing sheet and a skull mask as the centerpiece ("Untitled" 3, in Arbus 1972), for me re-creates the Danse Macabre, the Dance of the Doomed as they prepare to enter hell.[9]

For Arbus, these subjects exist at the very fringe of the known world. They mark the limits of the universe of rationality, order, security, intellectuality, creativity, sociability, restraint, and good taste within which she was raised and lived. She described her disgust and revulsion as she forced herself to meet these people on their own turf. For her, it was a trip to another world; it "was really like Hades" (Arbus 1972, 14). Her pictures were trophies from these hunting expeditions in hell that attempted to make the power of this experience present to her audience in the affluent world of the modern American art consumer and to produce anxiety in them.

What do people in the art world say about these photographs of the developmentally disabled? In

1995, twenty-three years after the publication of the original Arbus monograph, her estate for the first time published a portfolio of fifty-one photographs of people with intellectual disabilities entitled "Untitled." On its website, the publisher has the following description of the sixty-dollar volume: "*Untitled* may well be Diane Arbus's most transcendent, most romantic vision. It is a celebration of the singularity and connectedness of people and it demonstrates Arbus's remarkable visual lyricism" (Aperture Foundation 2011).

This description stands in some contrast to a 1995 review by Nan Goldin, who places an interesting and puzzling spin on the reality of the photographed individuals' experience of institutionalization. "The vision of a mentally disabled patient dressed as a ghost with a skeleton mask, or of a couple in a dunce hat and clown suit holding hands on a wide lawn under a dark somber sky, looks like Grimm's fairy tales. The people become characters in a medieval theater or a Pirandello play. Somehow these pictures describe the experience of being institutionalized, not from a documentary viewpoint but from the magical and symbolic realm where reality sometimes arrives" (1995). In concluding her review, Goldin returns to the theme of the artist as the gifted creator who provides the viewers with the opportunity for a truly unique experience. Speaking about Arbus's suicide, she suggests that perhaps in Arbus the audience faces an artist who truly plumbed the limits and perhaps even went beyond them. According to this art world rendering, to confront people with developmental disabilities is to plumb the limits of what one can bear.

Arbus and many of her colleagues commented that a person with a significant difference, including a disability, does not become a freak simply by going on the payroll at a sideshow; they are existentially freaks. Based on Arbus's own words and on what we know from her biography, it is clear that regardless of how well she got to know her subjects, their world was always the world of the freaks, and hers was always the world of art

9. This image can be found online at http://diane-arbus-photography.com and in Arbus 1972.

(Arbus 1972; Bosworth 1984). She bridged the gap in search of powerful images, but the two worlds always remained separate.

RICHARD AVEDON

Diane Arbus is likely the most important photographer to regularly include people with disabilities in her images. As noted, they are central to her work. But other art world luminaries also dabbled in photographing people with disabilities as subjects. In such photographs, these people are mere extensions of the photographer's approach and style.

Richard Avedon was a friend of Diane Arbus. Like many of the photographers who emerged as creative forces in the late 1950s and early 1960s art scene, Avedon mastered the craft of photography while working in the commercial sector of the medium. Until his death in 2004, he was regarded as one of the world's premier fashion and portrait photographers. A Google search of his images or a visit to his foundation's website provides a catalog of the most significant and familiar faces of the second half of the twentieth century.[10]

In his photographs, Avedon concentrated on his subjects' faces. Nowhere is this confrontation more clearly etched than in his series of portraits of his terminally ill father Jacob Israel Avedon ("Jacob Israel Avedon, Father of the Photographer," in Avedon 1976).[11] As presented in a 1974 exhibition of the artist's work, eight of these pictures in their square static format were enlarged to greater than life size and lined up on the wall of the Museum of Modern Art; they chronicled his father's physical deterioration and the increasing pain caused by an incurable and debilitating disease. Although the subject is the photographer's father, and he is dying, that relationship disappears from consideration as the viewer sees the subject's glazed eyes, the whitening of his hair, the loosening clothes, and the transformation of his face as the bones become more prominent.

At various times in his career, Avedon undertook extended personal projects separate from his contracted work. At times, his personal work is indistinguishable from his commercial assignments (Malcolm 1980). There is a similarity between these personal photographs of his father and his 1963 "Mental Institution" series, which builds on the theme of the human face with a number of intense close-up studies of personal agony. A frequently reproduced image from this portfolio captures an African American man in a paroxysm of emotion ("Mental Institution 9 East Louisiana State Mental Hospital, February 15, 1963," in Avedon 1964).[12]

Every aspect of this picture speaks of unbearable tension. The subject is not statically placed in the center of the frame; instead, his head runs on a diagonal plane through the frame. He is wrapped in a crumpled blanket; one edge of the wrap has torn off and straps the top of his head. The flecks of white in his hair make the viewer wonder about his true age. Just a small part of a tightly clenched fist emerges from the blanket. But the central focus is the muscular structure of his face and the veins in his forehead, which stand out in sharp relief brought on by the clenched and grinding teeth and the furrowing in the brow and eyes.

Like Arbus's pictures and those of other art photographers, these images of inmates in mental hospitals are not about the cruel institutional environment or about the suffering of a class of people with disabilities; they are about composition and style.

MARY ELLEN MARK

Mary Ellen Mark's body of work parallels Avedon's in a number of ways. She has received her

10. Avedon's website is at http://www.richardavedon.com.

11. Search the Internet using "Jacob Israel Avedon" to view the images of Avedon's father.

12. Also see http://www.richardavedon.com/index.php#mi=2&pt=1&pi=10000&s=6&p=5&a=2&at=0.

9.4. Mary Ellen Mark, from *Ward 81*, 1979.

greatest exposure through her portraiture work. This commercial work supports her in personal work as a photojournalist and documentarian with an art world following. She has produced a series of book-length photo essays on topics ranging from the work of Mother Teresa to the prostitutes of Bombay.[13]

In the late 1970s, the first of these book-length essays, *Ward 81* (Mark 1979), examined life on the secure women's ward at the Oregon State Mental Hospital. Like so many who have taken their cameras into mental hospitals, Mark emerged with images that seem to echo Arbus's experience of crossing into Hades. The pictures are art images, though. They concentrate on lighting and other aesthetic aspects of the work. Her subjects are prominent, but their institutional environment is not.

Mark's images continually present the viewer with the questions, "What is it within this person that led them to crumble?" and "How come I can endure?" One picture of three people standing in front of a soda machine at a dance in the institution (illus. 9.4; in Marks 1979, 64) seems to say that a lack of social adaptability is the answer to the first question. All three face squarely into the camera. In the center is a woman wearing a floral print dress and a crocheted vest. She blankly stares and stands as if at attention. In contrast to her rigid posture, the two men on either side of her seem contorted with discomfort. The eyes of the man on the right side are wide, almost dazed looking, and he has a forced, tight-lipped smile on his face. A bearded man in a dark sweater appears almost belligerent. His head is bent toward the woman and tilted slightly forward so that he has to look up, from under his eyebrows, at the camera. Here, as in so many pictures from mental hospitals, the cue to the internal state is in the eyes: they are glazed, dazed, or belligerent.

Many of the pictures in *Ward 81* demonstrate the uses of lighting—the photographer's central tool—to create a compelling and challenging image. One image is particularly revealing in this respect (illus. 9.5; in Mark 1979, 85). Three women and an almost invisible male figure are shown in a dark institutional hallway. The women in the background are secondary—they almost disappear into the shadows. Center in the foreground

13. See the listing of Mark's publications on her website at http://www.maryellenmark.com/books.

9.5. Mary Ellen Mark, from *Ward 81*, 1979.

is a woman with closely cropped hair, a patterned blouse, a white shawl, and a manacle on one wrist. Hidden in her shadow, a male figure seems to be adjusting her restraints. The use of flash from a low angle pulls the main subject out into space while creating a large, dark shadowing behind her. The light also catches an expression of utter exhaustion on her downcast face. This picture creates a disturbing mood of sinister foreboding. The photo essay provides no clue as to what fear is actually confronting this woman (Is she waiting to receive electroshock therapy?) other than the grouping of

this image with others that show people in various forms of restraint.

Although many of the photos taken in institutions present images of pain, another recurring theme is the escape or hiding from human contact. In one of Mark's pictures, a woman seems to be experiencing as much pain as the man in Avedon's picture, but here the emphasis is on separation (illus. 9.6; in Mark 1979, 73). The woman is behind the head of a bed staring at the ceiling with one hand over her mouth and a tearful expression on her face. The picture was taken with a wide-angle lens from the foot of the bed and creates the visual illusion of a white cone with the woman seated at the summit.

No photographic documentary text helps the viewer really understand the plight of the mentally ill in large public institutions. The subject's experience is removed from the context of his or her life and placed in the world of art.

EUGENE MEATYARD

A simple description of Eugene Meatyard's work can make it sound like a collection of silly little tableaux in which masks, dolls, and children are

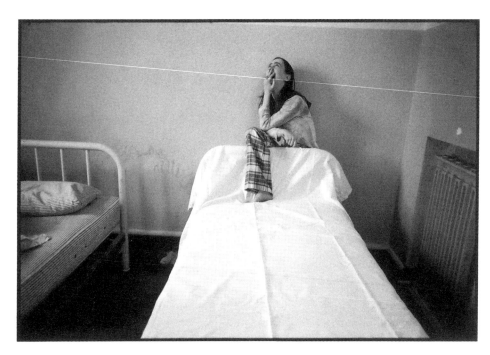

9.6. Mary Ellen Mark, from *Ward 81*, 1979.

brought together in old buildings, forests, or fields. Yet in the art world these pictures work as very serious, often disturbing visual probes into the human psyche (Coke 1991). Different from the images discussed so far here, his work is an example of the use of disability in surrealist and fantasy images. Although real disability appears only occasionally in Meatyard's photographs, he is a master at using grotesque masks and other devices within his finely orchestrated pictures to create the illusion of significant physical difference and deep-seated unease.

Like filmmakers who create horror movies, some photographers use disability in a surrealistic mode in their work. Meatyard capitalizes on physical difference to create a sense of foreboding in his contrived images. The image in a 1960 picture by Meatyard (in Meatyard 1970) offers a good example of this approach. In this very dark picture set in a stone entryway, a short figure sits leaning on the wall. The size and structure of this dark, clothed body indicates a child, yet the face is of a very old man with sunken eyes and deep wrinkles. The head is disproportionately large for the body. At the waist, the head and arms of a doll project from the figure's right hand.[14]

In addition to masks and lighting, Meatyard frequently makes use of controlled blurring. In his case, blurring is about psychological instability. In his 1962 "Occasion for Diriment," a short male figure in a light-colored, pullover shirt stands in front of a plank shack to the right of the frame. He wears a grotesque mask. On the left is a small girl waving her arms and bobbing her head in a rapid motion, which blurs all her features into a human face that roughly duplicates the deformity of the mask.[15]

Meatyard was also particularly adept at creating and using real people with disabilities in his strange images. In an untitled picture, the exterior of an old cabin and a dark doorway are the background. A one-handed man reaches out to what seems to be a woman's hand on the right. It is not clear, however, whether the latter belongs to a person or a mannequin (Meatyard, 1974, 9).[16]

LES KRIMS

Les Krims is typical of the generation that came to the forefront in the art world in the late 1960s and early 1970s. He, like many of his contemporaries, owes his identity as a photographer to the creative openness that emerged in the medium from 1960 on. He learned his craft in art school, teaches in a college art department, and sees himself as an artist who uses photography as his medium (personal communication from Krims to the author, 1974). The major influences on his work, surrealism and pop art, come from outside of photography (Rosenblum 1984). The principal photographic roots for his imagery include such unlikely sources as police and medical photographs and snapshots of hunting trips. Like Meatyard's pictures, some of Krims's elaborately staged images hearken back to the *tableau vivant* pictures of the nineteenth century (Coleman 1977). His pictures serve different purposes and excite diverse responses.

Many people with disabilities are present in Krims's strange and often abrasive images. In "Human Being as a Piece of Sculpture Fiction" (reproduced in Coleman 1977, 89), an African American man who has no legs is seated on a pedestal in front of three bay windows in a sparsely furnished room. The picture was made with a wide-angle lens, which distorts the space, enabling

14. This image can be found online at http://www.fraenkel gallery.com/index.php/artists/RalphEugeneMeatyard/romances /26.

15. This image can found online at http://www.metmuseum .org/works_of_art/collection_database/photographs/occasion _for_diriment_ralph_eugene_meatyard/objectview_zoom.aspx ?page=3&sort=6&sortdir=asc&keyword=meatyard&fp=1&d

d1=19&dd2=0&vw=1&collID=19&OID=190023049&vT=1 &hi=0&ov=0 and in Tannenbaum 1991.

16. This image can be found online at http://www.masters -of-photography.com/M/meatyard/meatyard_hands.html and in Meatyard 1974.

us to look down on the central figure and still take in the alcove containing his pedestal. The picture is printed on a high-contrast paper, which breaks down the image's continuous tone quality and emphasizes the negative's grain structure. The man on the pedestal grasps it tightly, leans forward toward the window, and screams. Like Avedon's picture from the mental institution, this carefully constructed tableau is a metaphor for loneliness and alienation. From Krims's perspective, however, the absence of legs is merely a convenient device with strong power.[17]

In 1971, Krims produced a set of photographs of dwarfs published as *Little People of America*. Jonathan Green attacks Krims in *American Photography: A Critical History 1945 to the Present* (1984) for his "juvenile" use of visual puns and jokes at his subjects' expense. Yet although Green is critical of certain aspects of *Little People of America* (see the example reproduced in Coleman 1977, 46), he hails it as opening up, albeit with a mocking attitude, previously taboo subject matter for the creative photographer. He accepts the underlying rationale for this type of work by articulating the mythology of the dwarf, which lends Krims's images credibility as an essay on the limits of full membership in the human community. "The dwarf became the dominant image for alienation, for the grotesque and the repulsive. He was the walking human contradiction: part myth, part person, the visual embodiment of all our cultural fears of disease, difference, and deformity. He was a creature known to exist but psychologically difficult to confront or acknowledge. The dwarf was the prototypical social outcast, partaking in human life without a normal human shape" (Green 1984, 120–21).

As has occurred so often in this discussion of the photographic image of people with a disability, Green locates meaning in the person in the picture.

From this perspective, the limits of existence are not the effect of social conditions; they are part of the person. For Green, the dwarf really is *the other*.

ROBERT D'ALESSANDRO

Robert D'Alessandro[18] has worked as a street photographer in the tradition of Winogrand. I saved Robert D'Alessadro's work until the end of the chapter because his motivation in producing the photos was similar to that of the photographer who leads the chapter, W. Eugene Smith, whose work documents the suffering caused by industrial pollution in Japan.

In a picture entitled "Fourteenth Street, NYC, 1971" (illus. 9.7; in D'Alessandro 1973), D'Alessandro shows us the front of an office of the New York City Department of Social Services. Three people with disabilities are on the sidewalk. To the left of the door is an American flag. An elderly man with a cane is bent over. A younger man who has no legs is seated on the sidewalk closest to the camera. Nearest to the door is a man in a wheelchair. This man and the man seated on the sidewalk are looking to the right as a number of nondisabled people walk rapidly toward them and into the picture. The tension created by the difference in pace and direction of the people with and without disabilities sets the tone of this image. There is a sense that the people with a disability are being swept away or trampled by the onslaught of fully ambulatory people.

Although there is a sense in which D'Alessandro is presenting a sympathetic image of the plight of the three men with disabilities, people in the art world argue that his primary concern was to create an intriguing image by showing these men as a counterpoint to the rapidly moving legs. This tension is indeed intrinsic to the image, but it reduces the people with disabilities to a visual component.

17. This image can be found online at http://www.les krims.com/leskrims2.html.

18. The Getterman Gallery in New York City carries D'Alessandro's work.

9.7. Robert D'Alessandro, "Fourteenth Street, NYC, 1971." © Robert D'Alessandro, 1972. Available at Gitterman Gallery.

In his book of photographs *Glory* (1973), D'Alessandro develops a highly personal surrealistic examination of how people use the American flag. The photos in that book are a product of the Vietnam era and are meant as a serious critique of America during that time. One of the most powerful images, "Flushing, NY, 1972" (illus. 9.8), takes viewers to the extreme of the conventions found in photographs of amputees by displaying the stumps of two severed limbs. The picture is done in the subject's living room. He sits in the center of the frame on a couch that is covered with the flag. The man, who has shoulder-length hair and is naked, has removed both of his prostheses. With his hands folded in front of him, he leans forward. The light coming through a window in front of him casts long, barlike shadows across the floor and the man's lower torso. Outside this area of bright light, the room recedes into deep shadows. In this picture, light, so often a symbol of freedom, is transformed into symbolic bars imprisoning this man. Art world commentary, however, does not focus on the plight of the veteran or others like him; it focuses on the aesthetics of the image.

Although one would not necessarily know from looking at D'Alessadro's images that he saw himself as a documentary photographer motivated to point out injustice in an effort to contribute to social change, that was at least in part how he saw his work. I did not know this until he shared the diary notes he wrote at the time he took the pictures in *Glory*. Prior to taking the pictures, he had served as a Peace Corps Volunteer in the slums of Brazil. He was back living in New York and trying to sort out his life. He spied the people pictured in "Fourteenth Street" from his apartment window. His mind raced back to Brazil, where the sight of

9.8. Robert D'Alessandro, "Flushing, NY, 1972." © Robert D'Alessandro, 1972. Available at Gitterman Gallery.

destitute people with disabilities on the streets was common. The American flag hanging out over the office jolted him into realizing that what he was seeing was not Brazil; it was the United States. "We don't have people in that situation here, do we?" he said to himself. Although not clear about what his discomfort with the scene meant, through his camera he wanted to tell people about the view that distressed him.

The circumstances surrounding the D'Alessandro picture of the amputee was quite different. D'Alessandro wanted to make a photograph that would very clearly show what the Vietnam War was doing to those who were fighting over there; he wanted to bring attention to their plight. He called the Vietnam Veterans Association, seeking disabled veterans. The person pictured in illustration 9.9, Billy, volunteered as a subject. Both of Billy's legs had been blown off by a land mine in Vietnam. When he first returned to the United States, he was active in the Veterans Against the War movement. He was one of the veterans who protested during the Republican National Convention in Miami in 1968 and had seen demonstrators beaten by law enforcement agents.[19] When D'Alessandro took the picture, Billy was fed up with America and preparing to move to Mexico. He eventually became a heroin addict and died of causes related to his addiction.

D'Alessandro laments that people in the art world have pushed aside the social content of his photographs to emphasize form and style. He understands that once a photograph becomes an art object, the photographer loses control of its meaning, but he identifies more with Eugene Smith than with those photographers anchored in the art world.

19. Although the demonstrations at the Democratic National Convention in 1968 were more widely covered by the press and most discussed, there were demonstrations at the Republican National Convention as well.

CONCLUSION

Critics and others try to answer the question why images of people with physiological and psychological differences proliferated in the art photography of the 1960s and onward. This trend certainly was not a nefarious plot by photographers against people with disabilities. The mere presence of people with a disability in the work of highly regarded photographers was enough for some to call these artists humanists. A more tenable answer is that this was a period when the "freak" became popular. Young people adopted the word freak to express their alienation from the dominant culture's lifestyles, mores, and values (Fiedler 1978). To be a freak was a badge of honor, a mark of rejection by a war-mongering and decadent society. Within the 1960s cultural framework, photographers who identified with the values of the counterculture photographed people whom they saw as being outside the dominant culture—freaks.

There is some validity in attributing the subject matter of pictures to the tenor of the times. The popularity of these images of "freaks" in the late 1960s and 1970s was likely related to the unrest of the time. However, many of Arbus's pictures, many of Avedon's confrontational portraits and his mental institution series, a large portion of Winogrand's work, most of Meatyard's pictures, and images by other photographers in this period were made before the emergence of a freak counterculture. In addition, the representation of people with disabilities in these photographs—in contrast to Smith's work—does not suggest that the photographers embraced these people as kin.

Forces were at work within the art world that need to be considered. A. D. Coleman connects the emergence of a new type of photographic imagery with the coming of a new generation of photographers who saw themselves primarily as artists, were well trained photographically, and had strong connections with the world of art. In many ways, these photographers were seeking an answer to the perennial question directed at photography: "But can you call it Art?" Stieglitz's answer forty years earlier needed to be reformulated.

The environment in which Arbus, Avedon, Winogrand, and many others formed their mature vision as artists was the relatively small world of the New York art scene in the late 1950s (see Bosworth 1984; Gablik 1984; Welch 1986). New York in the 1950s was a hotbed of photographic activity (Welch 1986). Many individuals who identified themselves as artists with a camera sought an approach that had the power of social vision yet would stand independent of the dominant perception of photography primarily as journalism. The perspective growing out of this environment and the endorsement by the photography department of the Museum of Modern Art under the directorship of John Szarkowski in the post-1962 period fostered the growth of the casting of people with a disability in most of photography (Szarkowski 1978).

Important in understanding the use of disability in art photography is the influential critic Harold Rosenberg's (1964) concept of the "Anxious Object." The Anxious Object is found in disturbing images, the grotesque, the weirdly fantastic, and the freak show. Rosenberg argues that the Anxious Object is one of the hallmarks of modern art. It is intended to provoke discomfort, uncertainty, and anxiety by challenging the viewer's expectations. By creating tension and ambiguity, an Anxious Object demands a response from the viewer. It seeks to subvert a routine way of looking and to challenge the viewer to rethink his or her way of thinking.

The reviews by Coleman, Colombo, and Green of the photographers discussed here make it clear that in the post-1960 period a substantial number of photographic artists made a conscious decision to use provocative subject matter to produce images that were upsetting and produced anxiety. For many of these photographers, people with disabilities were the provocative subject matter. The decision to use such people in this manner may not have been conscious or reprehensible. A picture of a dwarf or an amputee was synonymous with "a powerful image." That was by way of saying that the picture would be shocking.

The relegating of people with a disability to the role of provocateur was supported by the art world's definition of the artist. The artist, by definition, is uniquely qualified to challenge the public's preconceived perceptions in any way he or she sees fit. Of course, artists are not autonomous; they, like everyone else, are part of a culture that has stereotypes of people with disabilities. Like most of the general public, artists define people with a disability as fundamentally different. The only preexisting frame of reference that photographers have for understanding is their prejudices. Many of the artists in the period discussed here approached the disabled as creatures who inhabited the outer reaches of the known world, away from "normal" people and especially away from people like themselves who are defined as gifted.

In the period 1965–80, during which most of the photos I have examined were made, the images created by some of the world's foremost photographic talents served to reify the concept of people with a disability as the personification of the outsider. The images reviewed here communicate a message of fundamental difference, dependence, and segregation. Such a message flies in the face of the efforts by many people with a disability to gain recognition of their mutual interdependence, economic independence, rights, and integration.

10 Citizen Portraits
Photos as Personal Keepsakes

10.1. Young man who has cerebral palsy with family, ca. 1890. Cabinet card.

In disability photographs, the person with the disability and his or her physical or mental condition are central to the composition. This centrality is clear in freak show handouts, begging cards, charity publicity, eugenics texts' clinical portraits, and other genres. In addition to the deliberate and flagrant display of disability, other aspects of visual disability rhetoric are at work in these various genres.

It is not just photography of people with disability that employs specific visual conventions,

however. There is a different visual rhetoric for each category of human being. The way men are photographed, for example, is strikingly different from the way women are presented (Goffman 1988). For any particular cluster of people, substantial variation exists in how they are photographed: women, for instance, can be photographed as pin-ups, housewives in ads, and executives in corporate booklets. In this chapter, I look at photographs of people with disabilities in which disability photographic conventions are not employed or, if they are, they do not dominate the image. In other words, in these photos people with disabilities are photographed as ordinary members of the community—regular citizens and family members. The rhetorical devices of family, friend, and other typical membership roles trump disability photograph conventions.

When I say that in "citizen portraits" people with disabilities are photographed in the way people typically are, I do not mean to imply that their disabilities are concealed from the viewer. The impairment is visible, but it is not featured as it is in other genres. As in illustration 10.1, wheelchairs, missing limbs, braces, and other indicators of disability are taken for granted in the genre of citizen photography.

The images in this chapter, unlike the images in the other chapters, were produced as personal keepsakes to be placed in family albums, scrapbooks, and other special places where private and cherished memorabilia are safely stored. The photographers were by both professionals and amateurs. Although some of the images were shared, even sent through the mail, they were distributed privately to intimates, family members, and friends. They were not produced for commercial public relations, to solicit money, to sell, or for personal or organizational gain.

Illustration 10.1 is an example of what I am getting at. It shows family members who in the late 1800s had their picture taken at a local photographer's studio. The way they are arranged, their clothing, the bicycle, the backdrop, and how the son with cerebral palsy in the wheelchair is included echo family visual rhetoric, not disability conventions. It is this sort of photography that I examine in this chapter.

Since the late 1960s, there has been a progressive movement among professionals, parents, people with disabilities, and their spokespersons to promote the inclusion of people with disabilities in the life that everyone else participates in.[1] This movement has self-consciously produced a genre of photography of its own where people with disabilities are deliberately posed as "normal."[2] Social service agencies have been behind the production of these photos, but socially conscious businesses incorporate people with disabilities into their ads as well, showing them as a regular part of the business team. These images are designed to present people with disabilities in the most complimentary way. This self-conscious production of normality rendered photographs that resemble the images I discuss in this chapter, but, as you will see, they are considerably different. The images I focus on are natural, flow unselfconsciously from people's ordinary circumstances, and were taken by intimates and local photographers. They stemmed from people's natural involvement with family, friends,

and fellow workers, not from the arranged creation of inclusion by a human service and human rights social movement.

How do regular pictures taken within the frame of ordinary people, family, friends, workers, citizens look compared to the conventions of imaging disability examined throughout the book? When people are pictured in ordinary ways, they are in everyday settings—homes, gardens, public parks, stores, photo studios, at work and at play. They are also often pictured with people and animals with whom they have loving or close relationships—friends, family, fellow workers, and pets. In addition, inanimate objects that the subjects care about and that are part of their commonplace, nondisabled identity are part of the composition. Last, their apparel, grooming, and personal appearance are the same or similar to that of other citizens and family members. They dress in "regular" ways. I examine these dimensions in detail in this chapter.

SETTINGS

Pictures taken within the conventions of "ordinary people photography" are shot inside homes, in front of homes, on the porch, in backyards, and in other domestic locations. When taken away from home, they are in work environments, public places, and other common locations. Photographer's studios are also sites of ordinary people photography. Whether an amateur or a professional picture taker produced the image, the convention is to show the person in a typical, pleasant environment, one that establishes and promotes belonging for both disabled and nondisabled people.

Domestic Locations

Illustration 10.2 is an example of a person with a disability being photographed inside his home. The boy, who has Down syndrome, is sitting in a window seat. Note the décor—the patterned cushions, the lace curtains, and the potted plant. The spot where the photo was taken provides a positive

1. These ideas and policies originated with the concept of "normalization" (Wolfensberger 1972), providing the conditions that allowed people with a disability access to all aspects of a typical life, including housing, dress, and human relationships.

2. See Pietropaolo 2010 for an example.

impression of both the dwelling and the subject. Given the location and the pose, the photograph could have been taken of anyone, not just a person with a disability. Contrast this picture with the illustrations in other chapters, such as those taken in institutions or for eugenics texts.

Illustration 10.3 shows a man sitting at his desk. The wallpaper, curtain, oil lamp, rug, and pictures hanging on the wall convey the impression of a person's personal, intimate, and comfortable space. We see a man who happens to use a wheelchair sitting at his desk at home.

In illustration 10.4, a young man with a developmental disability is shown on the porch of his family's home. The picture was likely taken by a relative who was an amateur photographer. The subject is sitting in a rocker surrounded by plants,

common props used in photography in the early part of the twentieth century. The wooden screen door, the clapboards in the background, the bucket plant containers convey normal life. The inconsequential setting contributes to the image's ordinariness.

The setting is just as normal in illustration 10.5. Rather than being indoors, the woman in the wheelchair is on the edge of the family's cornfield. Farm family pictures taken on their own property with their crops is a visual cliché. Created as visual records of a family's farming success, such pictures were taken when a harvest was good. As you can see, the field in this picture is filled with robust corn.

10.2. Child with Down syndrome, ca. 1910. Photo postcard.

10.3. Man in wheelchair at desk, ca. 1908. Photo postcard

10.4. Developmentally disabled young man on the porch, ca. 1907. Photo postcard.

10.5. Woman in wheelchair with family in cornfield, ca. 1912. Photo postcard.

Work Settings

People also normally spend their time at work and so are photographed there. In illustration 10.6, a man in his forties is in a wheelchair in his office, surrounded by typical office furnishings. An open safe is on his right, the shelves behind him are filled with file holders and drawers, and he has pulled back from his desk for the purposes of the photo shoot, giving the sense that he belongs. His officemate is at a desk toward the back. His work environment is what defines the situation, not his disability.

Illustration 10.7 includes a farmer in a field at work harvesting his crop of hay. As at so many small family farms, the workers are either relatives or hired hands. The man is probably the owner of the farm and is in the field supervising the harvest. His crutch and missing leg are apparent, but the harvest is central to the picture, not the disability—as evidenced by the wide shot of the entire field and the inclusion of other figures.

Illustration 10.8 shows another ordinary work setting in which a person with a disability is present. Three men stand on the factory floor in front of a large machine as they pose for the photograph. The man with the amputated leg and a crutch is

10.6. Man in office, ca. 1910. Photo postcard.

10.7. Man standing in field, ca. 1909. Photo postcard.

not the subject of the picture. He is just one of three workers.

The group picture of workers standing outside their factories, offices, shops, and other vocational locations is a common photographic form. In some establishments, such pictures were taken yearly. Illustrations 10.9 is a good example of a work group photo. Given the high quality of the image, it was probably taken by a professional photographer. The setting is outside a shoe store in an unnamed Midwest town. The sales staff are lined up on the street, and the owner of the establishment is on the left, one step above the others. As we might expect for an owner, the man, who has crutches and only one leg, is holding the ropes that control the awning, and is better dressed than his employees. In worker group pictures, the boss is often placed in the center of the group; this

10.8. Man with missing leg in factory, ca. 1912. Photo postcard.

10.9. Group picture of workers with boss who has a disability, ca. 1911. Photo postcard.

man's position on the sidewalk, one step up, sets him apart not as a person with a disability, but as the person in charge.

In illustration 10.10, the musician on the left has an arm that is not fully formed, but that disability is not central to the photograph, as it would be in images of disabled musicians in freak show and begging photographs. The person here is pictured as part of a musical group—not as a "human wonder," but as an ordinary person doing an ordinary thing.

Schools and Civic Settings

Regular schools, social agencies, and such community facilities as libraries and churches are

10.10. Band with one player who has a deformed limb, ca. 1914. Photo postcard. Joel Wayne, Pop's Postcards.

additional places where people with disabilities appear in normal, everyday photos. Unlike institutional pictures in which people with disabilities are clustered together in segregated settings and dressed in uniforms, these photographs present the person with the disability as simply one of a group that also includes nondisabled peers. The placement of the person with the disability is sometimes dictated by the physical aspects of the setting, as in the class picture in illustration 10.11. Here the size of the platform on which the other children stand or sit is not large enough to accommodate the disabled child's wheelchair.

Illustration 10.12 is a high school senior class picture taken in front of the main entrance to the school. See how the young man second from the left in the bottom row, the person who is unusually short, is included.

The photo postcard of a large group of church members (illus. 10.13) taken on a Sunday after services includes a man with a disability in a wheelchair in the center. In such pictures, that location is most often occupied by the pastor, which might be the case here.

10.11. Class picture with one child in a wheelchair, ca. 1912. Photo postcard.

10.12. High school class picture including a young man with a disability, ca. 1915. Photo postcard.

10.13. Church group with man in wheelchair, ca. 1911. Photo postcard.

Studio Portraits

In the period of concern here, photo studios were places frequented by the general citizenry and by people with disabilities as well. Some photo studios were located on the top floors of buildings, where skylights provided the illumination needed for picture taking. Such places could be reached only by climbing stairs, making access for people with physical impairments difficult, but the number of studio portraits I came across of people in wheelchairs suggests that although accessibility might have been a challenge, it was not an insurmountable one.

The initial illustration that leads off this chapter (10.1) and illustration 10.14 show studio portraits of people with cerebral palsy in wheelchairs. The decorative backdrop and the props in 10.14 may seem unusual, but they are normal for photo studio pictures of the time. The subjects in the photographs were thus photographed in the same way as other citizens were.

Illustration 10.15 is a studio portrait of a teenage girl with a disability and a companion who is probably a family member or friend. Notice the seaside scenery in the back. Such backdrops were common in photo studios of photographers who specialized in resort tourist trade. The two pictured were likely vacationing in a coastal town, a place that people without a disability frequented, too. In another seaside vacation image (illus. 10.16), two buddies in period bathing suits strike casual poses while sitting on a paper moon studio prop. The man on the left is an amputee.

APPAREL

If you review all the illustrations in this chapter, you will see that people with disabilities appear in more or less the same attire and have the same grooming as anyone else. Of course, their appearance, as does anyone's, varies according to age, social class, status, and occupational group. In family and citizen pictures taken when people know they are going to be photographed, they dress up for the occasion, wearing their best or at least being sure to dress in conventional clothes that were clean and neat. Such clothing conventions are quite different from the conventions I discussed in earlier chapters, especially in freak photographs, horror movies, and asylum depictions.

10.14. Studio portrait of young man with cerebral palsy, ca. 1889. Cabinet photo.

10.15. Girl in wheelchair with companion in studio with seaside backdrop, ca. 1910. Photo postcard.

10.16. Buddies on vacation, ca. 1907. Photo postcard.

For many, the trip to the photo studio was a formal occasion. For middle-class men, it meant wearing a suit and tie. The man in illustration 10.17 follows those conventions as he faces the camera head on. Notice how his hair in neatly combed, and he wears a lapel pin. Although the pin is too small to inspect closely, it probably identifies him as a member of a particular church, civic, or Masonic organization. The fact that he is a double amputee is evident but not the focus of the portrait.

PHOTOGRAPHIC COMPANIONS

An important dimension of picturing people within normal conventions is the presence of other people with whom the person has meaningful relationships: fellow workers, family, friends, and other loved ones. You can see this dimension of normality in many of the illustrations I have already discussed, but there are many more to examine.

The most common group portraits are of people with family members. Illustration 10.18 resembles the first picture in this chapter. Both are studio portraits consisting of a family group surrounding a disabled family member. In this photo, a child in a wheelchair is comfortably situated in the center of the picture with his parents and sister in the group.

The same is true of the image in illustration 10.19 that includes a child with a disability, likely cerebral palsy, sitting on his father's lap. It is a studio portrait of a boy, his mother and father, and his two siblings. It clearly has many elements of a typical family portrait rather than being a picture

10.17. Studio portrait of amputee, ca. 1907. Photo postcard. B. Nelson Collection.

10.18. Family studio portrait, ca. 1898. Tintype.

10.19. Family portrait, ca. 1910. Photo postcard.

of a disabled person. Although this picture is dominated by family visual rhetoric, there are two elements that violate those conventions. The disabled son's footwear, the white knitted booties, and the fact that he is sitting on his father's lap are not typical of what a boy of his age would wear or how he would be posed for a family picture. Like the presence of wheelchairs, braces, and other visual indicators of disability, these elements violate typical photographic code, but their presence is not so intrusive as to change this picture's place in the category of a typical family photograph.

I have seen many photographs taken by amateurs showing people with disabilities as part of family and friendship groups. Illustration 10.20 includes a sightless girl in the front row and her blind mother in the second row (third from the right). The picture, likely taken by a family member, was shot at a family gathering. The individuals with disabilities intermingle with other family members in a way that suggests that they are not singled out for special treatment in either family life or family photography.

In a photo postcard that was probably taken by an amateur photographer, a mother and father and their two children are grouped outside their home in a rather formal and solemn pose (illus. 10.21). They have dressed up for the occasion and carried

10.20. Family photo with blind people included, ca. 1914. Photo postcard.

10.21. Family outside their home, ca. 1908. Photo postcard. Maslan Collection.

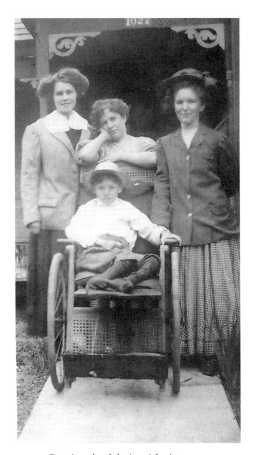

10.22. Boy in wheelchair with sisters, ca. 1910. Photo postcard.

10.23. Sisters, ca. 1900. Cabinet card.

10.24. Brothers, ca. 1898. Tintype.

10.25. Mother holding child with Down syndrome, ca. 1890. Cabinet card.

two kitchen chairs outside for the parents to sit on. The child on the left has Down syndrome. She is photographed, as are the others, as simply a part of the family.

In the picture of a young man in a wheelchair surrounded by his sisters (illus. 10.22), the subjects' social ties, casual postures, and smiling faces identify it as a family photo rather than a disability photo.

Duet images are also part of family photography—sisters with sisters, brothers with brothers. Illustration 10.23 captures a younger sister hugging her older sibling, who has a developmental disability. In illustration 10.24, two brothers pose in a formal studio setting. One brother's body is completely in view. The other, the one with an orthopedic disability, stands partially behind a table that he uses for support.

In the realm of typical family photography, it is common to have a parent pose with a child. Mothers holding young children are the most abundant of this type of portrait. The picture of a mother with her child with Down syndrome exemplifies the pose (illus. 10.25). Grandmothers are often pictured, too. In illustration 10.26, it is the grandmother who has a disability. Grandmothers also pose with their children and their children's children (illus. 10.27).

Older children with their disabled mothers are also common. Illustration 10.28 is a studio portrait of a middle-aged mother in a wheelchair posing with her daughter. Although it is difficult to make a diagnosis based on the photograph, the mother's gaunt appearance suggests tuberculosis.

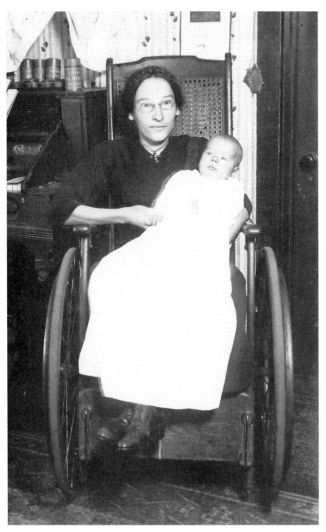

10.26. Grandmother in a wheelchair holding her grandchild, ca. 1908. Photo postcard.

10.27. Great-grandmother and family, ca. 1914. Photo postcard.

10.28. Mother in wheelchair with older daughter, ca. 1896. Cabinet card.

The daughter stands close to her parent, her body turned toward her. A feeling of closeness is created by her position, posture, and the way she holds her mother's chair gently, as if it were an extension of her loved one.

Photographs also reveal couple relationships, people who have disabilities in romantic partnerships with people who do not. Illustration 10.29 shows a middle-aged person in a wheelchair with a person we can assume from the pose and body language is either her husband or her boyfriend. See how they look each other in the eye, body language suggesting intimacy. From their facial expressions, you get the impression that they

10.29. Romantic encounter, ca. 1910. Photo postcard.

10.30. Woman in wheelchair with husband, ca. 1909. Photo postcard.

genuinely care for each other. They are photographed the way a typical couple would be photographed, and the woman's disability is incidental to the composition.

I have come across many pictures of elderly couples in which one of them is in a wheelchair, and both display caring gestures toward one another. Notice how in illustration 10.30 the man and woman are photographed to show their closeness as a couple. The women's arm extends over to her husband so that he can hold her hand. Although both are experiencing physical deterioration associated with old age, the image displays them in a positive way in which personal relationship is central.

PETS

During the first third of the twentieth century and continuing to a lesser extent later, people had their

pictures taken not only with human loved ones, but also with pets, mostly dogs and on occasion cats and other animals (Arluke and Bogdan 2010). Pets with their owners were a regular subject for photography. In illustration 10.31, a well-dressed young woman sits on the porch of her home. Her leg braces are inconspicuously visible where her long skirt ends. She reaches out to touch the dog, either to pet it or to assure that it does not run away before the shutter opens.

Including pets was not just a part of snapshot photography; people brought their pets to photo studios to sit for formal portraits as well. Illustration 10.32, showing a dog perched on a man's wheelchair, was clearly taken in a photographer's

10.31. Teenager in braces with her dog, ca. 1910. Photo postcard. B. Nelson Collection.

10.32. Man in wheelchair accompanied by his dog, ca. 1916. Photo postcard. B. Nelson Collection.

10.33. Siblings and puppy with boy in a wheelchair, ca. 1916. Photo postcard.

studio. In another picture, both the well-dressed siblings of the boy in the wheelchair and the adorable puppy help turn what might be a picture of a seriously ill child from a disability photograph into a family image (illus. 10.33).

These pictures of people with disabilities and their pets are not the first we have seen where people with disabilities are shown with animals. In the begging chapter, we saw animals, but, with the exception of the dog in illustration 3.20, they were used as working animals. Be they dogs or goats, they served their owners by providing transportation and in other ways facilitating their begging. The way the animals are pictured reinforced the centrality of disability in the images. Images of people with their pets in this chapter produce the opposite effect.

ORDINARY OBJECTS

Within the conventions of normal photography, in addition to living beings—family, friends, and pets—people are photographed with objects that are meaningful to their identity. Things such as books, toys and playthings, cars, and spinning wheels regularly appear. For working people, objects associated with their occupations—tools and equipment—are included.

The picture in illustration 10.34 was taken on the steps of these siblings' front porch. The girl on

10.35. Young woman with violin in wheelchair, ca. 1909. Photo postcard. Don and Newly Preziosi Collection.

10.34. Girl with disability on porch with doll, ca. 1916. Photo postcard.

the right wears a leg brace and a lift on one shoe, suggesting that she has polio. But note how the children are holding playthings; the younger sister has a teddy bear, and the older sister is holding her favorite doll. These objects promote the idea that the children are typical young people.[3]

In illustration 10.35, we see a young woman with a disability sitting in a decorative rattan

3. Note the person, most likely the children's mother, in the window behind the girls. She adds not only depth to the composition, but also the presence of the adult overseer.

wheelchair and photographed, as any person might be, with a musical instrument, a violin. There are freak photos of people performing with musical instruments, but these people are presented as human wonders rather than as normal students of an instrument, as this image suggests.

Although illustration 10.36 may be offensive to some because of the presence of a dead animal, I include it because it epitomizes normal photographic conventions. It was very common for hunters in the first third of the twentieth century to be pictured with their dead prey. Some of these photographs feature women, but the great majority are of men finishing the hunt, a symbol of male culture and manliness. Here a person of small stature stands holding a gun next to the buck he just shot.

It was common for US mail carriers who delivered the mail by horse-drawn wagon in rural areas to have a local photographer take pictures of them beside the objects associated with their occupation, the mailbag and the delivery buggy. They had this portrait taken for personal correspondence but also to give to patrons on their route near the holiday season. In illustration 10.37, an African

American US mailman, dressed in his occupational uniform, stands outside the Caledonia, Michigan, post office. He is holding the hand of a child and is standing next to his mailbag and horse-drawn rig. Upon close inspection, you can see that his left arm is missing.

Illustration 10.38, the last in this section showing people with objects, is another occupation-related photo postcard. It is of a farmer, Norman Brown, standing next to a complex yet primitive machine he built. Look carefully at Brown's left arm, and you will see that the lower part is missing and a metal prosthetic device is in its place. He unselfconsciously displays it. (The prosthetic is much more apparent in the original than in the illustration copy.) The card is postmarked "Beaver Dam, Wisconsin, 1913" and was sent to Brown's cousin to show her the "ditching plow" he had built over the winter. In the message written on the flip side, Brown brags about the machine and speculates that he will sell it for "nothing less than $600." Although Brown has an obvious disability, it is not mentioned on the card. Brown and his invention are front and center. As in other images of people with objects shown in this section,

10.36. Dwarf with dead deer, 1915. Photo postcard.

10.37. Amputee rural delivery postman, ca. 1908. Photo postcard. Aikenhead Collection.

10.38. Farmer with his ditching plow, 1913. Photo postcard.

attention is drawn way from the disability to the object, a plow.

CONCEALING DISABILITY

In the images reviewed in this chapter, the disability is apparent; no attempts were made to hide the person's missing limbs, wheelchair, braces, or other indicators of impairment. But what about pictures where the person conceals his or her condition? How do we know that some family pictures do not have a person who is hiding a disability?[4] What about conditions such as deafness, mental illness, retardation, and others where the nature of the disability may not be apparent? How should they fit into the analysis of visual disability?

I do not have answers to these questions, but I do have a photo that brought the issue to my

4. This is quite different than with begging cards, where we are not sure whether the person pictured has a disability or is only feigning one.

10.39. Brother and sister in front of their home, 1909. Photo postcard.

attention, the picture of a brother and sister at the front steps of their home (illus. 10.39). Both have toys. He holds a bugle and a drum, and she has her hands on a doll carriage filled with dolls. Neither child appears to have a disability. In another photo postcard (illus. 10.40), however, we see the same youngsters a few years later. They are still in front of their home, and she still has a carriage with her dolls, but he is not holding toys. Careful inspection shows that the boy does not have a right arm. In addition, he has either a cleft pallet or a demonstrable scar on his upper lip. In the first photograph, his disabilities seem to have been successfully and purposefully hidden with his toys, whereas in the second he unself-consciously reveals them. Should we think of hiding a disability as a normal part of family visual rhetoric?

CONCLUSION

I end this chapter with a compelling photograph of a mother with her two children taken in a photo studio (illus. 10.41). It has all the elements of a typical family photo. The dress, the people, the location, the body language, the props are all there.

10.40. Brother and sister shown in illustration 10.39 four years later, ca. 1913. Photo postcard.

10.41. Mother with children, ca. 1909. Photo postcard.

The child on the left appears to have Down syndrome, but that may be a misdiagnosis. She might just have some of the physical characteristics we associate with that condition, but not the condition itself.[5] If she does have a disability, the picture is a wonderful illustration of how the visual significance of a disability is muted when a photograph is taken using normal family photographic conventions. If the child does not have the condition, it is a good illustration of a photo using family conventions. Either way it points out the power of photographic context in setting the scene and in leading the viewer to an interpretation of a person's characteristics.

5. On the back of this postcard, the phrase "Down's Syndrome" is written in pencil, but I am not sure who wrote it or if the diagnosis is accurate.

11 Conclusion
Just a Beginning

In this book, I have shown you amusement world freak photographs, beggars' cards, poster children, asylum representations, art photography, advertisements, clinical photographs, movie stills, ordinary family and citizen photography, and more. I have discussed and demonstrated an approach to analyzing pictures of people with disabilities that places the images in the context of the times and places of those who produced those images. As I have emphasized, the producers operated with a set of assumptions that were part of the organizations and institutions to which they belonged. The images were an outgrowth of their social location.

My goal was not to cover every genre of disability photography or all the permutations within the genres discussed. I have only started the job of systematically scrutinizing the wide range of historical photographs of people with disabilities. As I did the research for and wrote this book, other genres of disability photographs that I had overlooked became apparent. Either I did not have enough images to explore these topics, or in my judgment they were not important enough to warrant a full chapter. Before I close, I introduce some of these genres to you. In addition, there are images that I came across that were too complex to place in genres. I discuss some of these and warn readers to be cautious in analyzing how people with disabilities are pictured.

TOWN CHARACTER PORTRAITS

I came across images that at first glance looked like begging cards. The subjects of these images did not strike poses that evoke pity as those pictured in begging cards would do. On closer inspection, they suggest another genre of disability photography, "town characters." The people in the images I am referring to were considered peculiar by others in their community. Although today they would likely be referred to as "disabled," they were not seen that way when the pictures were taken. In most cases, they did not use the images to solicit money; rather, the photographers who took the portraits most likely sold them for their own profit.

The people I am referring to were quasi-celebrities in their communities. They could be seen about town. Some had personalities that drew attention. Some lacked the basic skills needed to function fully as ordinary community members. Although they were viewed as peculiar and in most cases as inferior, they were embraced as "one of us." They were protected from those who might do them harm and had a special role and position in the town's hierarchy.

Most embraced the role of local character, but some seemed to be oblivious of their status. The photo portraits taken of them by local photographers were sold to tourists as souvenirs and to local citizens as keepsakes.[1] More integrated into local

---

1. In my collecting, I overlooked the range of photos that might fit into a "local characters" genre because I dismissed them as irrelevant to what I considered appropriate for the book. Rethinking these photographs, I see now that local characters were pervasive throughout the United States, especially in small towns and perhaps even in urban areas.

communities than freaks, more financially independent than beggars, but not exactly fully normal community members, town characters deserve to be singled out for study.

I came across a number of portraits of "local characters" featured on photographic postcards who would be labeled mentally ill today. One such person was an upstate New Yorker who was the subject of a number of real photo postcards, Huckleberry Charlie (Bogdan 2003, 184). Charlie was a common sight in the northern reaches of New York State's Adirondack region (illus. 11.1). His full name was Charles R. Sherman, and he was the son of wealthy parents. Locals were sympathetic to his condition, amused by his antics, and appreciative of the goods he sold. Charlie was a local eccentric who, in addition to his family inheritance, supported himself by selling newspapers and local products such as sauerkraut, horseradish, and, when in season, huckleberries. He was known for his nonsensical, riddlelike talk and for his unconventional dress and song. Locals held mixed opinions about whether he was crazy, intellectually disabled, or just wildly eccentric. In spite of his oddities, he was part of the community. He spent much of his time hanging around Pine Camp, a military training camp that is now the US Army's Fort Drum.

Another town character, a person who likely had psychiatric problems, was a man whom a photo postcard identifies as "Horace" (illus. 11.2). His portrait is an engrossing studio shot of a person who apparently lived on the streets of a small town in the Midwest. The message on the back of the card suggests that Horace was a regular part of community life, but because of some unknown trangression he became "unwelcome everywhere." The message goes on to describe Horace as "one of God's poor under normal creatures" and hopes that the Supreme Power will look after him.

Dan McCuin lived with his brother near Plymouth, Vermont, the town in which President Coolidge was born and raised. McCuin seemed to

11.1. Huckleberry Charlie at Pine Camp, New York, ca. 1908. Photo by Henry Beach.

embrace the title "the Smallest Man in New England." From descriptions and pictures, it appears that McCuin's small size was probably caused by an underactive thyroid gland, a condition often associated with developmental disabilities. Individual portraits of him exist, but the most widely circulated images were of McCuin posing with President Coolidge (as in illus. 11.3). The picture here was published in newspapers throughout Vermont, some captioning the shot, "The Biggest Man in the Country Shaking Hands with the Smallest." The postcards of McCuin with the President were produced by a local photographer

11.2. "Horace," ca. 1910. Photo postcard. Joel Wayne, Pop's Postcards.

11.3. President Calvin Coolidge with Dan McCuin, ca. 1923. Photo postcard.

and sold by him as well as retailed through stores (Greene 1997, 31).[2]

A town celebrity of a different sort was "Captain M. V. Bates." Rather than being small in stature, he was extremely tall—in circus terminology, a giant (Bogdan 1988, 206). Bates's status as a town celebrity was not just a function of his extreme height. His life as a sideshow exhibit contributed to his local fame. Bates appeared in the sideshows of the most well-known circuses of the time in his preretirement life. He married Ann Swann, another sideshow giant, and they were exhibited as the tallest couple in the world. In the late 1800s, they went in search of

a community in which to settle. They bought a farm and became citizens of Seville, Ohio, where they were integrated into the local community. After his wife died, Bates married a daughter of the Seville Baptist Church pastor. Bates is shown in illustration 11.4 attending the fair at Seville a few years before his death in 1919 at eighty-one years of age.

"Town character" Mike Shanahan (illus. 11.5) was a sightless upstate New York regional celebrity who was the subject of at least four different photo postcard views (Bogdan 2003, 50). In each, he is pictured with a guide dog, animals that Shanahan must have trained himself, given that the formal instruction for such animals did not start until World War I. (In the four pictures of

2. McCuin did not seem to use his cards as beggars used their pictures. He lived as part of the community, did odd jobs, and helped his brother around the house.

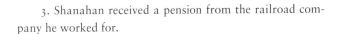

11.4. Captain Bates, ca. 1910. Photo postcard. Maslan Collection.

11.5. Mr. Shanahan with his famous dog, ca. 1909. Photo postcard.

him I have seen, two show a black dog, and the other two have a white dog.) In the photo postcard shown here, Shanahan is selling newspapers at the small Benson Mines town railroad station. As he sold papers, he engaged people in small talk. His paper selling was as much a way of socializing around town as it was a way of supporting himself.[3] He hung out mainly at the town depot waiting for trains to arrive. The railroad coincides with his biography. Prior to being blinded in a railroad accident, he had worked for the railroad. According to what I could find out, although Shanahan sold newspapers, he himself did not sell his photo postcard portraits. They were available on postcard racks at retails stores in and around the town of Benson Mines.

I have provided only a few examples of local characters here but have not discussed the photography involved. This genre of photography is an example of an unexpected topic emerging from my research. These photographs of "town characters" introduce the important role that people with disabilities played in some communities. The topic is almost absent in discussions of the history of disability.[4] These characters provide an interesting example of inclusion, albeit a form that might not

3. Shanahan received a pension from the railroad company he worked for.

4. The following are exceptions: Groce 1986 and Langness and Levine 1986.

be appealing to current advocates of inclusion of people with disabilities into community life (Bogdan 1992).

RELIGION AS A GENRE

A number of chapters in this book touched on religious themes. For example, beggars often framed their appeals with religious arguments, as did some charity campaigns. I have not pursued photos with religious themes or produced by religious organizations as a major genre of disability photography, but the religious mode of presenting people with disability deserves further attention.

The need to explore religious themes was made evident not only in begging and charity photographs, but also in other images I came across. The photo in illustration 11.6 was obviously taken in a

11.6. Boy with cerebral palsy sitting in front of Christmas tree, ca. 1912. Photo postcard.

home during the Christmas season. The child is in front of a holiday tree with his gifts displayed. It appears to be a standard family holiday view, but in this case the child with a disability, cerebral palsy, is awkwardly sitting in a stiff wooden chair that does not accommodate the contours of his body. His awkward, uncomfortable, unsmiling pose does not correspond with normal family photographic conventions. There is another aspect of the picture that is incongruent with a typical portrait. In addition to gifts, there is a prominently displayed statue of the Virgin Mary standing with the adult Jesus. I have examined many images of typical children in front of the Christmas tree, and I have never seen religious statues such as this one other than in nativity scenes. Were the child's parents seeking religious comfort, a blessing, by including the statue in the scene? Was its presence linked to the son's disability? Perhaps the difficulty in assessing the picture is that it may better fit a genre as yet not developed—picturing disability from a religious perspective.

FOREIGN VIEWS

In this book, I have dealt almost exclusively with picturing disability in the United States. By examining a limited number of images produced in Europe, however, I could see that there are differences both in subject matter and in the approach to photographing people with disabilities. What was particularly striking to me was the number of photographs related to disabled veterans injured in World War I.

I have also seen many foreign postcards showing indigenous people from colonized areas of the world. Westerners' might describe some of the subjects as having disabilities. These postcard views were almost exclusively produced by Western expatriates as souvenirs to send home. Studied now, they might be an important source for understanding how colonized people with disabilities were represented by their colonizers.

One of the most heralded expatriate photographers who worked in Central Africa was Casimir

Zagourski (Bassani and Loos 2001; Geary 2002). In addition to photographing people with disabling conditions, he photographed people who because of tribal custom altered their children's bodies to meet their culture's beauty standards. In the 1930s, he extensively documented the Mangebetu people of what is now the Democratic Republic of the Congo. The canon of beauty for the Mangebetu at the time was elongated skulls. The heads of infants were compressed by means of wrapping thin ropes of raffia around the skull to produce the ideal look in adulthood. The freak show presentations of people with microcephaly, as shown in chapter 2, were derived from stories of the head-binding practices in Africa—for

instance, by the Mangebetu. The juxtaposition of these images and the image of the Mangebetu woman in illustration 11.7 provides a vivid contrast of photographic depictions and cultural interpretations of head binding.

Studying the global dimensions of disability photography would help us put American representation of disability in a larger comparative context.

DISABLED VETERANS

I did not purposely seek out images of US disabled war veterans, nor did I come across many in my research. I briefly discussed and exhibited images of World War I veterans in chapter 3 on begging cards and in chapter 4 on charity campaigns.

Chapter 4 also showed US presidents and their wives pictured with soldiers who had been injured during war. These photographs suggest another area of study, however—government publicists' use of disability photography to promote patriotism during times of war as well as photojournalists' picturing of soldiers with disabilities.

Illustration 11.8 is of a government-issued printed postcard. It shows men working in an artificial-limb shop in a government hospital toward the end of World War I. The government production of war images that bring attention to soldiers with disabilities is a double-edged sword. On the one hand, such images may evoke patriotic sentiments by graphically showing the government's efforts to support veterans. On the other hand, they can dramatically show the suffering caused by war and raise questions in people's minds about war policy.[5]

Other military images that came to my attention were of Civil War veterans. In some cases, they were participating in Grand Army of the Republic reunions or were residents in old-age

11.7. Mangebetu woman, ca. 1931. Photo by Casimir Zagourski. Photo postcard.

5. See Beth Linker's fine book *War's Waste* (2011) for a discussion of the government's role in the rehabilitation of World War I veterans, the controversies surrounding its role, and its use of disabled veterans in propaganda.

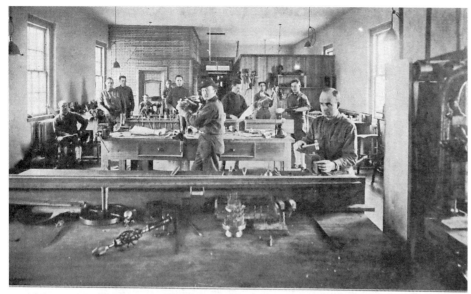

ARTIFICIAL LIMB SHOP, U. S. A. GENERAL HOSPITAL No. 10, BOSTON, MASS.

11.8. Government artificial limb shop, ca. 1918. Printed postcard.

11.9. Grand Army of the Republic members in Veterans Home, ca. 1911.

homes that served the veterans. Illustration 11.9 shows the interior of such a facility. These images are different from other institution pictures in a number of ways. As you see in the illustration, the men are dressed in their military uniforms. Their identity as soldiers outweighs their status as institution residents. In addition, the picture is not dominated by institution staff or routines of institutional life. There is no attempt to show off the facility, as in other institutional pictures reviewed in chapter 5.

The photo shown in illustration 11.10 was taken outside a Veterans Home. Note the patriotic display of flags. Most of the men in the picture are wearing clothing that relates to their military service. One aspect of this picture that was surprising to me was the integration—both Caucasian and African American men are pictured.

11.10. Outside view of home for Grand Army of the Republic veterans, ca. 1909. Photo postcard.

AFRICAN AMERICAN AND OTHER NON-CAUCASIAN SUBJECTS

Illustration 11.10 brings up another important topic not addressed in this book—images of African Americans and other non-Caucasian Americans with disabilities. Non-Caucasian Americans are underrepresented in this book and in the images I surveyed. When they do appear, they are in group photos. Illustration 10.37 of the African American mail carrier is the only image in the ordinary photo genre where a non-Caucasian person is the main subject. The only individual portrait of an African American person I came across is shown in illustration 11.11. Pictured is an old man with crutches who appears to be poor. One of his legs has been amputated and the other disabled. To the man's right is a small garden pick. Because there is no caption or writing on the message side of this photo postcard, it is impossible to determine the context in which it was produced. It is most likely a family portrait.

I do not know why I found so few photographs of non-Caucasian people who have disabilities. Was it the result of the way I searched or where I searched, or were not that many images of non-Caucasians with disabilities produced? Starting early in the twentieth century, photography was

11.11. African American man with crutches, ca. 1910. Photo postcard.

widely available to a range of people in the United States. Many portraits of African Americans and other non-Caucasians are available on the antique photograph marketplace, but few of them include people with disabilities. This puzzle needs exploration. Knowing who was and who was not photographed and why is an important aspect of studying photographic images.

OTHER GENRES

There are other genres that need exploration. In the chapter on art photography, documentary photographers were mentioned several times. Their work needs more exploration. In the clinical photo chapter, mug shots were mentioned, and they, too, might be explored. I have also not treated newspaper photographs, specifically those accompanying news stories that feature people with disabilities.

VISUAL CONUNDRUMS: EXPANDING THE ANALYSIS

Most pictures are easy to place into one specific genre or another of disability photography discussed in this book, but others contain peculiarities or visual conundrums. I share some of these more complicated images with you to suggest that the analysis of photographs is complex and to add a cautionary note to those who would develop quick classification schemes and automatically place particular disability images in specific categories. These images also suggest other dimensions of disability photography yet to be explored.

At first glance, illustration 11.12 appears to be of the type we looked at in the chapter about citizen and family. A second look, however, causes reason to question that judgment. There is no caption or writing on the back of the photo postcard to help us put the picture in context. What are we to make of the people in the picture? One is a lanky, disheveled man in dirty, ripped clothing, with sloping shoulders and an expressionless face. Next to him

is a well-dressed, somber man sitting in an elaborate wicker chair. Is the standing man mentally disabled? What is the relationship between the two men? Are they relatives? Brothers? Friends? Does the standing man work for the other? Or perhaps the picture is staged—that is, the two were in a theater production and came to a photographer's studio in costume. The way the disheveled man's overalls are ripped seems to be too excessive to be natural. But look at his hands. They are working man's hands, with one finger adorned by a dirty bandage, not the hands of an actor. If we speculate that the two are relatives and the tall man is mentally disabled, how would the photo fit with our

11.12. Studio portrait of two men whose relationship is unknown, ca. 1912. Photo postcard. Joel Wayne, Pop's Postcards.

discussion of conventions for photographing where disability is trumped by normality?

In illustration 11.13, we see a picture that is difficult to place in any of the schemes presented. Perhaps this image fits best in the genre of local character, but perhaps not. "Blind Willie's" role as a gospel preacher is apparently central to his status, but the fact that he is blind is highlighted in the presentation of his name. Although not a local character in the sense of the others discussed earlier in this chapter, he was nevertheless a local celebrity beyond his role as an evangelist. I came across a number of images of people with disabilities who were musicians. Perhaps the realm of performers with disabilities deserves further exploration and even a separate genre.

The family portrait in illustration 11.14 provides another puzzle. The composition resembles that of a typical family studio portrait, with the father in the middle sitting in a wheelchair surrounded by children and wife. The children on the right affectionately touch his chair. But at least two aspects of the picture bring into question whether we are looking at a standard family portrait or at one using those conventions for begging. The uniformly glum faces resemble the pity poses seen

11.13. Blind Willie, ca. 1912. Photo postcard.

11.14. "Henry Novak—Frozen in Storm Jan-29–09," ca. 1910. Photo postcard.

in the begging cards. The caption reinforces this impression: "Henry Novak—Frozen in Storm of Jan-29-09." That caption would never appear on a photo taken for personal use or to share with intimates. That caption would be used only if the picture's purpose was to solicit contributions. The photograph was probably composed using family conventions as a strategy for eliciting sympathy in a begging strategy. Perhaps it belongs in another category that I have not developed, or it might be classified as a mixed-genre photo.

SEVERE AND PROFOUNDLY DISABLED PEOPLE

Although a few of the images in this book are of people who might be classified as having severe impairments, most do not. The reason is simply that I did not find many aside from images in medical textbooks. The only others I have come across are shown in illustrations 11.15 and 11.16. Both appear to fit into the family photograph category, pictures taken of a family member to have as a keepsake or to be placed in a family album. But they are not easy to interpret.

Illustration 11.15 is of a child with very visible hydrocephaly. He appears in the backyard of his home dressed for the photographic occasion with long stockings and an attractive jacket. His hair has been carefully combed, his hands are intertwined, and his small chair is covered with a brightly printed, flowered fabric that fits with the natural foliage surrounding the child. When I first saw the picture, it caught me off guard—I was taken aback and reluctant to engage with it. I had never seen a family photo of a child with such a demonstrable disability. The child's large head dominated my attention. After I looked at the photo over time, the child's disability became less dominate. I came to see it as a picture of a child who might never measure up to the common standards of a lovely looking person, but who was loved. It is difficult to interpret the caption "Master Handsome," but I came to see it as a family member's sincere expression of both

what he or she hoped the boy would be and how he or she saw him. Although his profound disability might grab our eye and dominate our viewing, seeing a photo like this one over time diminishes the salience of the person's impairment. The changing meaning of the photograph suggests that the context in which the photo is viewed as well as the individual viewer's evolving relationship with both the subject and the image need to be taken into account in analyzing disability photographs.

I was also reluctant to confront the photo in illustration 11.16, yet I was drawn to it. It is difficult to understand the meaning of this photo postcard to those who took it and kept it. The image is of a person with a profound disability,

11.15. "Master Handsome," ca. 1909. Photo postcard. Matthews Collection.

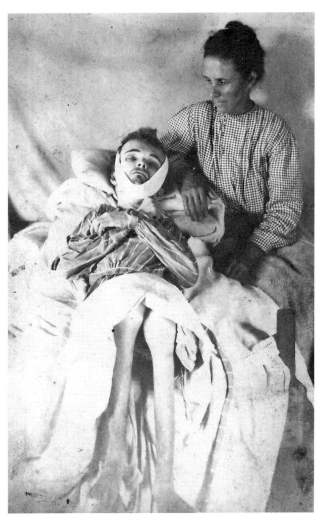

11.16. Severely disabled person with loving other, ca. 1908. Photo postcard.

a fragile young man with emaciated body. He is with a woman much older than he, his mother or a caretaker. Note the body language. She sits close to him, with her arm touching his head. For me, the photograph illustrates the power of an image to pose an unsolvable mystery while at the same time drawing the viewer into an attempt to get to the bottom of understanding the human condition. It demonstrates how photographs can capture the subject as well as the viewer.

FINAL THOUGHTS

My goal for this book was to present disability photographs from the 1860s to the early 1970s in a

way that showed how they fit into the lives of those who produced them. I have accomplished this objective in part. Each chapter looks at depictions of disability in terms of the context that generated them, but the analysis has stayed closer to the photos and their producers than some might like. The larger social forces that shaped these images have not been examined. The evolution of human services and capitalism in the United States and the relationship between the private sector's and the public sector's responsibilities to people with disabilities needs to be examined to understand the disability charity images as well as other depictions reviewed. The history of the human-service professions in the United States has to be studied in order to understand the production of the images discussed in the chapters on charity, clinical depictions, and asylum photographs. Industrialization, urbanization, and the growth of the urban middle class have to be taken into account to understand the family's inclusion of people with disabilities in their pictures. Racism, sexism, anti-immigration, and other negative social *isms* must be examined to understand image production. Development of the advertisement and entertainment industries needs to be understood to grasp what was behind the production of advertising that used people with disabilities and of freak show photographs. Last, how the change in photographic technology influenced the kinds of pictures taken of people with disabilities needs to be explored.

This book has focused on the past. All the images reviewed were in tune with the culture in which they were produced and were a product of the times and transformations taking place then. By analyzing old photographs, my colleagues and I hoped to develop a deeper understanding of the historical experiences of people, both those pictured and the picture takers.

Patterns of representation are easier to identify by looking backward than by looking at present-day representations. Nonetheless, an approach similar to the one used here might be taken in analyzing the images of disability being produced today. Such images would include depictions created by people who are involved in the disability rights movement, in advertising, by various professional organizations, by press photography, and in the personal photographs that grow out of family and other close relationships.

References ∾ Index

References

A. A. Marks. 1906. *Manual of Artificial Legs.* New York: A. A. Marks.

Apel, Dora, and Shawn Michelle Smith. 2008. *Lynching Photographs.* Berkeley: Univ. of California Press.

Aperture Foundation. 2011. "Diane Arbus: *Untitled,* Photographs by Diane Arbus." Retrieved from http://www.aperture.org/books/browse-by-photographer/a-c/diane-arbus-untitled.html.

Arbus, Diane. 1972. *Diane Arbus.* Millerton, NY: Aperture.

———. 1995. *Untitled.* New York: Aperture Foundation.

Arluke, Arnold, and Robert Bogdan. 2010. *Beauty and the Beast.* Syracuse, NY: Syracuse Univ. Press.

Asma, Stephen T. 2001. *Stuffed Animals and Pickled Heads: Culture and Evolution of Natural History Museums.* New York: Oxford Univ. Press.

Avedon, Richard. 1964. *Nothing Personal.* New York: Atheneum.

———. 1976. *Portraits.* New York: Farrar, Straus, and Giroux.

Barr, Martin W. 1904. *Mental Defectives: Their History, Treatment, and Training.* Philadelphia: Blakiston.

Barr, Martin F., and A. B. Maloney. 1920. *Types of Mental Defectives.* Philadelphia: P. Blakiston.

Bassani, Ezio, and Pierre Loos. 2001. *Zagourski: Lost Africa.* New York: St. Martin's Press.

Baynton, Douglas C., Jack Gannon, and Jean Bergey. 2007. *Through Deaf Eyes: A Photographic History of an American Community.* Washington, DC: Gallaudet University Press.

Becker, Howard S. 1982. *Art Worlds.* Berkley: Univ. of California Press.

Bjornsdottir, Inga Dora. 2010. *Olof the Eskimo Lady: A Biography of an Icelandic Dwarf in America.* Ann Arbor: Univ. of Michigan Press.

Black, Edwin. 2003. *War Against the Weak: Eugenics and America's Campaign to Create a Master Race.* New York: Four Walls Eight Windows.

Blatt, Burton, and Fred Kaplan. 1966. *Christmas in Purgatory: A Photographic Essay on Mental Retardation.* Boston: Allyn and Bacon.

Bogdan, Robert. 1988. *Freak Show: Presenting Human Oddities for Amusement and Profit.* Chicago: Univ. of Chicago Press.

———. 1992. "Delbert Ward: Community Acceptance of a 'Simple' Farmer Accused of Murder." *Disability, Handicap, and Society* 7, no. 4: 303–20.

———. 1998. *Exposing the Wilderness.* Syracuse, NY: Syracuse Univ. Press.

———. 2003. *Adirondack Vernacular.* Syracuse, NY: Syracuse Univ. Press.

Bogdan, Robert, Douglas Biklen, Arthur Shapiro, and David Spelkoman. 1982. "Media's Monster." *Social Policy* 13, no. 2 (Fall): 32–35.

Bogdan, Robert, and Sari Biklen. 2007. *Qualitative Research for Education.* 5th ed. Boston: Allyn and Bacon.

Bogdan, Robert, and Ann Marshall. 1997. "Views of the Asylum: Picture Postcard Depictions of Institutions for People with Mental Disorders in the Early 20th Century." *Visual Sociology* 12, no. 1: 4–27.

Bogdan, Robert, and Todd Weseloh. 2006. *Real Photo Postcard Guide.* Syracuse, NY: Syracuse Univ. Press.

Bosworth, Patricia. 1984. *Diane Arbus: A Biography.* New York: Knopf.

Bremner, Robert H. 1988. *American Philanthropy.* 2d ed. Chicago: Univ. of Chicago Press.

Carlson, Elof Axel. 2001. *The Unfit: A History of a Bad Idea.* Cold Spring Harbor, NY: Cold Spring Harbor Laboratory Press.

Chivers, Sally, and Nicole Markotic. 2010. *The Problem Body: Projecting Disability on Film.* Columbus: Ohio State Univ. Press.

Chorover, S. L. 1979. *From Genesis to Genocide: The Meaning of Human Nature and the Power of Behavior Control.* Cambridge, MA: MIT Press.

Christie's Auction House. 2009. "Tomoko in Her Bath," Minamata, Japan, 1972. Sale information: Sale 2279, the Miller-Plummer Collection of Photographs, Oct. 8. Retrieved from http://www.christies.com/LotFinder/lot_details.aspx?intObjectID=5236759.

Coke, V. D. 1991. "Ralph Eugene Meatyard." In *Ralph Eugene Meatyard: An American Visionary*, edited by Barbara Tannenbaum, 79–82. New York: Rizzoli.

Coleman, A. D. 1977. *The Grotesque in Photography.* New York: Summit.

Crookshank, Francis G. 1924. *The Mongol in Our Midst: A Study of Man and His Three Faces.* New York: Dutton.

D'Alessandro, Robert. 1973. *Glory.* New York: Elephant.

Davenport, Charles B. 1911. *Heredity in Relation to Eugenics.* New York: Henry Holt.

Davies, S. P. 1930. *Social Control of the Mentally Deficient.* New York: Crowell.

Dennett, Andrea Stulman. 1997. *Weid Wonderful: The Dime Museum in America.* New York: New York Univ. Press.

Diamond, Hugh W. [1856] 1976. "On the Application of Photography to the Physiognomic and Mental Phenomena of Insanity." In *The Face of Madness: Hugh W. Diamond and the Origin of Psychiatric Photography*, edited by Sander S. Gilman, 19–24. Secaucus, NJ: Citadel Press.

Dotterrer, Steven, and Galen Cranz. 1982. "The Picture Postcard." *Journal of American Culture* 5, no. 1: 44–50.

Dwyer, Ellen. 1987. *Homes for the Mad: Life inside Two Nineteenth-Century Asylums.* New Brunswick, NJ: Rutgers Univ. Press.

Elks, Martin. 1992. "Visual Rhetoric: Photographs of the Feeble-Minded during the Eugenics Era." PhD diss., Syracuse Univ.

———. 1993. "The 'Lethal Chamber': Further Evidence for the Euthanasia Option." *Mental Retardation* 31, no. 4: 201–7.

———. 2005. "Visual Indictment: A Contextual Analysis of *The Kallikak Family* Photographs." *Mental Retardation* 43, no. 4: 268–80.

Fadner, Fredric. 1944. *The Gentle Giant.* Boston: Bruce Humphries.

Ferguson, Philip. 1994. *Abandoned to Their Fate: Social Policy and Practice toward Severely Retarded People in America.* Philadelphia: Temple Univ. Press.

Fernald, Walter E. 1912. "The Burden of Feeble-Mindedness." *Journal of Psycho-Asthenics* 17, no. 3: 85–99.

Fiedler, Leslie. 1978. *Freaks: Myths and Images of the Secret Self.* New York: Simon & Schuster.

Fine, Gary. 2004. *Everyday Genius: Self-Taught Art and the Culture of Authenticity.* Chicago: Univ. of Chicago Press.

Francher, Raymond E. 1987. "Henry Goddard and the Kallikak Family Photographs: 'Conscious Skullduggery' or 'Whig History'?" *American Psychologist* 42: 585–90.

Gablik, Suzi. 1984. *Has Modernism Failed?* New York: Thames & Hudson.

Garland-Thomson, Rosemarie. 2001. "Seeing the Disabled: Visual Rhetoric of Disability in Popular Culture." In *The New Disability History*, edited by Paul Longmore and Lauri Umansky, 335–75. New York: New York Univ. Press.

———. 2002. "The Politics of Staring: Visual Rhetorics of Disability in Popular Photography." In *Disability Studies: Enabling the Humanities*, edited by Sharon L. Snyder, Brenda Jo Brueggemann, and Rosemarie Garland-Thomson, 56–73. New York: Modern Language Association.

———. 2004. "Integrating Disability, Transforming Feminist Theory." In *Gendering Disability*, edited by Bonnie Smith and Beth Hutchison, 73–104. New Brunswick, NJ: Rutgers Univ. Press.

———. 2009. *Staring/How We Look.* New York: Oxford Univ. Press.

Geary, Christraud. 2002. *In and out of Focus: Images from Central Africa, 1885–1960.* Washington, DC: Smithsonian Institution, National Museum of African Art.

Gerber, David. 1992. "Volition and Valorization in the Analysis of the 'Careers' of People Exhibited in Freak Shows." *Disability, Handicap, & Society* 7: 14–19.

Gifford, Denis. 1973. *A Pictorial History of Horror Movies*. New York: Hamlyn.

Gilman, Sander S. 1982. *Seeing the Insane*. New York: Wiley.

Glaser, Barney. 1978. *Theoretical Sensitivity*. Mill Valley, CA: Sociology Press.

Glaser, Barney, and Anselm Strauss. 1967. *The Discovery of Grounded Theory*. Chicago: Aldine.

Goddard, Henry H. 1912. *The Kallikak Family: A Study in the Heredity of Feeble-Mindedness*. New York: Macmillan.

———. 1914. *Feeblemindedness: Its Causes and Consequences*. New York: Macmillan.

Goffman, Erving. 1959. *The Presentation of Self in Everyday Life*. Garden City, NY: Doubleday/ Anchor.

———. 1963. *Stigma*. Englewood Cliffs, NJ: Prentice Hall.

———. 1988. *Gender Advertisements*. Rev. ed. New York: HarperCollins.

Goldberg, Vicki. 1991. *The Power of Photography*. New York: Abbeville Press.

Goldin, Nan. 1995. "Review: *Untitled*—Diane Arbus." *Artforum* 34, no. 3 (Nov.): special section.

Gould, Stephen J. 1981. *The Mismeasure of Man*. New York: Norton.

Green, Jonathan. 1984. *American Photography: A Critical History 1945 to the Present*. New York: Abrams.

Greene, J. R. 1997. *Calvin Coolidge: Plymouth Vermont*. Dover, NH: Arcadia.

Grob, Gerald. 1983. *Mental Illness and American Society, 1875–1940*. Princeton, NJ: Princeton Univ. Press.

Groce, Nora. 1986. *The Town Fool: An Oral History of a Mentally Retarded Individual in Small Town Society*. Working Papers in Anthropology. New York: Wenner-Gren Foundation.

Gulick, W. V. 1918. *Mental Diseases: A Handbook Dealing with Diagnosis and Classification*. St. Louis: Mosby.

Hales, Peter Bacon. 1984. *Silver Cities*. Philadelphia: Temple Univ. Press.

Haller, Beth. 2010. *Representing Disability in an Ableist World*. Louisville, KY: Advocado Press.

Haller, Mark. 1963. *Eugenics: Hereditarian Attitudes in American Thought*. New Brunswick, NJ: Rutgers Univ. Press.

Harris, Neil. 1973. *Humbug: The Art of P. T. Barnum*. Chicago: Univ. of Chicago Press.

Hevey, David. 1992. *The Creatures Time Forgot: Photography and Disability Imagery*. London: Routledge.

———. 2006. "The Enfreakment of Photography." In *The Disability Studies Reader*, 2d ed., edited by Lennard Davis, 367–78. New York: Routledge.

Hollander, Russell. 1989. "Euthanasia and Mental Retardation: Suggesting the Unthinkable." *Mental Retardation* 27, no. 2: 55–61.

Holmes, Arthur. 1912. *The Conservation of the Child: A Manual of Clinical Psychology Presenting the Examination and Treatment of Backward Children*. Philadelphia: Lippincott.

Katz, Michael B. 1990. *The Undeserving Poor: From the War on Poverty to the War on Welfare*. New York: Pantheon.

———. 1996. *In the Shadow of the Poorhouse: A Social History of Welfare in America*. Tenth anniversary ed. New York: Basic Books.

Kevles, Daniel. 1985. *In the Name of Eugenics: Genetics and the Uses of Human Heredity*. New York: Knopf.

Knoll, James. 1987. "Through a Glass, Darkly: The Photographic Image of People with a Disability." PhD diss., Syracuse Univ.

Kozloff, Max. 1979. *Photography & Fascination*. Danbury, NH: Addison House.

Krims, Les. 1972. *Little People of America*. Buffalo: Les Krims.

Langness, L. L., and Harold Levine. 1986. *Culture and Retardation: Life Histories of Mildly Mentally Retarded Persons in American Society*. New York: Springer.

Laughlin, H. H. 1914. *The Legal, Legislative, and Administrative Aspects of Sterilization*. Eugenics Record Office Bulletin No. 10B. Report of the Committee to Study and to Report on the Best Practical Means of Cutting off the Defective Germ-Plasm in the American Population. Cold Springs Harbor, NY: Cold Springs Harbor Laboratory Press.

Linker, Beth. 2011. *War's Waste: Rehabilitation in World War I America*. Chicago: Univ. of Chicago Press.

Lombroso, Cesare. [1911] 2006. *Criminal Man*. Durham, NC: Duke Univ. Press.

Ludmerer, Kenneth M. 1972. *Genetics and American Society: A Historical Appraisal.* Baltimore: Johns Hopkins.

Malcolm, Janet. 1980. *Diana and Nikon: Essays on the Aesthetic of Photography.* Boston: Godine

Mallory, Michael. 2009. *Universal Studios Monsters: A Legacy of Horror.* New York: Universe.

Marien, Mary Warner. 2006. *Photography: A Cultural History.* New York: Harry N. Abrams.

Mark, Mary Ellen. 1979. *Ward 81.* New York: Fireside.

McDaid, Jennifer Davis. 2002. "'How a One-Legged Rebel Lives': Confederate Veterans and Artificial Limbs in Virginia." In *Artificial Parts, Practical Lives,* edited by Katherine Ott, David H. Serlin, and Stephen Mihm, 119–46. New York: New York Univ. Press.

Meatyard, Ralph Eugene. 1970. *Ralph Eugene Meatyard.* Lexington, KY: Gnomon.

———. 1974. "Meatyard." *Aperture* 18 nos. 3–4 (special issues).

Metropolitan Museum of Art. 2006. "Paul Strand: Blind (33.43.334)". In *Heilbrunn Timeline of Art History.* New York: Metropolitan Museum of Art. Retrieved from http://www.metmuseum.org/toah/works-of-art/33.43.334.

Mihm, Stephen. 2002. "'A Limb Which Shall Be Presentable in Polite Society': Prosthetic Technologies in the Nineteenth Century." In *Artificial Parts, Practical Lives,* edited by Katherine Ott, David H. Serlin, and Stephen Mihm, 282–300. New York: New York Univ. Press.

Miller, George, and Dorothy Miller. 1976. *Picture Postcards in the United States, 1893–1918.* New York: Clarkson N. Potter.

Millet, Ann. 2004. "Exceeding the Frame." *Disability Studies Quarterly* 24, no. 4. Retrieved from http://dsq-sds.org/article/view/881/1056.

Mitchell, Michael. 1979. *Monsters of a Gilded Age.* Toronto: Gage.

Morel, B. A. 1857. *Traite des degenerescences physiques, intellectuelles et morales de l'espece humaine et des causes qui produisent des varieties maladives.* Paris: Bailliere.

Morgan, John J. B. 1928. *The Psychology of Abnormal People: With Educational Applications.* New York: Longmans.

Noll, Steven, and James W. Trent Jr., eds. 2004. *Mental Retardation in America.* New York: New York Univ. Press.

Norden, Martin. 1994. *Cinema of Isolation: A History of Physical Disability in the Movies.* New Brunswick, NJ: Rutgers Univ. Press.

Ott, Katherine, David H. Serlin, and Stephen Mihum, eds. 2002. *Artificial Parts, Practical Lives: Modern Histories of Prosthetics.* New York: New York Univ. Press.

Parr, Martin, and Gerry Badger. 2004. *The Photobook: A History.* Vol. 1. New York: Viking Press.

Paterson, Donald G. 1930. *Physique and Intellect.* New York: Century.

Pietropaolo, Vincenzo. 2010. *Invisible No More: A Photographic Chronicle of the Lives of People with Intellectual Disabilities.* New Brunswick, NJ: Rutgers Univ. Press.

Popenoe, Paul. 1929. *The Child's Heredity.* Baltimore: Williams & Wilkins.

———. 1930. "Feeblemindedness Today." *Journal of Heredity* 21, no. 10: 221–30.

Popenoe, Paul, and R. H. Johnson. 1918. *Applied Eugenics.* New York: Macmillan.

Pressey, Sidney L., and L. C. Pressey. 1926. *Mental Abnormality and Deficiency.* New York: Macmillan.

Rafter, Nicole Hahn. 1988. *White Trash: The Eugenic Family Studies, 1877–1919.* Boston: Northeastern Univ. Press.

Reeves, H. T. 1938. "The Later Years of a Mental Defective." *Journal of Psycho-Asthenics* 43: 194–200.

Reilly, Philip R. 1991. *The Surgical Solution: A History of Involuntary Sterilization in the United States.* Baltimore: Johns Hopkins.

Rose, David W. 2003. *March of Dimes.* Charleston, SC: Arcadia Press.

Rosenberg, Harold. 1964. *The Anxious Object.* New York: Horizon House.

Rosenblum, Naomi. 1984. *A World History of Photography.* New York: Abbeville.

Rothman, David. 2002. *The Discovery of the Asylum.* Rev. ed. New York: Aldine.

Sandell, Richard, Jocelyn Dodd, and Rosemarie Garland-Thomson. 2010. *Re-presenting Disability: Activism and Agency in the Museum.* New York: Routledge.

Saxon, Arthur H. [for Lavinia Warren]. 1979. *The Autobiography of Mrs. Tom Thumb*. Hamden, CT: Archon Books.

Schweik, Susan. 2009. *The Ugly Laws: Disability in Public*. New York: New York Univ. Press.

Scott, Richard. 1969. *The Making of Blind Men*. New York: Russell Sage Foundation.

Serlin, David. 2004. *Replaceable You: Engineering the Body in Postwar America*. Chicago: Univ. of Chicago Press.

Sessions, M. A. 1917. "Feeble-Minded in Ohio." *Journal of Heredity* 8, no. 7: 291–98.

Shuttleworth, George E., and W. A. Potts. 1916. *Mentally Deficient Children: Their Treatment and Training*. 4th ed. Philadelphia: Blakiston.

Siebers, Tobin. 2010. *Disability Aesthetics*. Ann Arbor: Univ. of Michigan Press.

Smith, J. David. 1988. *Minds Made Feeble: The Myth and Legacy of the Kallikaks*. Austin, TX: Pro-Ed.

Smith, W. Eugene, and Aileen Smith. 1975. *Minamata*. New York: Holt, Rinehart, and Winston.

Snyder, Sharon L., Brenda Jo Brueggemann, and Rosemarie Garland-Thomson, eds. 2002. *Disability Studies: Enabling the Humanities*. New York: Modern Language Association.

Stange, M. 1978. "Photography and the Institution: Szarkowski at the Modern." In *Photography: Current Perspectives*, edited by Jerome Liebling, 65–81. Rochester, NY: Light Impressions.

Szarkowski, John. 1978. *Mirrors and Windows: American Photography since 1960*. New York: Museum of Modern Art.

Talbot, Eugene S. 1901. *Degeneracy: Its Causes, Signs, and Results*. London: C. Scribner.

Tannenbaum, Barbara, ed. 1991. *Ralph Eugene Meatyard: An American Visionary*. New York: Rizzoli.

Taylor, Steven J. 2009. *Acts of Conscience: World War II, Mental Institutions, and Religious Objectors*. Syracuse, NY: Syracuse Univ. Press.

Tredgold, Alfred F. 1908. *A Textbook of Mental Deficiency (Amentia)*. New York: William Wood.

———. 1916. *Mental Deficiency (Amentia)*. New York: William Wood.

———. 1929. *Mental Retardation*. New York: William Wood.

———. 1947. *A Textbook of Mental Deficiency (Amentia)*. Baltimore: Williams and Wilkins.

Tredgold, Alfred F., and Kenneth Soddy. 1956. *A Textbook of Mental Deficiency*. Baltimore: Williams and Wilkins.

Trent, James W., Jr. 1994. *Inventing the Feeble Mind: A History of Mental Retardation in the United States*. Berkeley: Univ. of California Press.

Welch, M. 1986. "After Evans and before Frank: The New York School of Photography." *Afterimage* 14, no. 1: 14–16.

Williams-Searle, John. 2001. "Cold Charity: Manhood, Brotherhood, and the Transformation of Disability, 1870–1900." In *The New Disability History*, edited by Paul K. Longmore and Lauri Umansky, 157–86. New York: New York Univ. Press.

Wolfensberger, Wolf. 1972. *The Principle of Normalization in Human Services*. Toronto: National Institute of Mental Retardation.

Index

Page numbers in italics denote illustrations and table.

ROBERT BOGDAN, Distinguished Professor Emeritus in Sociology and Disability Studies at Syracuse University, lives in rural Vermont, where he writes about the application of visual sociology to disability studies and other subjects.

MARTIN ELKS received his PhD in intellectual disabilities and disability studies at Syracuse University. He is unit manager of disability client management and individual service packages for the Department of Human Services, Victoria, Australia.

JAMES A. KNOLL is the chair of the Department of Early Childhood, Elementary, and Special Education at Morehead State University in Kentucky. He received his PhD in special education from Syracuse University. One of his main research interests is the inclusion of people with disabilities in schools and the community.